Bad Moon Rising

by

Stephen Pickering

North Country Press

Bad Moon Rising

ISBN 978-0-945980-98-8

Library of Congress Control Number: 2015939571

Cover photo by Sara Pickering
saraelizabethphotographymaine.weebly.com

North Country Press
Unity, Maine

Hope you got your things together.
Hope you are quite prepared to die.
Looks like we're in for nasty weather.
One eye is taken for an eye.

-John Fogerty

DEDICATION

To my dad, Archie Pickering, for telling me at a very young age that I could do anything I wanted as long as I put my mind to it.

To my mom, Anita Pickering, for showing me that his words were true.

Chapter One

Sam took a breath and his mouth began to form the words that his thoughts had not and would not release. Carl gripped the steering wheel with both hands as he stared at the taillights of his father's Ford pickup. They were moving at a sedate forty miles per hour but Carl's knuckles were white as he drove his '69 Roadrunner.

"Leave it alone," Carl said.

"But I didn't. . . ."

Carl cut off his little brother's words. "You were going too," he said. "Just leave it alone," Carl repeated as his own thoughts screamed inside his head. They were screaming to be let out. The three walked into their home together like survivors of some epic battle.

"They got stuck on the soft shoulder on the Fish Creek Road," Arnold said to his wife. "I had to pull them out." She didn't notice the still wet blood on the sleeve of his insulated denim jacket. She didn't think the dazed and subdued demeanor of the boys was unusual. She was sure that Arnold had not been pleasant when he found them and she didn't dare ask about Carl's black eye. The three never spoke about the incident though Carl had nightmares for several months with the first beginning that night.

Just three hours earlier Sam Peterson had no way of knowing that his young life was about to change direction. Like most 14-year-old boys he had not yet plotted a course for his life. He lived one minute at a time and worried about what happened when it happened. Sam was only five foot four inches tall and weighed a hundred pounds soaking wet. He had long blonde hair which accentuated his feminine features and hazel eyes. One would call Sam pretty. Not the description he wanted. He compensated by dressing like he spent the weekend at Max Yasgur's farm with three hundred thousand of his closest friends. He wore torn bellbottom jeans, black T-shirts and Converse Low-Tops with no socks. Sam's parents were not impressed but he was a good kid and they tolerated his taste in clothing. It worked for Sam.

"Sam," his mother called out. "Will you take care of the trash for me?"

"In a minute," he said. "I'm doing my homework."

Anne smiled in disbelief but Sam was actually doing his freshman geometry homework, something he normally put off until just moments before the class was to begin. He was sitting at his small desk that was manufactured by rapists and murderers in the Thomaston State Prison wood working shop. His parents gave all three boys desks from the prison last Christmas. New desks, in their new rooms, in their new house, life was good.

Sam shared a sparsely furnished room with his 11-year-old brother Darren. The room had two beds, two bureaus, two desks and one closet. Sam's thoughts bounced from parallelograms to Janis Joplin, Jim Morrison, Jimi Hendrix and John Lennon. These four fueled Sam's dreams of excitement and fame. He didn't realize that he had surrounded himself with senseless death and wasted opportunities. Yet, before this year would be over, three of the four would be gone and Sam nearly got to wherever they were going before them. Sam's door was open and he could hear Carl, his 17-year-old brother, trying to explain to their mother why he didn't need to take Sam with him when he went to see his friend, Gary Grover.

Anne Peterson was a striking woman. Tall with dark brown hair, almost grey eyes and fair skinned. She had just received her teaching degree the hard way. She took classes at night and on weekends during the regular school year and day classes in the summer. She did it in five years and graduated with high honors. Not bad for a mother of three with a part-time job picking out crabmeat for a local seafood dealer.

Anne thought that if she made Carl take Sam with him, Carl would at least try to stay out of trouble for fear his brother would tell on him. What Anne didn't realize was that Sam worshiped his brother and never would betray Carl's trust. As added insurance, Carl threatened to beat the living shit out of Sam if he ever told Mom and Dad about his occasional indiscretions. Anne also didn't realize how many times she nearly lost two sons instead of one when she sent Sam along with Carl. Tonight would be one of those nights.

Carl Peterson was the antithesis of Sam. Six foot one, a muscular one hundred and seventy pound three-sport athlete, short blonde hair and sharp blue eyes. Carl wore straight leg black jeans, cable knit sweaters and brown penny loafers. He was nothing like the prep school student he looked like. Though very intelligent he lived hard and fast and was well on the way to discovering that alcohol might be a cure-all for all of life's woes. Alcohol was something that would control the rest of his life. Of course what was about to happen was going to seize his entire being and never relinquish it. Not even alcohol would be able to flush away the memories of March 17, 1970.

Carl had been drinking beer since he was 13 years old. His parents didn't suspect anything until he was 16 years old when he crashed his car and the deputy found beer bottles in the back seat. Anne also suspected that Carl may have been experimenting with marijuana. That's what parents call it when they find out their child is using drugs. Experimentation, a phase, something they will grow out of. Carl wasn't experimenting. He had it figured out and he liked it.

Anne called out, "Sam. Your brother is going to Stonington and he would like you to come along."

"Right," Sam said to himself, or did he say it out loud? Sometimes you can't tell. Sam knew Carl didn't want him to come along but Carl and his friends had gotten used to Sam being there and they learned to trust him.

3

"Yeah sure mom. I'll be right there," Sam called back. Sam heard the front door slam as Carl left and the next sound he heard was Carl's Roadrunner starting. It seemed to start hard but Carl explained to Sam that the 383-cubic-inch engine had a very high compression, 10:1, whatever that meant. Carl said that was the reason it seemed to start hard but when it did start it was music to Sam's ears. Even their father was impressed. As Carl explained, the 383 had 1967 GTX 440 heads. The camshaft had a high lift and long duration. Carl said this meant more fuel to the engine and more power. It had a Holley 850 cfm, double pumper, four barrel carburetor with mechanical secondaries mounted on a stock cast iron intake manifold. It had Hooker headers that dumped into two-and-a-half inch dual exhaust with little Thrush mufflers. Arnold Peterson, the boys' father, loved the car and was scared to death at the same time. It was a killing machine in the wrong hands and Carl seemed to be proving to anyone who saw him drive the medium blue Plymouth with the flat black hood that his were the wrong hands.

Sam approached the passenger side of the big square Plymouth and smiled as he listened to the slow labored idle of the engine. It was one of those quiet afternoons. It was the kind of quiet that comes just before a storm. So quiet you can hear the flapping of a bird's wings or the sound of a cat's tongue as it laps milk from a dish. If not for the low rumble of the powerful motor Sam would have likely heard the deer chewing on cedar boughs just 50 feet into the woods from where he walked. There was no predicted storm on the horizon, at least not one caused by converging weather fronts. As Sam slid onto the black vinyl bench seat Carl grasped the long, chrome-plated, strangely bent gear shift lever, put the blue beast into reverse and slowly backed out onto Route 15.

"Where are we going?" Sam asked. Sam was eager for a ride in his brother's car and did not think about why he was actually there.

"Shut up," Carl said. Carl was annoyed that Sam was sent along to keep an eye on him. Sam was cool about the drinking and driving fast. He actually seemed to enjoy the driving fast. Today was different. Carl's friend, Gary, didn't like having the "little punk" along. Gary especially didn't like Sam around when he was making a sale of marijuana to Carl. You couldn't trust "little punks" no matter whose brother they were. Carl revved the 383 to about 3,500 rpm and quickly released the clutch. The Plymouth violently squatted in the rear as if it were a cat about to pounce on its prey. The front end lifted as the torque of the powerful motor tried to twist the car in two. The Mickey Thompson 60 Series rear tires made a weak little squeak as the car was catapulted south on the narrow two-lane country road. Carl liked the fact that the Roadrunner hooked up so well. Most guys with powerful cars liked long smoky burnouts like the drag racers on television did to heat up their tires before a race. Sam was fond of burnouts too and the feeling of being slammed into the seat as the car launched was pretty cool, he thought. Carl, with blinding speed, slammed the shifter into second. This caused the rear of the car to slide to the right and the Mickey Thompsons began to smoke. This would have caused Sam to fall over in the seat but he was used to this maneuver by now and he clutched the armrest with one hand and braced his other on the seat. Sam couldn't suppress the big grin on his face. One day when Carl was in a good mood he had actually let Sam drive the Roadrunner. Carl patiently explained the nuances of gas pedal and clutch release and compensating for the violent torque with the steering wheel. Carl told Sam, "If I can see your hand move, you're shifting too slowly." The engine rpms built quickly and Carl wasted no time muscling that long, bent, chrome shifter into third gear. This gear change caused the rear of the Plymouth to snap to the left and Carl managed to control the direction change and had the car pointing straight again. The 140 mph speedometer shot past 90 mph as they reached the sweeping left turn in the road. The big square car seemed to plow into the corner like it wanted to dig a hole into the pavement. Sam wasn't very impressed with this part as it always seemed that they would leave the road and crash into the trees. The trees were menacingly close to the edge of these rural roads and their leafless limbs seemed to reach out trying to pull the car into their dark and unforgiving home. Carl managed to overcome the laws of physics and keep the trees waiting for another chance on another day. Carl let off the gas, shifted easily into fourth gear and let the speed drift down to 50 mph for the rest of the trip to Mountainville. Yeah, their mom thought they were going to Stonington, but Stonington actually had a police department and Gary did not want them snooping around his "business". The plan was to meet Gary at the Walker Estate near the Haystack Mountain School in the Mountainville section of Deer Isle.

This was a short but exciting ride for Sam. The excitement, if you could call it that, would not end with the ride in his brother's muscle car.

Carl gently shifted down through the gears as he turned down the dirt road that led to the Walker Estate. The branches of the large spruce trees that lined either side of the road created a canopy that blocked the now receding daylight. The dirt road became a tunnel that separated two different worlds. Sam and Carl left the world of the average and the normal and entered the world that was usually the domain of the privileged and carefree. Carl drove slowly as if he were letting a thoroughbred race horse cool down after a hard run. The Roadrunner was indeed a thoroughbred and the Walker Estate used to have a stable of riding horses so this was as it should be, Sam thought. Sam especially liked the Walker Estate. Not for its 6,400 square feet of living space, its three field stone fireplaces, the eight bedrooms, six bathrooms and a huge screened and covered porch overlooking Southeast Harbor and Whitmore Neck. Sam had never been inside the sprawling estate and seen the two stainless steel kitchens with its three dining rooms, its maple and oak floors and the magnificent double staircase that looked as though it should have been in an English palace rather than a summer cottage in Deer Isle. At 14, he wouldn't really have noticed the fine architecture and ornate wood trim. Sam had heard his father call the place a summer cottage. To Sam, cottage meant a structure that was a little bigger than a camp. The Walker Estate was nearly six times bigger than the home he and his family shared. He liked this place because his father used to come here as a boy and mow the huge lawn and tend to the riding horses. He liked being in this place and imagining his father at the same age as he. Sam wondered or tried to imagine what his father thought about life in general at 14 years old and more specifically, did his father's expectations as an adolescent match the results that he achieved as an adult or did they fall short. He wondered if the Korean War, that eighteen month detour in his father's life, changed his planned course. He wondered if the Vietnam War would be over before he turned eighteen. It certainly seemed as if it would last long enough to swallow up his brother Carl, who would be eligible for the draft in four months. Sam's fear of fighting in a war in a foreign land was normal enough. What wasn't normal was that he and Carl were about to get a firsthand look at what happens in war; what can happen when your very existence is at stake; what can happen when a soldier's training takes over and puts the normal human mores and rules that govern civilized lives into a little locked safe for just a few minutes. Just a few minutes that would undoubtedly alter Sam's and Carl's future. The future that they hadn't planned yet but surely had thought about. They would be unable to do anything but watch, with no control, as the course of their lives was perversely rerouted by driving down the tunnel between two worlds.

Carl carefully backed the Plymouth around the corner of the boathouse. Carl wanted to be able to see who was coming down the driveway before they saw him. The owners surely wouldn't arrive until after Memorial Day but he didn't know how often the caretaker checked on the place. He could quickly escape parked this way. He knew his car would be recognized but at least he would have time to come up with a story as to why they were there. Besides, they were only trespassing and there weren't even any signs prohibiting that. Screw the people from away. Carl would roam around Deer Isle wherever he liked. This was his home. Not many could say that their families had lived here for ten generations. He was entitled, at least that's the way he saw it.

Carl had tuned the radio's AM dial to WMEX in Boston. That seemed so odd to Sam. The only radio stations that played rock music for Maine listeners in coastal Hancock County were in Boston, Massachusetts. WMEX and WRKO. A five-hour drive from Deer Isle but less than 150 miles across the Gulf of Maine. "Badge" by Cream had just started. A short song but the opening bass riff played by Jack Bruce totally enthralled Sam and he could do nothing else for the next couple of minutes but listen. Carl liked music just fine but he liked beer more. He reached under the seat for that last bottle of Michelob that he had saved from last weekend's six pack. Not being twenty-one didn't stop Carl's ability to acquire beer. All you needed was to know someone who was of legal age and willing to break the law for you. They were easy to find in Deer Isle and Stonington. The biggest hurdle was having money. Isn't that always the biggest hurdle in any endeavor? It certainly seemed that way. Today, Carl's beer money was being converted to pot money. Carl and his friends saw pot as a harmless recreational drug and they saw no danger in using it. Peace, love and dope had been the mantra as the 60s ended. The mantra did not include money. You needed money if you wanted dope and the people in the dope business were more dangerous than the drug if you got between them and the money.

Eight new Ford pickups with two men in each truck were just now crossing the light green suspension bridge that connected the mainland to Little Deer Isle. It almost looked like a parade but there was nothing festive about this group. They were the dark clouds of the impending storm crossing the Eggemoggin Reach.

It was twenty-five minutes before four in the afternoon. Gary was not going to be there until four thirty. Normally Carl would have driven around awhile before arriving at the Walker Estate, but gas had just gone up to thirty cents a gallon and the Roadrunner got only seven miles per gallon. Carl needed to conserve his cash. He lived off the money he earned with his father lobster fishing in the summer. He had an occasional weekend job in the winter working on a scallop dragger or loading trucks at the Co-op. He preferred not to work in the winter but he would have to work full time soon enough.

Carl reached over and turned up the volume. "Love Me Two Times" by the Doors was playing and Carl loved the Doors.

Sam said, "I like this song too." Sam sounded like a puppy dog trying to get his master's attention.

Carl laughed, "You don't even know what the song is about."

"I do too!" Sam stated indignantly. What the song is about, Sam thought to himself. What did he mean by that? It's a cool song. What more is there? Carl chuckled to himself. Carl wasn't about to explain blowjobs to his little brother. Not that Carl had experienced that sexual pleasure but he was aware of the concept. Gary Grover had bragged about Naomi Findlay's expertise in that particular sexual act. Gary had done a lot of things that Carl hadn't. Well, if you believed Gary's stories and Carl was inclined to believe about anything Gary said. Sam summed up Gary with one word. Asshole. Arnold Peterson felt the same way as Sam about Gary but neither had ever heard the other use that particular word. They both used it quite often but not in the brief exchanges between father and 14-year-old son. That was as it should be but very soon the prospect of Sam hearing his father refer to someone as an asshole would be so minutely insignificant compared to what Sam and Carl were about to witness from their father.

Fontella Bass was in the middle of belting out "Rescue Me" when they both noticed a new Ford F300 Camper Special four wheel drive pickup emerge from the tree lined driveway and make its way slowly in to the large semi-circular parking area. It was a pale yellow truck with a camper secured in the body. It was a cloudy afternoon and the sun was beginning to set but there was enough light to see that the two men in the truck weren't from Deer Isle. The Rhode Island license plate should have been their first clue but all the two boys noticed were the two men staring back at them. The men had long hair drawn back into ponytails. The driver had a long scruffy beard and the passenger had a more neatly trimmed beard. Carl took the last swallow of his beer, slid the empty under the seat and prepared to leave.

Frank Silveira was the passenger in the Ford truck and John Silveira, Frank's brother, was driving. Frank was the president of an outlaw motorcycle club known as The Slayers. They were over six hours from their Warwick home but they were not lost.

"Somebody supposed to be waiting for us?" John asked.

"No," Frank said. Frank's "no" was cold and ominous. John knew not to pursue it further. John also knew that whoever was parked in the blue Plymouth was not going to have a good evening. "You and O'Shea can greet our visitors," Frank said.

Chapter Two

Frank had been here just five weeks ago on a very cold ground-hog day. Frank was hired by a capo of the Patriacha family to find a suitable off-load site for the delivery of 10,000 pounds of marijuana. Frank was told that the organization wanted to explore the feasibility of using locations along Maine's three thousand miles of coastline. Frank had checked out several locations from Cundy's Harbor near Brunswick to the Washington County fishing village of Cutler. The United States Coast Guard had so many strategically placed stations in Maine that it was difficult to find a location that wasn't under their constant watchful eye.

Being the president of an outlaw motorcycle club wasn't a vocation, it was kind of a hobby. Not to say that the members did not enjoy certain benefits, but one needed a regular job to keep the IRS happy and the FBI uninterested. Frank and John actually owned a drywall company and did quite well. It didn't hurt that the organization they were affiliated with exercised a sizable control over the unions that handle the assignment of construction jobs in the greater Providence area. The price of their job security was errands such as he was on now. After six trips and two months of research Frank settled on Deer Isle. The island was connected to the mainland by a suspension bridge built in 1939. It was an impressive sight as its long slender roadway arched over the Eggemoggin Reach like a lime green rainbow.

Frank returned to Deer Isle on Monday, February 2, 1970 at nine thirty in the morning driving a rented, silver 1970 Ford Thunderbird. The car reminded Frank of a Navy destroyer escort. It handled like one too. It had plenty of power but it floated and plowed like his old ship in rough seas. It was a cold and cloudy day but that was normal for New England in February. According to the news on WRKO, Punxsutawney

Phil had not seen his shadow that morning. Spring would be here soon. So inspired was the disc jockey at WRKO that he brightened up the airwaves with "Summer In The City" by the Cowsills. Frank turned the radio off as he pulled in to the first real estate office he came to in Deer Isle Village. The large colorful sign read End of the Rainbow Realty. Frank thought that was lame but it was the first agency he had seen and he was tired of driving. He wondered if Dorothy and Toto were going to greet him. Frank had cleaned himself up from his usual outlaw biker look for the trip. Frank had left his leather and club colors at home. He was dressed in nicely pressed grey Haggar slacks, a very business-like white Burlington shirt that was covered by a not quite warm enough brown London Fog overcoat. He was wearing the obligatory LL Bean boots. Clothes do make the man but it is difficult to hide a three-inch scar that traveled from just below his right ear lobe towards his chin. Extortion can be a messy business and the scar was a reminder of one of the very rare occasions that Frank ended up on the bad end of a bad deal. The temporary winner of that negotiation disappeared forever a week later.

Frank did indeed clean up well. His classic Portuguese features on a muscular five foot ten inch frame were warmed by a very charming smile. He shaved his beard and his long thick black hair was carefully combed into a pony tail by his sister.

"What's the occasion?" Maria Santos asked with the voice of a teasing younger sister.

Frank's reply was stern and final, "You don't want to know."

Maria did not live the life her older brother did and she really didn't want to know if it had anything to do with that gang of thugs he hung out with. Maria actually thought Frank had met someone nice who would change his life. A sister can hope and she would never give up on Frank's redemption. Maria saw her two younger brothers the day before they left on "a business trip" with Frank. She had no idea what they would be doing and didn't want to know. She did see them a week later but not in the setting that families look forward to.

The long-sleeved shirt covered the abundance of tattoos that normally would put off the average real estate broker. Most real estate brokers, no matter what the location, are more receptive to affluence and tattoos are not representative of affluence. Several of Frank's tattoos included the words "death" and "kill" along with several naked women. Frank thought it best to keep them covered.

It was ten degrees above zero outside but Julia kept the office a very warm seventy-five degrees inside. Julia was a twenty-seven-year-old bundle of energy. She was passionate about everything and her energy and drive were contagious. Most found her personality endearing but some found it annoying. The latter usually had more to do with professional or personal jealousy. Her clients loved her and were as loyal as a hunting dog. She worked very hard for her clients and she was fun to be around. Julia was five foot three inches tall and tipped the scales at 116 pounds. She had a rich mane of auburn hair that she usually kept in a pony-tail. Her emerald green eyes captivated men and women alike. Julia had a plain gold band on the ring finger of her left hand. She wasn't married, not even engaged. This was her safety net intended to keep unwanted propositions to a minimum. Bruising the male ego could be bad for business. Frank hadn't noticed the green eyes yet or the gold band. Not that the gold band would have deterred Frank. Julia was wearing a nearly see-through white blouse and a white lacey bra that barely held in her ample breasts. Frank's gaze worked its way down to the black skirt that was supported by gorgeous slender legs and then back up, briefly stopping at her breasts and then locked onto those incredible green eyes.

"Hi there! What can I do for you today?" Julia addressed Frank in a welcoming but professional tone.

13

I can think of several things and they have nothing to do with real estate, Frank thought. "I need to rent a home on the water for the month of March. It should be secluded and have an all tides deep water dock," Frank said.

"Great. A man that knows what he wants," Julia said as she walked towards the filing cabinet that contained the listings that also could be available for rent. Frank noticed that there was a lot of collateral movement in her short walk across the small office.

"I usually get what I want too," Frank said with a hint of lechery in his voice.

"I bet you do," Julia said with a flirty smile. Julia approached Frank with her left arm cradling several file folders against her breasts. Julia did get uncomfortable when men stared. Even though her blouse was almost see-through and the top button was unbuttoned it didn't mean she was advertising. It meant she was showing off and that was Julia's second favorite pastime. Julia's favorite pastime was flirting. It didn't hurt business either. Occasionally, an insecure wife would be put off. Julia was quick to recognize the signs and would resort to a more conservative approach. The wives appreciated her change in demeanor and business usually was not adversely affected. Her right hand was outstretched in anticipation of a handshake.

"Julia. Julia Henderson. I'm very happy to meet you," she said with innocent charm. Frank reached out with his right hand, gently grasped her delicate hand and pulled it towards his mouth as he leaned forward and kissed the back of her hand.

"Charlie Richards and the pleasure is all mine," he replied in a tone drenched with lust. If my sister could see me now, Frank thought. Julia felt her face flush and also noticed a tingling sensation in another location of her body.

Charles Richards was born on April 2, 1944 and died in the same hospital he was born in on April 7, 1944. All you needed was a little research time at the city hall and five dollars for a copy of a birth certificate. That five dollar purchase could allow you to get a driver's license, a checking account, a social security number and a passport. A new identity anytime you needed it. Frank needed it for this job. What he didn't yet know was he would need another to survive the aftermath of this job. He could never be Frank Silveira again, and never is a very long time.

Julia invited Mr. Richards to sit at her small conference table at the front of the office. Mr. Richards is how Julia planned on referring to this dangerous man. Julia's idea of danger was a man she couldn't handle and to Julia that could be very dangerous indeed. Julia wouldn't know until long after Mr. Richards left Deer Isle that her instincts were correct. Her instincts didn't warn her how dangerous he really was. She was only worried about potential sexual advances and how to fend them off without offending Mr. Richards. The only way to accomplish that was turn down the flirt and turn up the business woman. Some guys just don't get it, Julia thought. Actually no guy gets it at first and it takes a while for the big head to educate the little head in the ways of women. Most men never graduate from that class and Frank, or Mr. Richards as he was today, never even signed up for the course.

Julia, who was standing across the table from Mr. Richards, spread four dog-eared manila folders on the table in front of him.

"Here's what I have," she said. "Look through these and see if there is anything you like." Julia had the tone of a school teacher now. Unfortunately, Mr. Richards was staring down the very revealing opening in her blouse that was even more pronounced as she bent at the waist. Frank almost said out loud, Yeah, I see what you have and I like them both just fine, thank you. He kept the thought to himself but with a sly smile he responded, "I'm sure you have what I want."

15

Jesus H. Christ! Julia thought with certain frustration that was bordering on anger. Can't he give it a rest? Julia's very controlled and professional voice did not betray her thoughts.

"I'm sure we can accommodate your needs in one of those folders." She smiled as she stood up and walked to her desk. She sat down, buttoned the top button of her blouse and thumbed through the Rolodex. Julia was not scared but she didn't know what she was feeling. It was like an alarm was going off and she should pay attention. She wasn't going to call anyone but she wanted the numbers handy. She stopped at the P. Maine State Police – 1-800-555-7381 and 555-2121. She also had Trooper Dan Gervais' home phone number listed on this card. Julia thought the 800 number would take a while to dial, the 555 number was the regional dispatch center in Orono and there was Dan in Surry. If I call Orono they would have to find someone and send them, probably Dan. If I call Dan at home and get him he's most likely not working and it would be precious time wasted as he explained that I needed to call someone else. Dan would probably respond whether he was working or not. He was a nice man and appeared to be a very dedicated trooper. Julia closed the Rolodex and mumbled softly, "This is ridiculous. I'll be fine with this guy."

Mr. Richards turned in his chair and said, "You talking to me?"

Julia responded with a laugh, "I'm sorry. I talk to myself sometimes when I go over my to do list." Whatever tingle or excitement she felt a few minutes ago wasn't going to come back anytime soon. Frank noticed the now buttoned blouse. I guess I came on a little strong, he thought. But she seemed so friendly in that don't-you-want-to-screw-me sort of way. Oh well. I could have been wrong but I doubt it. Men never thought they were wrong in their interpretation of the signals women send out. The women were just confused, not the men.

"Oh," Mr. Richards responded as he turned back and continued to study the second folder.

Julia's office was relatively small but efficient. It was on the first floor of a two and half story building. It had the original 100-year-old hardwood floors that creaked under the foot falls of its many visitors. The wainscoting was painted white and helped lighten up the otherwise poorly lit area. Julia's oak banker's desk was in front of a large window that overlooked Northwest Harbor. The view was beautiful but it was to Julia's back. She felt that her customer's would take in the view as they talked and it would solidify their resolve to purchase property on Deer Isle. On the second floor was an apartment that Julia was currently renting to the elementary school principal and her husband. He worked as an accountant at Barter Lumber Company. No kids and no pets equaled great tenants. They paid the rent on time too. The attic was mainly for storage and it had an outside wooden staircase that Julia had installed the same summer she bought the building five years ago. Yes, at the young age of twenty-two she managed to save enough money cleaning homes for summer people that she could come up with a down payment for the mortgage on the building. It didn't hurt that her father was the branch manager of the local bank, but it was still done by the numbers. Julia's main advantage was that she didn't receive the usual scrutiny that most first time young borrowers did. In the opinion of the branch manager, Dad, she was not a bad risk. The building was also worth more than the money borrowed for it and that was the bottom line, now wasn't it. Julia had just received her real estate broker's license when she bought the building and hung out her shingle. The name was easy, Over the Rainbow Realty. No big secret meaning there. Julia loved the song made famous by Judy Garland in The Wizard of Oz and it gave the suggestion that anyone coming through the doors of her business would find their pot of gold. The pot of gold would be the property that they were looking for and couldn't live without.

The staircase to the attic was a financial boon and Julia had intended it to be. The attic had a large dormer and balcony at the rear of the building. This location overlooked the beautiful Northwest Harbor and had views of western Penobscot Bay including Pickering Island. She installed a small bathroom and a kitchenette in the attic, or loft, as she called it in her brochures that attracted the rich artist wannabes from away. Real artists couldn't afford the rent but every once in awhile she would give a sincere and obviously talented artist the opportunity to rent the loft at a much reduced rate. This usually meant receiving a beautiful work of art to hang on the wall at Dad's bank.

The window behind her desk had about the same view as the loft, just no balcony. On the wall behind where Mr. Richards was seated were several nautical charts spliced together that depicted the area from Frenchman's Bay east of Mount Desert Island to Owl's Head just south of Rockland. Many of Julia's clients were recreational boaters and they reveled in pointing out all the places they had sailed in Penobscot Bay. Julia used the charts to show prospective buyers where the properties that were available for sale were located. There were double meanings in almost every aspect of Julia's life and she often had trouble distinguishing between what she did and what she meant. It was even harder for the people around her.

"This looks promising," Mr. Richards said as he got up from the table and walked to the nautical-chart-covered wall. Julia joined him at the wall and had to move in close and cock her head sideways to see which listing Mr. Richards brought with him.

"The Walker Estate," she said. "A very nice place and it does have everything you need."

Julia noticed that he was wearing nice cologne. At least he looks good and smells good. Too bad he's such an ass Julia thought ruefully. She pointed out the location on the chart. She already had a red push pin on the spot as she did for the rest of her listings. Julia would paint the end of the pin white and then write a number on the painted white area. This number would correspond with a number on the listing file. Julia was organized and efficient. That translated into successful.

"The Walker Estate is kept heated year round and the caretaker keeps the driveway clear all winter. I can show it to you now if you like," Julia said.

"That would be good. We can take my car," Mr. Richards said. His tone indicated that taking his car was more than a suggestion. It was like there was no choice but he wanted to sound polite.

Julia replied coolly, "If you don't mind, I'll take my car and you can follow me."

Mr. Richards responded with an insincere smile and a friendly tone that did not match his fake grin, "Oh no. I insist. The only way I'm going to remember how to get back to this place is drive it myself without any help other than your directions."

Either he's getting ahead of himself or I already have a deal, Julia thought—we haven't even talked price yet.

"Find your way back?" Julia asked.

"Yeah," Mr. Richards responded with a puzzled look on his face. "You weren't planning on showing me around again when I come back in March, were you?"

"No!" Julia said, sounding just a little flustered. "But you haven't seen it yet and we haven't even discussed the price."

"If the place is as it appears to be on paper and if you accept cash then we have a deal," Mr. Richards said in the manner she had heard her father speak while he conducted bank business. "I'm sure the price will be reasonable," he said sincerely.

Julia's father had told her that she would have days like this and not to question it. "Just go with it," he would say "and put your money in my bank." Julia grabbed her dark green knee length Maine Guide winter coat and walked to the door.

"Well. Let's go then," she said without a care in the world. Frank went outside first and as Julia locked the office door he started up the Thunderbird. He rushed back around and opened the cavernous passenger door for Julia. Frank wasn't being a gentleman. He had learned that when a woman entered a car with a short skirt on that they didn't have a lot of control of how high the skirt went up as they sat down into the car seat. So, if the gentleman was standing there holding the door open then he would likely be treated to a nice view of the woman's thighs. Frank stood on the front fender side of the door and held it open by the top of the window. Julia stepped in one leg at a time as most people do. As she sat she pulled her coat closed, this action covered her legs down to her knees. Did I ruin your view, you lousy shit? Julia did not say this out loud but she wanted to. She figured out what was happening as soon as he opened the door for her. She pressed her knees together and stared out the window. Thanks for nothing, Julia, Frank said to himself dejectedly as he closed her door.

"Just give me directions to the place as if you weren't going with me," Mr. Richards requested. "If I miss it you can tell me then."

"OK," Julia said. God, he's anal about this finding his way around stuff, Julia thought. It must be a man thing. "Make a U-turn here, turn right on Route 15, turn left at the Mobil Station, you'll go about a mile and a half where you will bear right at the sharp corner where the water comes up to the road. Don't go straight there or you'll end up on the Fish Creek Road. Continue on about a half mile and look for a big red mailbox on the right with "Walker" written on it. If you come to a sign that says Haystack Mountain School you've gone too far." Julia imparted the directions to Mr. Richards quickly as if to challenge him to get it right the first time.

"Thanks," Mr. Richards said.

Julia thought the Thunderbird was a nice car but she was happy with her blue Ford Maverick and its sneaky little 302 V-8 motor. Julia surprised a lot of the island boys with her "Mustang in disguise". Julia's father admonished her for "raising hell" like some delinquent. She was an adult and a business woman and should carry herself that way. Julia agreed with what he was saying but she was just having fun and saw no harm in it. The Peterson boy with the blue Roadrunner was the only person that complimented and appreciated her driving ability. Of course he could afford to be gracious. She lost sight of his Plymouth in the first mile of their seven mile race. To make it worse, he was sitting on his fender waiting for her at the Sunset Post Office, the agreed-upon finish line of the impromptu race. He was a cocky kid but polite. That was the day she had inadvertently destroyed the ego of a 14-year-old boy. The three of them, Julia, Peterson and his little brother were admiring her 302 motor and comparing it to Peterson's 383. The problem was she thought Peterson's little brother was a girl. "It's nice to see young girls who know about cars," she said to Samuel Peterson. He didn't take it well and stalked back to the Plymouth and sat down. Sam's brother saw the humor in it and told her not to worry about it. Julia felt terrible and would formally apologize someday.

Mr. Richards turned the right directional on and turned on to the driveway to the Walker Estate.

"That was easy," he said. "Good directions."

Julia did not respond. Mr. Richards put the big car in park and got out. Julia didn't wait for him to open her door. It was just as well because he walked down the weathered boardwalk to the dock. He didn't even glance at the house. Julia unlocked the house and went inside to turn up the heat. Normally she would have walked to the dock with her new client but it was bitterly cold and the wind was blowing off the water which made it feel much colder. Frank stood at the end of the dock. A small chain was fastened to both sides of the rail to prevent people from walking off the end into the water. The ramp and float had been taken up for the winter. It wouldn't be needed. Frank saw that there was about a foot of saltwater ice that extended over one hundred yards away from shore. That would not be a problem in March. The temperature would be warmer and a couple of good blows from the southwest would clear out the winter ice. At high tide the dock was about six feet above the water. The deck of the vessel that would be using the dock was eight feet above the water. The nautical chart at End of the Rainbow Realty showed that there was more than enough water even at low tide to accommodate Frank's needs. Perfect, Frank thought.

Frank joined Julia who was waiting for him in the foyer of the huge house.

"Would you like to look around?" Julia asked with no inflection in her voice whatsoever.

This hadn't gone well at all, Frank thought. "Sure," he said.

Julia glided from room to room explaining this and that like a professional tour guide. Frank half listened. If everything went well he wouldn't even have to go inside when he came back. Julia left her coat on. Not that it was cold inside she just didn't want to deal with Mr. Richards' advances. He followed her up the wide staircase. Even the heavy winter coat couldn't conceal the back and forth hip movements that were exaggerated by climbing stairs. I hope you enjoyed the show cause that's all there is, Julia thought to herself. I guess that is all there's going to be, Frank mused to himself. Oh well. Another time and another place Julia and things would be different, Frank told himself. Frank had been known to take what he wanted but this was business and there was more at stake here than getting laid.

"I'll take it," Mr. Richards said. "I'll need it for the entire month of March."

Julia stated that the terms would be fifteen hundred dollars for the rent and fifteen hundred dollars for the security deposit.

The deposit would be returned after an inspection of the property by Julia and all the keys returned.

"No problem," Frank said. "Where do I sign?"

"We will have to go back to my office to fill out the contract," Julia informed Mr. Richards.

"Well, let's go," he said as he went out the door. Julia turned the thermostat back to fifty-five degrees and locked the front door. Mr. Richards was not waiting at her door but it was open. Julia climbed in and they left. He didn't care about the house. He didn't listen to a thing I said. He checked out the dock and that was it. Julia was trying to figure out what Mr. Richards was up to and she didn't think it had anything to do with renting a house. Nothing happened, she reassured herself. He had every opportunity to overpower me. Julia kept telling herself that this was the dumbest thing she had ever done and hoped she would survive to tell the story. Julia was mad at herself for being in this situation. This man was a walk-in, no appointment; she did not tell anyone where she was going and broke her own rule about using her car. Stupid. Stupid. Stupid.

Julia actually let out an audible sigh of relief as Mr. Richards pulled up to her office.

"You OK?" he asked.

"Oh yeah," Julia didn't realize the sigh was that loud. "I just remembered that I had invited my parents over for supper and I haven't been to the store yet." That was actually true.

"Oh," he said. "I thought you were relieved that you were nearly done with me." Mr. Richards got out of the car before she could respond. Julia got out and unlocked the office as Mr. Richards patiently waited. Julia went in first and he followed. She sat at her desk and Mr. Richards sat in the chair next to the desk, facing her and to her right. He did not take in the view from her window. His eyes were locked onto hers and the contempt or maybe even disgust was uncomfortably apparent.

Julia paused, "I'm sorry, Mr. Richards, if I gave you the wrong impression. I've been a real estate broker for five years and I did everything today they teach you not to do," Julia explained. "In this business there are survival rules that a female and some males must follow or they could end up in a bad situation. I was afraid I had put myself in a bad situation today. You are a very charming man and this deal seemed too easy to be true. Do you understand?"

Frank thought for a second, yeah lady you certainly screwed up today. You are one lucky girl, he said to himself. Frank was preparing to leave Mr. Richards behind.

"Oh sure," he said. "I understand completely. Forget about it. As for the deal. I knew what I wanted, you had it and the price was right." Now let's get this over with before I change my mind, Frank, the real Frank, thought to himself.

Julia filled out the contract while Mr. Richards went to his car and returned with a small leather bound black briefcase. Mr. Richards popped the locks with his thumbs and took out three $1,000 stacks of ten $100 bills. Julia couldn't help but notice that there was much more money in the briefcase. Mr. Richards flashed a quick smile as Julia counted the thirty $100 bills. He signed the contract. She handed him a receipt and a carbon copy of the contract. Julia explained that on the morning of March 1st she would put the keys in an envelope with Mr. Richards' name on it in the drop box on the outside wall of her office.

"That will be fine," he acknowledged. They both stood at the same time.

Julia offered her hand, "Nice doing business with you. I hope you enjoy the Walker Estate."

Frank let her hand just hang there. Screw you bitch, he said to himself. Julia weakly let her hand drop back to her side. "Nice doing business with you too. I'll be back for my deposit," Frank said.

He turned and left the office. Julia was now doing what she should have done when that man first arrived in her office. She was shaking with fear and thanking God that she was okay.

Chapter Three

Carl was just about to let out the clutch and drive out of their hiding spot when the second truck appeared through the tree line. Same make, model and camper only this one was green and the two men in this truck looked a lot like the first two. The Plymouth's radio was playing "Sympathy for the Devil" by the Rolling Stones. Neither boy heard it. Their gazes were transfixed on the driveway as the semi-circular parking area filled with eight identical, except for a few color variations, Ford trucks with two men per truck. Someone tapped the back of his hand on Carl's door window. It startled him and his foot slipped off the clutch causing the Plymouth to lurch forward and stall. Sam heard a decidedly unfriendly laugh outside his door.

* * *

Arnold Peterson stood on the washboard of the fishing vessel *Two Boys* and then gingerly jumped to the float as Neil Jones brought the forty foot lobster boat that was rigged for scalloping squarely alongside the float. Arnold secured lines to the stern and bow cleats. Arnold was thirty-eight years old and in the physical condition of a twenty-five-year-old. He had what was once a slender and sturdy six-foot frame. The frame was still sturdy but Arnold had a little beer gut going on. He had powerful arms that came from hauling water soaked wooden lobster pots day in and day out. Arnold's own boat now has a hydraulic pot hauler but he used to haul pots by hand. His hands were massive and they were even bigger now from the permanent swelling that comes from immersing them in cold seawater every day. He had thinning brown hair and his bright blue eyes gave a hint of the quick wit and sense of humor that waited behind them. Those same eyes also hid the scars of combat in that God forsaken place that is called Korea. Arnold and Neil were happy to be back but they still had a lot of work to do. The work day was already into its thirteenth hour and they still had another hour of work before Arnold could begin the ten mile drive up the island to his less than a year old home. Arnold and Anne used to live less than a mile from where Arnold moored his boat. The house had spectacular views of the western bay but it was old and small. He wanted more room for his three boys and a nice kitchen for Anne with all the modern conveniences. He felt bad that a dishwasher was not in the budget. The budget wouldn't include a garage and workshop either. His workshop would be in the basement. Arnold was sure that the dishwasher and the garage would be a reality someday. The two men unloaded the forty-five gallons of scallops in small white pails. They had had a great day, probably the best in a couple of seasons. They had found a piece of bottom that was thick with scallops. "This is just like raking blueberries," Neil had said with a smile after they hauled the drag up for the third time.

Neil grabbed the water hose that was plumbed through the water cooled exhaust manifolds of the huge 455-cubic-inch Buick engine that powered the *Two Boys*. The water was about one hundred degrees when it reached the end of the hose. Neil washed the debris that was left inside the boat on the deck from the many dumps of the six foot wide scallop drag. The debris consisted of broken shells, moss, seaweed, small rocks, mud and a host of living or once living creatures that inhabited the bottom of Penobscot Bay. It all washed out the scuppers at the stern of this sturdy wooden vessel in a warm stream of water. Arnold placed the gas nozzle into the fuel tank and continued washing down the deck and bulkhead. The fifty gallon fuel tank took thirty-five gallons to top it off. Arnold laid the nozzle on the float and followed the fifty feet of black hose back up the ramp to the pump. Norm Wallace already had the slip made out. Thirty-five point six gallons at twenty-six cents per gallon.

This came to nine dollars and twenty-six cents. Gas for the fishing boats was always cheaper than at the gas stations in town, a benefit that the fisherman took advantage of for their cars and trucks as well as their boats. Arnold took the slip from Norm and calculated in his head that the gas cost a little over three gallons of scallops. The sun was nearly down as Neil brought the *Two Boys* back to the mooring. As Neil pulled alongside the large mooring buoy he put the boat's transmission in neutral, picked up the six foot gaff, an inch and a half diameter pole with a stainless steel hook on the end, hooked the buoy and its rope and pulled it on to the washboard in one gliding motion that looked more like a choreographed dance than the mundane working procedure that it was. Neil had done this thousands of times. Neil stepped up unto the washboard, a foot wide deck that surrounds the perimeter of the boat. Neil quickly made it to the bow and pulled the mooring chain on to the bow deck, hand over hand, and rested the chain in the bow cleat on the starboard side. He put the loop down over the T shaped post in the center of the bow. The boat was secure. Neil half walked half crawled back down the narrow washboard. He had reached the opening in the wheel house and took the last step before he stepped in. A wave rocked the boat as Neil was putting his left foot down. He was thrown off balance by the wave and his boot lost its grip on the wet washboard. He fell backwards as his arms flailed in the cold March air as he tried to regain his balance. Arnold had been tidying up the bulkhead area and getting the tools and equipment ready for the next day when he saw Neil start to fall. He jammed the scallop shucking knife that was in his right hand into his coat pocket and moved forward in an instant. He would say, if anyone asked, that it seemed like his feet were nailed to the deck. Neil's right hand grabbed the small decorative rail on the edge of the wheel house. It slowed his fall for a second and then he lost his grip. Arnold lunged towards Neil and with his right hand grabbed a fist full of

Neil's heavy insulated coat. Arnold's left hand clutched the edge of the wheel house. The only part of Neil's body that was in contact with the boat was the heel and calf of his right leg. The rest of his body was horizontal over the bay as Arnold held him in what seemed like suspended animation. Arnold pulled Neil's two hundred and twenty pound, six foot three bulk onto the deck with a violent jerk powered by all the strength he could muster. Neil managed a weak smile and said, "That would have been cold." Arnold returned the smile and said, "Come on. Let's go. Anne's making chowder out of that haddock we caught yesterday and I'm hungry." No maudlin expressions of appreciation or humble your welcomes. As far as they were concerned it didn't even happen. If you thought about the dangers of being a fisherman in Maine you wouldn't leave your home. A lot like thinking about combat, Arnold thought.

***

Carl thought about locking his door but the thought was as close as he got. Both doors were opened at the same time, from the outside. Carl was greeted by John Silveira and Sam's doorman was James O'Shea.

"Well, what do we have here? A couple of queers?" John taunted.

"That's what it looks like to me," James sneered.

"Who are you calling a queer?!" Sam said with as much fear as bravado.

"You, sweetie," James said as he pulled Sam from the car by his ear lobe.

Sam let out a yelp like a dog whose tail had been stepped on. Carl had let Sam wear his Boston Celtics ball cap and the cap fell to the ground as he was yanked from the car. O'Shea scooped up the hat and said, "Thanks for the souvenir."

Carl turned to reach for his brother as John struck Carl on the side of his face with a brutal back hand slap. The blow stunned Carl and Sam was already gone from his view. What is happening? he thought. Who are these assholes? John reached in and grabbed Carl by the crotch squeezing Carl's testicles so hard that Carl thought he would pass out. Carl did not cry out. Carl had never shown pain or discomfort when that was what the person inflicting the pain wanted. Arnold used to punish the boys with a leather belt. Carl would never give his father the satisfaction of knowing that it hurt. This actually worked to Carl's advantage. If the action had no result then there was no need for the action. Carl's reaction to the pain was to punch John as hard as he could. Carl was a strong young man and his punch caught John square on the bridge of the nose shattering the boney part of his nose and the left edge of John's right eye socket. The blood flow was instantaneous and John released his grip, staggered and fell backwards. John was struggling to remain conscious but everything was fading like he was looking into a dimly lit narrow tunnel. Carl climbed out of the car quickly and turned to help his brother when he saw a bright piercing light and for a brief instant he felt an excruciating pain at the back of his head. Carl was unconscious before he hit the ground. Sammy Sangelo clubbed Carl in the back of the head with the butt of a Mossberg 12 gauge shotgun.

Gary and Naomi were just turning onto the driveway to the Walker Estate when Naomi yelled, "Look out!" Gary instinctively slammed on the brakes causing the black 1966 Chevy II coupe to skid to a stop on the gravel inches from the chain that was suspended between the two large spruce trees at the entrance to the Walker Estate road. Ralph Costa, John and Frank's cousin, could see car headlights where he had just put up the chain. He was about 50 feet away standing in the shadows of the spruce trees that lined both sides of the narrow driveway. Costa thumbed the safety to the fire position on the Ithaca M37 Featherlight 12 gauge shotgun he was carrying.

There was still a little daylight left but it was dark on the tree-shadowed road and he could see legs in the headlights and heard the chain rattle. Costa heard a car door close and saw the headlights disappear. He put the shotgun back on safe. Costa didn't like being in the Maine woods by himself. Give him a dark alley on a deserted street in East Providence any night. That is where Costa was most comfortable. Not in these damn woods. God only knows how many bears or wolves were watching him and planning their next meal. Costa flipped the safety back to fire and left it that way.

"That chain wasn't there yesterday," Gary said to Naomi.

"Carl must have gone to your house looking for us when he found this place locked up," Naomi responded.

"Nah. He wouldn't go there," Gary said. "He knows I don't deal at my parents' house."

"Let's take a ride around the island. He'll turn up," Gary confidently told Naomi as the introduction to "You Can't Always Get What You Want" by the Rolling Stones began playing through the tinny-sounding speaker in the dashboard.

* * *

Arnold didn't notice that the interior light didn't come on when he opened the door to his truck. He did notice the click, click and then nothing when he turned the ignition key. "Hey Neil!" Arnold yelled across the parking area. "I need a jump."

"Be right there," Neil responded. "You got cables?"

"Yep," Arnold answered. What's going to happen next? Arnold wondered to himself. Arnold had no idea what else was in store for him this evening. He was going to have to confront circumstances that no father could imagine or deal with but Arnold wasn't most fathers.

***

Julia Henderson had been out of the office all day finalizing a real estate sale in Ellsworth. She did some shopping at Britt's Department Store on High Street and with her commission check firmly in hand she drove to Morang's Ford in Southwest Harbor to look at a 1970 Mach 1 Mustang. All she did was look though. She had had her blue Maverick for only six months and decided that it would not be a good financial decision to trade now. It was fun shopping though and putting the Mustang through its paces. She enjoyed making the sixty something salesman nervous when she was driving seventy miles per hour out through the winding roads in Manset. On her way home Julia stopped at the office to update the file on her latest sale. As she left she looked at the drop box. She had checked the box every day since the first of the month and the key was still there. "What was up with that guy?" she thought. She opened the box expecting the envelope to still be there and it almost startled her when she saw it was gone. She felt a shiver of anxiety come over her and then go away as quickly as it came. "Welcome back, Mr. Richards. Enjoy your stay," she said sardonically to no one there. Julia got in her car and drove home. This day is done and tomorrow will bring something new, she thought to herself. It always did but Julia would not be prepared for what this new day would bring.

***

Arnold pulled into the driveway of his modest but new ranch style home. He felt very proud that he was able to provide for his family and give them a lifestyle with no financial worries. They were by no means rich but they did not want for anything essential either. This was a big deal to people who grew up during the Great Depression. He was especially pleased that he was able to help Anne get her teaching degree—a promise he made to her eighteen years ago on their wedding night and one he vowed to himself that he would keep. "Great," Arnold said to himself. "This isn't good." Arnold noticed that Carl's car was not in the driveway. The boys, all three of them, were to be home at supper time. It was a time for families to interact, discuss their days if they liked or just be together in the same room at the same time doing something they all liked—eating Anne's good cooking. That's what strong and emotionally connected families did. This was even more important to Arnold as of late because it seemed that Carl was breaking that connection. The only exception to the tradition was during high school sports but the basketball season was over and baseball wouldn't start for another week.

Arnold was awakened from his disappointment by the smell of the haddock chowder and homemade biscuits. Yesterday he and Neil discovered a five pound haddock as they dumped the scallop drag for the fifth time that day. This was a rare and unexpected pleasure. Neil owned the boat and could have claimed the prize for himself. Neil was also a fair and sporting type of man and he appreciated having someone as reliable and hard working as Arnold aboard his boat. "I'll flip you for it," Neil said as he pulled a Kennedy half dollar from the pocket of his oilskins or foul weather gear as the US Coast Guard approved label had described them when he purchased them at the Co-op. The bright yellow outer garments they wore over their clothing were basically heavy duty rain coats and pants. They kept them dry and therefore warm. The name oilskins came from the whaling days. "Tails," Arnold called out as Neil flipped the bright silver coin into the sunlit air. The coin twirled and sparkled in the bright sun as it rose and then descended to Neil's waiting right hand. Neil slapped the half dollar onto the sleeve of his left arm. He slowly moved his hand away and smiled as he saw John Fitzgerald Kennedy's profile looking back at him.

"Tails it is," Neil called out with a laugh.

"You're kidding," Arnold said. "I never win at that game."

"Well, you did this time," Neil said with a satisfied grin on his face. Arnold promised Neil a thermos full of Anne's fish chowder and they went back to work laughing and laboring on Penobscot Bay.

***

An eighty foot eastern-rigged steel-hulled dragger out of Gloucester, Massachusetts, named *The Other Woman* was twenty miles south of Deer Isle, Maine, and would pass through the very patch of ocean the *Two Boys* had occupied earlier that day. *The Other Woman* had covered twenty-seven hundred miles of ocean since they had left the port city of Santa Marta, Colombia, South America seven days ago and the captain and his four-man crew were anxious to get home. They would make a quick stop in Deer Isle and then home to Gloucester.

***

The pleasant smells from the kitchen caused Arnold to smile but the smile quickly disappeared when Arnold saw Anne's red eyes and tear-streaked face. He didn't notice the happy welcome home he was receiving from his cute, dark haired, brown eyed, nine-year-old son, Darren.

"What's Carl done now?" Arnold calmly asked.

"I don't know. He and Sam left around three thirty to see Gary Grover. . ."

"That useless shit," Arnold interrupted. "There's no good reason for Carl to be around him."

"It's not like that," Anne explained, "Gary has Carl's catcher's mitt and Carl needed it to get ready for baseball season."

"Bullshit," Arnold responded.

33

"Arnold. Please. Darren's right behind you," Anne carefully pointed out to Arnold. Arnold turned around and saw Darren's wide eyes looking up at him. "Carl said they would be back by five and I had him take Sam along so he would come back on time," Anne explained. "I'm so worried. Something has happened. I know it."

Arnold hugged Anne. "Don't worry. I'll find them," Arnold, now calmer, promised. Arnold turned back toward the door, tussled Darren's thick dark brown hair and left. Anne watched as the taillights disappeared into the dusk.

Arnold knew Gary's reputation and figured there was more than a glove being exchanged. Arnold hadn't even taken the time to get out of his boots. He hated to see Anne so upset and wanted to get the boys home so she could stop worrying. He drove to his friend Ronnie Grover's home in Stonington. Ronnie was Gary's father. Ronnie had been a hell raiser when he was younger but nothing like Gary. Gary was just plain trouble. At least that's the way Arnold saw it. Gary's black Chevy was parked in the driveway but Carl's car wasn't there. Ronnie answered the door and was surprised to see Arnold.

"What's up, Arnie?" a puzzled Ronnie asked. Arnold hated the nickname Arnie. Ronnie, who was actually Ronald, was the only person who called him Arnie.

"I'm sorry to barge in at supper time, Ronnie," Arnold said sincerely. Arnold could smell Judy Grover's crabmeat casserole and hated to interrupt their family time. "Carl and Sam were supposed to be with Gary this afternoon and they aren't home yet."

"I'm sorry Arnie, Gary and I arrived home at the same time. Five o'clock I think," Ronnie said. "He was alone, too. I didn't ask him but I figured he had been at his girlfriend's house."

Ronnie sounded a little protective but understood Arnold's concern. Gary had been a handful for Ronnie and Judy for four years now and it was clearly a losing battle to keep him on the straight and narrow. Ronnie turned away from Arnold and yelled out, "Gary! Get your ass out here, now!"

Gary sauntered into view and started to speak, "What the hell is your prob ... Oh, hi, Mr. Peterson." Gary's attitude changed as soon as he saw Arnold and he did not make eye contact with his father. He knew he was in a world of shit for speaking to his father that way in front of Mr. Peterson.

"Do you know where Carl and Sam are?" Arnold asked. I knew Carl would bring Sam along, Gary thought to himself. I'm glad I didn't find them. Gary was convinced that one of these days Sam would narc him and Carl out to their parents.

"I haven't seen 'em," Gary said nonchalantly. Arnold just stared at Gary. Gary looked down as he shuffled his feet.

"Listen you lying little shit," Ronnie said as he addressed his son. "This is serious so stop dicking around and tell Arnie where his boys are."

Gary's thoughts were jumping back and forth between the truth and a believable lie. A believable lie needed some truth to work and Gary was a master of the art of lying.

"Carl asked to meet me in Deer Isle and bring his glove," Gary offered. Carl wanted Gary to bring a dime bag of pot too. Gary didn't think Mr. Peterson needed to know that part.

"Where?" Arnold asked.

"The Walker place," Gary volunteered. Another truthful statement. Gary was on a roll.

"You mean the Walker Estate on the Sunshine Road?" Arnold asked.

"Yeah. You know the place?" Gary asked, trying to be engaging.

"Why there? Whose idea was that?" Arnold fired back.

Gary told Arnold, "It was Carl's idea. Something about his car burning too much gas to drive all the way to Stonington." That should have sounded believable. Both responses were lies. Carl had wanted to meet at Atlantic Avenue Hardware but Gary did not want to do "business" in Stonington and it was

Gary that had suggested the Walker Estate. Gary had been there often making out with Naomi. It was a perfect spot to be and not be seen.

"Go on," Arnold prodded.

Mr. Peterson should have been a cop, Gary thought. "We got there, Naomi and me, about quarter after four but the road had been chained off," Gary truthfully explained. "We drove around looking for them but Naomi had to go home. I dropped her off and came home. Dad and I got here at the same time," Gary said as he looked for support from his father. Ronnie said nothing. Arnold was not sure what part was true and what part wasn't.

"Thanks, Ronnie," Arnold said as he turned to leave. "Do you want me to come with you?" Ronnie asked. Not meaning it and knowing he would be turned down.

"No, thanks," Arnold said as he went out the door. As the door closed, Arnold was sure he heard the sound of a big hand hitting the back of someone's scruffy-haired head. Arnold smiled.

Arnold knew where the Walker Estate was. Arnold had grown up less than a mile down the road and used to mow the lawn and tend to the horses for the Walkers. He hadn't been there since 1949 when he graduated from McKinley High School. Not since he was drafted and sent to Korea in 1951. Korea, Arnold thought. I could have gone my entire life without ever knowing where the hell that was. Arnold was awarded two Purple Hearts, a Bronze Star and two Silver Stars. All of the medals came with fancy written proclamations describing Arnold's heroism. Heroism. Arnold laughed to and at himself. All he ever did there was try to stay alive. He didn't look for action—it found him. He wasn't interested in being the hero that saved lives. He just couldn't leave anyone in need behind. It all happened so fast and 18 months later he was back in Deer Isle digging clams for a living, then as a stern man on a friend's boat and then working his own boat. Soon Korea was a bad dream and nothing more. Arnold got lost in his Korean nightmare on his way to the Walker Estate. The nightmare didn't end until he was half a mile from his home. Arnold looked at his watch. It was twenty after seven. He had lost an hour since he left Ronnie Grover's. Arnold looked in his rearview mirror and recognized the headlight and parking light combination of Carl's Roadrunner. Where did the time go? What had happened? Arnold was frightened for the first time since he returned home from war.

Chapter Four

If Arnold had seen a psychologist, the doctor would have said that Arnold might have experienced a fugue state. The doctor would have used layman's terms and told Arnold that he experienced a temporary amnesia. The doctor would have explained that less than one percent of the population actually experiences this phenomenon. The doctor would have added that people who had suffered through some traumatic event like war were more likely to experience a fugue state if some new stressful event was introduced to their daily routine. This doctor's visit would not have helped Arnold because he still wouldn't know where he went, though he remembered that he was going to the Walker Estate to look for his boys. Arnold did not remember what he had done during that hour. Carl and Sam had not said a word and they went along with his explanation of them being stuck. He had never dared to ask them and it scared him to think about what they might have seen. The newspapers and television news gave a fairly accurate description of what had happened at the Walker Estate sometime during the evening of Tuesday, March 17, 1970. "Is that what I can't remember?" a frightened and confused Arnold Peterson thought.

If Ronnie Grover had gone along with Arnold he would have seen his friend commit acts of violence that no one would believe possible. No one who hadn't been to war that is. Grover would have found it difficult to repeat what he would have seen but he would repeat it as anyone would have. Grover's story would have sounded like this:

Arnold parked at the head of the Walker's driveway, turned off the headlights and stopped the engine. Arnold saw that the chain was old but the Master lock was new and the wrapper was still on the ground. Arnold carefully stepped over the chain and walked only fifty feet when he encountered a rough-looking man holding an Ithaca 12-gauge with a magazine as long as the barely legal 19-inch barrel. Ronnie would have seen Arnold's eyes as they wildly darted from side to side like a hunted animal looking for an escape route. Ronnie would also have seen a calm come over Arnold's face as he transformed into the hunter. Ronnie would not know just by watching Arnold but Arnold was now in Korea, he was experiencing the smells, the sounds and sights of war.

Arnold felt the short and relatively dull scallop shucking knife in his pocket. It was a homemade tool that Arnold had fashioned from a stainless steel kitchen butter knife. The blade was shortened and rounded at the end. The handle was now wrapped in several feet of white adhesive tape to fatten it up to make it easier to grip. The blade did not have a very sharp edge. It was designed for prying more than cutting. It would cut but it would be a ragged cut. He had quickly put it there to empty his hand so he could keep Neil from falling into the frigid bay. Arnold was not thinking about this. His only thought was that he was grateful to have a weapon. Soon he would have a much more formidable weapon. Ralph Costa was too easy. Arnold had not been in combat for over eighteen years but he was back now and it was like he had never left. What a wonderful and dangerous place your mind can be.

Arnold picked up the Ithaca from where it had fallen. Costa's eyes were staring at the tree limbs above his face. They didn't register as an image in his brain. Costa was dead. For all Costa had known he may have been attacked by a wolf. It had happened in the blinking of an eye. His throat was ripped open much the same way a wolf would kill its prey. Costa never liked being in the woods alone. He would have been told that there are no wolves in Maine if he had known who to ask. That wouldn't make any difference to Costa now. The medical examiner would tell the investigating detectives that Costa's assailant would likely have some of Costa's blood on their clothing.

Arnold checked the action of the shotgun. There was one in the chamber and the magazine tube looked to hold eight more rounds. Arnold pressed his right thumb against the shotgun round that was visible in the magazine and pushed. It would not move. The magazine was full. He hoped it would be enough. The round in the chamber was a one ounce rifled slug. He would have to assume that the rest were also and aim accordingly. He would not have to be as careful with buck shot as the pellets spread apart quickly and would cover a wider area. A slug on the other hand had the diameter about the size of a nickel and it didn't get any bigger until it hit something.

Arnold's brain had already made the adjustment from the bladed weapon to the firearm as he carefully covered the next 300 yards under a dark and cloudy March sky.

O'Shea did not let go of Sam's earlobe until he had dragged Sam to the dining room and sat him down in one of the twenty ornate wooden antique chairs at the dining room table. Frank had already unlocked the house and turned on a few lights. The lights were mainly for the benefit of the approaching ship they were waiting for.

"Where's John?" Frank asked.

"I don't know," O'Shea answered. "I thought he was behind me with the other kid." Sammy rushed into the room still carrying the Mossberg but now the stock was broken and splintered.

"John is hurt bad!" Sammy blurted out. "There's blood everywhere!"

"What the hell happened?" Frank asked calmly as he looked at the girlish looking boy in disbelief.

"The other kid sucker punched him," Sammy said now, a little more controlled. Frank had that effect on his followers.

"Where's the kid?" Frank asked, expecting Sammy to say that the kid had run off into the woods. Frank did not have a lot of confidence in his crew. They were okay as long as there were no problems. Sammy held up the shotgun showing the broken stock to Frank.

"He won't be waking up anytime soon," Sammy bragged. "Maybe never," he added for Sam's benefit, though it was a definite possibility considering how hard Sammy had hit Carl.

The three men started for the door to check on John and the other kid. What were they doing here? Frank thought. No matter how well you plan there is always something unseen to screw things up. You can't plan for it. You just have to deal with it when it happens. Frank was trying to decide how to deal with this and that would be an easy decision as soon as he saw his brother.

"Where are you going, fool?" Frank said to O'Shea. "Stay here with the girl," Frank added before O'Shea could answer him. Frank didn't really think Sam was a girl—he was just being mean. Sam was too scared to care what Frank called him. He was scared for Carl. He couldn't imagine anyone surviving a blow to the head so hard that it shattered the stock of a gun. It now occurred to Sam that he would probably die. O'Shea turned around and threw the Celtics hat at Sam, hitting him in the face and then dropping to the floor. Sam hoped he wasn't crying. He was so scared he couldn't tell. Carl would be disappointed if Sam cried. Carl always told him to never let anyone know that they were hurting you. That was easy for Carl to say but—he would try.

It had been only two maybe three minutes since John had been unconscious. He was lying on his back and the bleeding from his nose had run down into his lungs. The lungs filled and John had drowned. The medical examiner would later point out to the investigating detectives that the non-lethal injury would not have killed John Silveira had he landed on his side or face down. Not that it would have made any difference to John. He was going to die one way or the other.

Frank could not believe what had happened. He was struggling to keep his cool. If he fell apart the rest of the crew would also. This was a trial run that would turn into several higher paying jobs if this one went smoothly. John was dead. Killed by some punk kid.

"Is the kid still alive?" Frank asked Sammy.

"Yeah. He's breathing but he's still out," Sammy said.

"Get him in the house," Frank ordered. "He and his little friend will be going on a boat ride."

"What about John and the kid's car?" Sammy asked.

"Leave John be for now," Frank said with a hint of sorrow in his voice. Frank was thinking how he was going to explain this to his sister Maria and John's wife Patty. Frank was glad his parents weren't alive. He was especially glad his father was dead but his mother wouldn't have taken this well and Frank would be to blame as this was his deal and he was responsible for everyone here. "When we're done we'll put John in the Roadrunner and I'll drive it back to Rhode Island. You will drive the truck John and I came in," Frank was on auto pilot now. Business first, grieve later. Sammy placed his broken shotgun on the hood of the Roadrunner and lifted Carl over his shoulder and did the fireman's carry to the house. Frank followed them in, watching Carl's bleeding head bob up and down as Sammy carried him up the steps to the house. Enjoy your swim, punk, Frank said to himself. Sammy plopped Carl on to the dining room table in front of Sam. Sam was crying now. Sorry, Carl, Sam thought. Frank told James and Sammy to stay with the boys.

"Get some rest. The load will be here anytime now," Frank called out to the rest of his crew. Vinnie Sliwa wouldn't hear him and Frank's words would be the last Patrick O'Halleron would hear. Arnold had silently dispatched them both with the efficiency of an emotionless machine. The perfect soldier.

Arnold had come up behind Vinnie as he was relieving himself onto some tree limbs. Without hesitation Arnold thrust the butt of the Ithaca shotgun into the base of the skull causing the brain and the brainstem to separate. This was the equivalent of turning off a light switch. No power, no light. Vinnie had essentially been turned off. He was dead before he hit the ground. The medical examiner would marvel at what a clean and simple injury Vinnie had received but would not be able to offer as to what the weapon was or how it was used. It didn't matter. Based on the rest of the deceased at the Walker Estate it would be safe to classify Vinnie's death as a homicide with the cause being blunt force trauma.

Patrick heard the sound of Vinnie's body landing on the ground and walked in his direction to see what had happened. Arnold stood in the shadow of the rear of the truck Patrick had been driving. When Patrick was close enough to touch, Arnold hit Patrick much the same way he struck Vinnie only this time the target was Patrick's larynx. The blow fractured the larynx and partially obstructed the airway. The force and the surprise of the assault caused Patrick to fall over backwards. As Patrick fell, Arnold pounced on him and at the same time bringing the shotgun barrel and fore stock against his throat. Patrick struggled briefly but Arnold pushed down with both hands as he thrust his body up bringing his knees down onto the shotgun. Patrick stopped breathing and his heart stopped a couple of minutes later. Patrick could not see his killer's face in the darkness but he did feel his warm breath on his own face. Frank's voice telling them to get some rest was the last thing his brain processed. Patrick didn't have time to wonder why he was being killed. During the autopsy the medical examiner would point out the imprint of a gun sight on Patrick O'Halleron's throat to the detective with him. The detective took several photographs and they were compared to each of the firearms collected at the Walker Estate. The mark on Patrick's neck would match the rear sight of the Ithaca shotgun. There were three sets of latent prints on the Ithaca shotgun. One latent was identified as belonging to Frank Silveira, one latent print was identified as belonging to Ralph Costa and the other latent prints belonged to an unknown person. This would remain a mystery until they had a known set of prints to compare the unknowns to. It was up to the detectives to find the person who belonged to the unknown prints. That was going to prove to be a tall order.

***

The haddock chowder had cooled and Anne was pacing the kitchen floor. Darren was watching Walter Cronkite. He had no idea why he was watching the news but he did know that things weren't well in the Peterson home. A smiling reporter was telling him about the World's Fair in Osaka, Japan, and how the last two days attendance had exceeded expectations. He listened as some unseen voice narrated the new images on the television screen. An American flag, a South Vietnamese flag, and a North Vietnamese flag were depicted. Each flag had captions next to them. Killed. Wounded. Missing. The numbers that corresponded with the American flag were much smaller than the numbers with the other two flags. Nine-year-old Darren surmised that this was a good thing. If there were flags at the Walker Estate it would now show four killed for the Slayers with one wounded and one missing for the Petersons. Those numbers were about to change.

***

Frank backed up the truck he and John arrived in parallel to the boardwalk trying to be careful not to drive onto it. Frank stopped at the dock and unloaded the lights, cables and wheeled ramps. He thought he saw lights on the horizon. Is that the load already? Frank thought. He supposed the dragger would come in with lights off but he wasn't sure. Frank worked quickly. This needed to be over soon.

Arnold stopped and was crouched like a baseball catcher. He was looking, listening and even smelling. He was looking for more enemy combatants. He could hear the gravel crunch under the weight of a person walking towards Arnold's location. Arnold gently laid the Ithaca on the ground. Arnold could see the red orange glow of the cigarette as the man took a long drag on it. Anthony "Tony" Silveira had arrived with Ralph Costa and was walking up the driveway to see how he was doing. Arnold could smell the cigarette smoke. Arnold did not move a muscle. Anthony, Frank's youngest brother and now his only living brother, would have surely seen Arnold had Arnold moved. Arnold didn't until Anthony was about to step on him. Arnold sprang straight up like a pheasant that had been flushed from his hiding place. As he rose he cradled Anthony's neck with his left forearm and grabbed Anthony's right shoulder with his left hand. Arnold grabbed a hand full of Anthony's hair and pulled him back sharply. Anthony's cigarette tumbled out of his mouth and down his coat to the ground. Arnold immediately pushed forward hard and held him tightly in this position as he backed up and laid Anthony on his back at the same time. Anthony tried to grab at Arnold's arm but didn't have the strength to lift his arms. This offensive maneuver worked flawlessly. The choking action cut off the blood flow to the brain and pinched off his wind pipe. If this procedure is done for less than ten seconds all you do is render your victim unconscious briefly and he is no worse for wear when he wakes up. If you hold this position for the forty-five seconds that Arnold did the victim will die a relatively merciful death. Anthony was only twenty-one years old. The medical examiner would look at the classic injuries associated with this type of strangulation and inform the detective that the assailant had some sort of police or military training. The possibility that he was a martial arts student would also be discussed.

Arnold's heart rate was normal, maybe even a little slower. His breathing was regular and controlled though he wasn't consciously controlling it. Arnold wasn't consciously controlling any of his actions. What had started out as father looking for his sons had turned into a search and rescue mission that required neutralizing anything or anyone that inhibited that goal with extreme prejudice.

Arnold surveyed the circular parking area. There were five more nearly identical trucks all equipped with campers. Arnold noted that the two trucks he was crouching next to were the same as the others. Arnold's eyes registered that they were new Ford F300 Camper Specials with campers in their rear bodies. The colors blended with the darkness and caused them to look the same. Arnold's brain translated the images into military vehicles. The contradiction of what he saw and what his brain told him they were was pushed away somewhere in his psyche by some other Arnold who was functioning at some other time and place over eighteen years ago. Ronnie, had he been there, would have been troubled at how easily and methodically Arnold eliminated the obstacles. Those obstacles were human lives that were being snuffed out like so many candles. Ronnie had never been in combat. He wouldn't have understood. Something inside Arnold had taken his military training and combat experience and combined it with the desire and primal need to protect his children. Discipline and the sense of duty normally controlled battlefield actions and decisions. Protecting one's children changed any need to show restraint or mercy. Arnold was on a mission that could have only one acceptable result. He could not fail. He also couldn't see Frank's truck through the two hundred feet of darkness parked by the dock. Arnold now cradled the shotgun in his arms again.

He walked low and slowly through spruce trees that lined the edge of the parking area. The tree trunks had been pruned to a height of about seven feet. The ground beneath them was continuously raked and there were only a few errant tree limbs on the ground from the last storm. This gave the area a neat and manicured look. It was not a natural look but it reminded the people from away who owned these beautiful secluded homes of the trees in their upscale neighborhoods and their city parks designed by college educated architects. This area was easy walking but the only cover it provided was shadows and darkness.

No one was looking in the trees. Frank's crew did not expect trouble. They were prepared in case some rivals heard about the load and had designs on hijacking it. Almost without exception someone would talk where they shouldn't have talked, someone would hear what they shouldn't have heard and someone would get the idea to try what they shouldn't try. That is what all their firepower was for and that is why Frank rarely told his crew where they were going and what they were doing until they were on their way. If the police arrived in the form of an organized raid, they would drop the firearms, surrender and not say a word ever until they talked to their lawyers. The first rule you learn in the business of crime, "No good can come from talking to the police." If one or two cops stumbled onto their operation then they would have some options and none of the options would be good for the unfortunate protectors of the civilized world.

Arnold approached the third vehicle in the line. He could see the glow of a cigarette that two men were apparently sharing but he did not recognize the smell that wafted from the partially rolled down windows. The men had their truck AM radio playing loud enough to hear what his sons called music. It was loud enough to cover any sounds that Arnold made as he approached. It was not music to Arnold's ears but it was familiar and it supported his resolve to find his boys. *"But if you go carrying pictures of Chair-man Mao, You ain't gonna make it with anyone an-ny-how. Don't cha know it's gonna be...alright"* Where are Carl and Sam? Arnold's thoughts begged to know. He couldn't see Carl's car yet but he could see lights on inside the house. The five trucks were between Arnold and the house and the house must be where his boys were.

Arnold was focused on the chrome door handle of the truck. The Ithaca shotgun was in his right hand and he gripped it in the firing position with his trigger finger outside the trigger guard. Costa had set the safety to the fire position and Arnold left it that way. Arnold reached for the door handle with his left hand. "Hey!" a voice shouted about ten feet in front of Arnold. Percy Adamson yelled out to the figure he saw crouching by the truck that Arthur Costigan and Carmine Palermo were sharing a joint in. Arnold quickly raised the shotgun up and grabbed the fore stock with his left hand. He did not use the sights. There was no time. He locked both elbows against his side and aimed with his arms and body. Adamson fumbled for the Colt Arms, chrome plated, .357 caliber revolver that was secured in a cowboy style holster on his right hip. He had managed to move his coat out of the way and unsnap the strap holding the revolver securely in place when he was blinded by the muzzle flash of the Ithaca shotgun. Adamson heard the deafening roar of the blast and felt the burning sensation as the slug pushed between the sixth and seventh rib fracturing them both. The slug impacted his heart and it exploded like a water balloon. The slug flattened slightly and tore out of Adamson's upper back nicking the edge of his left shoulder blade. The shoulder blade diverted the slug's trajectory slightly and its now jagged edge brought pieces of Adamson's clothing with it as it left his stunned and dying body. The slug only traveled about two and half feet when it hit Charlie Hancock in the throat and impacted his spine lodging there after severing the spinal cord. The two men had decided to join Costigan and Palermo and encourage them to share their marijuana. Instead, Adamson was lying under the neatly pruned trees dead and Hancock was just behind him face down. He felt no pain. He was just waiting to die. His nose was pushed into the moist rich soil and he could smell all the plants and creatures that had died there before him.

It would take the medical examiner two and a half days to determine, from the autopsies and what the detectives saw at the scene, that Adamson and Hancock had been killed with the same slug. Dr. Harry McSweyn, Chief Medical Examiner for the State of Maine, would smile and congratulate himself, "The Warren Commission could have used me," he told Det. Aronson as they worked together. Right. The detective thought to himself sarcastically.

Arnold worked the sliding shotgun action back and forth ejecting the empty cartridge and loading a new one. Costigan and Palermo were slow to react. The marijuana was already affecting their nervous systems and their brains were slow to process what was happening and more importantly what was about to happen. Palermo was the first to react. He reached for the Colt .45 Model 1911 semi-automatic pistol that he had placed on the dashboard of the truck earlier. Palermo had also been a soldier in Korea. Neither man knew it but both Palermo and Peterson had been treated in the same MASH unit at the same time. It was Palermo's first visit and he was treated for a bullet wound to his left thigh. It was Arnold's second visit. He had shrapnel from a mortar removed from his back. There would be no war stories or reminiscing this night or ever for that matter. Palermo's hand reached the pistol at the same time Arnold squeezed the trigger on the Ithaca for the second time over a period of less than six seconds—the time it took Arnold to stand, cycle the action on the shotgun, pull the driver's door open and point the gun at Costigan's head. The next round in line was also a slug as they all turned out to be. This had been Ralph Costa's deer hunting weapon of choice. It had a short barrel like a carbine with rifle sights and it was light and easy to carry. It had a terrible recoil but was not too bad if you were ready for it. Arnold was ready.

The slug impacted Costigan's left temple area. The top of Costigan's head blew straight up and hit the headliner of the truck as the slug smashed its way through the skull and penetrated the brain. Almost the entire brain was evacuated as the slug traveled on its way. The slug started to tumble as it exited what remained of his head and ricocheted through the rear window of the truck, striking and cracking the window of the camper before dropping into the truck body. There it rested, its job done. Detectives would find the slug a week later as they removed the gutted camper shell from the truck. The medical examiner would point out that Costigan's injury was a close contact wound due to the burns and stippling on the remaining skin and hair. "No shit, doc," Det. Aronson said. "Tell me something I don't already know." Det. Aronson had seen his share of close contact shotgun wounds in his fifteen years as a trooper and detective. Most were suicides but they all looked about the same. Dr. McSweyn just grunted and went about his work.

A large amount of Costigan landed on Palermo. He was the oldest of the crew by more than ten years. He had seen a lot and survived a lot, both in war and at home in southern New England. Palermo either didn't notice or wasn't fazed by being spattered with the brains and blood of the man he had shared a joint with just seconds earlier. Maybe it had happened before. Arnold had experienced it on more than one occasion all those years ago. Only they had shared a cigarette, not a joint.

Palermo was bringing the gun around and managed to fire it once harmlessly out the windshield before he could bring it to a more accurate aim at Arnold. Arnold had already cycled the action on the shotgun and needed only to adjust his aim a few inches before he released the third slug from the chamber of the shotgun. Just a slight squeeze of the trigger and the firing pin was released from its restraints. The pin impacted the primer at the end of the cartridge. The primer would explode igniting the gunpowder. The gunpowder would burn very rapidly in its confined location and the explosive gasses that were created would force the slug out the barrel of the shotgun at a speed of around 1,600 feet per second. The end of the shotgun barrel was only three feet from Palermo's head. It didn't take long for the slug to reach Palermo's brain. It was so fast in fact that Palermo didn't hear the gunshot nor did he see or feel the muzzle blast. The slug entered the right frontal lobe causing the skull to break away in several pieces and as it passed through the brain it took most of the right side with it. The slug then blew through the door window reducing it to little crimson-covered sparkly pieces of glass in the dirt driveway. The slug traveled another ninety-five feet as it lost its energy. It dropped and bounced on the grassy lawn a few feet from Carl's Roadrunner. The detectives would find the slug with a metal detector two days later. They would also notice the unusually wide tire impressions where the Roadrunner had been parked and driven across the lawn. Had the Roadrunner driven over the slug they could have accurately proved that the car had been there before Palermo was killed. The Roadrunner's left rear tire missed the slug by eleven inches.

Frank was startled by the first boom of a shotgun. He turned to look towards the parking area and he heard a second boom and then a more muffled but clearly large caliber gunshot and almost at the same time, a third boom. By the third shotgun blast Frank was lying flat on his belly on the dock.

Sammy Sangelo was sitting on the toilet off the kitchen near the rear of the house.

He had eaten some pizza in Portsmouth, New Hampshire, on the way to Deer Isle and it hadn't agreed with him. He was experiencing violent cramps and diarrhea. O'Shea was screaming at him to get back to the dining room. Carl had regained consciousness only to awaken to O'Shea pointing a pistol-sized double barreled sawed off 16 gauge shotgun at him. Frank had teased O'Shea, calling it a girl's gun. It was small and light. Easy to conceal and a sixteen gauge cartridge filled with number one buckshot would take care of any problems O'Shea encountered. Carl was groggy but he was alert enough to realize that Sam was okay and things were going to shit outside. Carl eased off the table and sat in the chair to Sam's left. Carl never took his eyes off O'Shea. By the look in O'Shea's eyes things weren't going to be much better inside. Sammy had heard the shots but he just couldn't bring himself to get off the toilet until his body was done emptying its bowels. Sammy convinced himself that some of the crew was just acting stupid. He sat there and hoped he was right.

Ronald Manson and his twin brother Donald Manson scrambled out of their truck and took cover at the rear of the camper. Both men had Browning 9mm pistols out and ready. John Sikes and Edward Horsley exited their truck at the same time and inched their way back, using the vehicles for cover, to where the Manson brothers were hiding—hiding from some unknown violent intruder. Arnold saw Sikes and Horsley briefly but it was too dark to see the sights on his shotgun. He wanted to wait for a better opportunity. He couldn't afford to waste a shot. As he moved toward the four men he saw Charlie Hancock's body behind Adamson's body. Arnold felt a sense of comfort in his good fortune and was happy that luck was still with him. "Luck"? The image of the twirling half dollar briefly entered his consciousness and then quickly disappeared. Arnold was not distracted.

O'Shea walked to the dining room window, trying to see what was happening. O'Shea was back lit by the lights in the dining room and made a very easy target. Arnold leaned onto the hood of Adamson's and Hancock's truck. He used the lights of the dining room to line up his front and rear sights. He slowly brought the shotgun back to the left until the sights disappeared in O'Shea's silhouette. Arnold had aimed the shotgun at what target shooters would call center mass or the center of the largest area of the target. If Arnold's aim was true that would mean the lower end of O'Shea's sternum. Arnold squeezed the trigger for the fourth time. The slug crashed through the window pane and struck O'Shea just below the right side of his rib cage. It tore through his diaphragm and knocked every last molecule of air from his lungs. It destroyed most of his liver before exiting the muscles of his back and his heavy denim coat. Carl and Sam wouldn't notice but the slug landed on the floor and skidded to a stop under Carl's chair. O'Shea fell to the floor and immediately curled into a fetal position. He couldn't catch his breath for almost a minute and by the time he did he had lost so much blood he fell unconscious. He wouldn't actually die for another ten minutes.

Carl and Sam looked at James O'Shea in horror. They had no idea what was going on and had no way of knowing that they were the reason for the carnage. Carl turned to Sam who was just staring at O'Shea while his lower lip quivered. "We've got to get out of here now," Carl said to Sam. Sam looked at Carl without speaking and stood up and started for the foyer.

Frank had just gotten to his feet and reached for the .45 Colt pistol in his shoulder holster. "Shit! Shit! Shit!" Frank said out loud to no one. When Frank's right hand found the empty holster he remembered he had given it to John when John went to check the blue Plymouth. John was only carrying a Walther .380 caliber pistol. It's a good up close weapon if you hit the right vital organ. Frank wanted him to have a harder hitting weapon just in case the occupants of the Plymouth were a problem. Frank hit the deck again when he heard the shot that felled O'Shea. Frank didn't know that Arnold could not see him or know that he was even there.

Arnold was aware that he had only five rounds left like a mother is aware of how many children she has. He was confident in his skills and he knew what he had to do. Arnold brought the shotgun to his shoulder and sighted down the barrel. The sights were barely visible but not enough to line them up properly. He would have to aim and shoot on instinct and with his body as well as his eyes. He held the shotgun firmly and charged to the rear of the truck where the four men were hiding. The Manson brothers, Sikes and Horsley had their guns ready but they weren't ready for Arnold. The end of the barrel of the shotgun eclipsed Horsley's pale face. Arnold squeezed the trigger and cycled out the old cartridge and cycled in the new cartridge. The slug went through Horsley's left eye socket, out the back of his head and grazed the left side of Donald Manson neck before disappearing into the darkness behind them. Donald Manson flinched when he was struck with the slug and accidently shot John Sikes in the right butt cheek with his 9 mm Browning. Sikes got out a half a scream when Arnold's sixth shot hit Sikes in the chest shattering his sternum, causing bone splinters to lacerate his heart, aorta, pulmonary arteries and veins, lungs, esophagus and liver. Arnold's seventh shot hit Donald Manson in the groin effectively removing his penis and right testicle. The left testicle was left hanging all alone. The slug also removed most of the prostate gland and rectum. Donald would go in and out of consciousness for an hour before he bled to death. He tried to crawl to the dock. He made it fifty feet down the boardwalk. Arnold's eighth shot was another chest shot that severed Ronald Manson's aorta from his heart. Ronald was a big man and the slug had a long way to travel. The slug exited his back, smashing a vertebra, and lodged in the lining of his heavy insulated coat.

Frank was stunned. Four booming shots in less than four seconds. He could hear Donald Manson's high pitched screams fade to sobs. The medical examiner would point out to Det. Aronson that Donald Manson would have been saved with prompt medical attention. As Det. Aronson surveyed Manson's injuries, he pointed out to the medical examiner that Manson probably would have been just as happy to have died. Dr. McSweyn looked at Det. Aronson with a puzzled expression and then glanced at Manson's lone testicle. "I suppose you're right," he said with a smirk.

Frank was starting to panic. He was talking to himself. Come on. Get a grip. How many shots? Come on. One, two-three, four, five-six-seven-eight. Eight shots. There are fourteen guys up there so there must be six left. Six guys and me. We can get through this. Frank made his way to the house.

Carl and Sam could see the muzzle blasts of the shotgun and saw the four men fall. They also saw the silhouette of the man doing the shooting. Sam said, "That guy is wearing rolled down hip boots." The kind of boots that clam diggers and fishermen wear. They fold the tops of boots down over themselves at the knee for comfort when they are not working. "I see them," Carl responded. Carl also thought he knew the man wearing them. He hoped he was right because that would mean they would be safe. He also hoped he was wrong. The boys started for the door when Sangelo screamed for them to stop. Carl and Sam turned towards Sangelo at the same time. Sangelo was holding his unzipped and unsnapped jeans up with his left hand and trying to tuck in his shirt tail with his right hand.

They both noticed that Sangelo had no gun. Like synchronized swimmers they turned together and ran for the door. Sangelo lunged for O'Shea's 16 gauge shot gun that was lying on the floor next to his body. O'Shea was not dead yet but was on his way. Sangelo's pants dropped to his knees as he stood up.

Arnold had met the boys running out as he was running in. The three stopped and looked at each for a second. Sam saw something in his father's eyes that was different. He would later describe it, much later, as vacant and lacking the warmth and caring that was normally there. Sam would also notice that those familiar eyes would be back by the time they got home.

"Go to your car," Arnold said. It was their father's voice but didn't sound the same. "Stay in the shadows," he added. They went out, obeying his commands. He went in.

Frank made his way to the kitchen windows. He could see past the kitchen and into the dining room. Why the hell does he have his pants down? Frank wondered. Frank watched as Sangelo brought up the sawed off 16 gauge shotgun as if to prepare to fire. Frank could not see what Sangelo saw. Arnold burst into the room, brought the Ithaca to bear on Sangelo and shot him in the heart. Frank jumped at the sound of the shotgun blast and saw Sangelo fall over backwards. Frank could see Arnold clearly now. Even at this distance and looking through a window he could see Arnold's piercing blue eyes. Frank would never forget those eyes. Arnold had fired the last shot but checked the action to be sure and then went back outside. Arnold carefully walked over to where the four men had been. Arnold counted three. He didn't look closer for Donald Manson. Arnold carefully laid the Ithaca onto the hood of the Manson brother's truck. The Ithaca and Arnold's soul had been as one for about ten minutes. Arnold whispered a thank-you to the piece of steel and wood and made his way to Carl's car. Frank had been watching Arnold but was unarmed and did not confront him.

A spotlight lit up the darkness and it was coming from the dock. Frank turned, ran towards the dock and tripped over Donald Manson and crashed onto the boardwalk jamming several splinters into his hands. Frank looked back at Manson. The spotlight made strange shadows on Manson's face, giving him an otherworldly look. He would be in that other world soon. "Frank. Help me," Manson said weakly. Frank got back to his feet and heard the Roadrunner start. Frank looked at the dragger as it was pulling broadside to the end of the dock. He looked back at Manson. His eyes were closed. Frank turned and ran towards the dock. He was almost there when heard a bleating sound like a lost sheep. It was Donald Manson. "Don't leave me, Frank," he called out. The two men on the deck of the vessel could not hear Manson's pleas over the din of the diesel engines at idle.

Arnold saw the broken shotgun on the hood of Carl's car. He picked it up and tossed it over the driver's side fender. He didn't see it bounce off John Silveira's head to the ground, but Carl saw it. Arnold opened the passenger door and told Sam to get in the backseat. Sam scrambled up over the seat and flopped into the back. Arnold sat down and looked straight ahead. Carl eased out the clutch and the 383 gasped but didn't die. Carl slowly drove across the lawn and towards the opening in the trees where the driveway began. Carl's gaze wandered to the shattered window of Costigan's and Palermo's truck.

"Who were they, Dad?" Carl asked with a subdued and soft voice. Like the voice he had when he was ten and his father was the only person who knew everything about anything.

A cold and matter of fact voice responded, "The enemy."

Carl depressed the clutch and put his foot on the brake and stopped at the chain. Arnold got out of the car and walked back down the driveway to where Costa's body lay. The only sound Arnold could hear was the slow, rhythmic idle of the 383 engine. Sam got on his knees and turned to look out the rear window. He could not see his father. The fear that had just started to disappear was now starting to grip Sam once again. Arnold found the key to the Master lock in the second coat pocket he checked. Arnold walked back into Sam's view and Sam slid back into the seat and began to sob.

"Stop it, Sam," Carl said sternly but with compassion. "We're OK. We're gonna be OK."

Carl was struggling to believe his own words but they did reassure Sam. Arnold unlocked the lock, dropped the chain and motioned for Carl to wait as he moved his truck. Arnold started the Ford and shifted the truck into reverse and backed onto the shoulder. As he backed up headlights flooded his rearview mirror. The bright light jogged a memory. It was that sparkling and twirling half dollar again now on its way down. This time it was a few seconds longer and then Arnold was back in his private war.

The bright headlights were coming from Osnoe Haskell's 1964 light blue Dodge Dart and the blue Dart was headed for the rear of Arnold's now stopped truck. Osnoe was so drunk that he thought Arnold's tail lights were on the paved road and started to steer for them. When some part of Osnoe's functioning brain realized that the tail lights weren't moving he jerked the Dart back into the right lane. The Dart's skinny bias plied retread tires strained and squealed as they fought to maintain traction on the black pavement. Despite Osnoe's best efforts the car continued all the way across the road and into the ditch. Osnoe was slow to register that this did not feel right but managed to steer the Dart back onto the road. He had slowed to about 15 mph and he was cussing to himself about that damn-fool truck being stopped in the middle of the road. He thought he recognized the truck as the one that belonged to Arnold Peterson. He didn't notice Carl's Roadrunner still parked on the Walker Estate driveway. Carl saw Osnoe's wide and panicked eyes as the Roadrunner's headlights lit up the inside of Osnoe's car. Carl had seen enough drunks to tell that Osnoe was shit-faced. By the time he got home, Osnoe Haskell would have no recollection of this event. Osnoe's weaving tail lights were still in view as Arnold got out of the now idling truck and walked to the chain. Arnold put the chain and lock back as Costa had left it a few hours earlier. Arnold walked back down the driveway and placed the key back in the same pocket of Costa's coat that he had removed it from. Arnold noticed Costa's wide and surprised dead eyes looking at nothing. Arnold felt nothing.

Chapter Five

Frank leaped from the end of the dock like an Olympic hurdle medalist. He had previously removed the chain but he still had to clear the edge of the hull that rose almost three feet higher than the dock. Frank had accomplished this with several inches to spare. His feet hit the slippery deck and skidded out from under him as he landed on his back. Frank got up quickly and briskly walked to the port side main deck door of the two-deck wheel house. He disappeared inside.

The two men on the deck looked at each other. One said, "I guess things aren't going to go as planned."

"That's what I was thinking," the other man responded. They had no idea.

Frank scrambled up the ladder to the helm area. Capt. Jackson Lowe, owner and captain of fishing vessel *The Other Woman*, greeted Frank, a man he was meeting for the first time, "There appears to be a problem?" it sounded more like a question than a statement of fact. It was actually an understatement of a very horrible fact.

"You have to cast off now. Make for Provincetown and we will off-load there," Frank nearly screamed his request that seemed more like an order to Capt. Lowe. Capt. Lowe gave orders on his ship. He did not take them.

"Where's my money?" Capt. Lowe asked calmly.

"Money! Screw the money. We have to get out of here," Frank blurted out incredulously. How could he worry about money at a time like this? Slow down, Frank thought to himself. He didn't see what I saw. Frank got his composure and explained that he and his crew had been ambushed and that Frank was the only survivor. Capt. Lowe listened and didn't trust Frank. Capt. Lowe didn't trust any of these thugs that he had to deal with but he did like their money and South America is a nice vacation spot in March.

"I tell you what," Capt. Lowe said calmly. "I'll prepare to head for Provincetown and you can go get my money."

"I can't go back there," Frank said with a definite sound of fear in his voice.

"You expect me to get it?" Capt. Lowe responded with a cruel smile. Frank did not say another word. He turned to leave the helm and took a portable emergency lantern from its cradle on the bulkhead. Frank stepped through the door and carefully climbed down the ladder. The ladder is actually steep metal stairs. They are called ladders on a ship. Frank wouldn't care what they were called as long as he made it back and was able to climb them again.

Frank walked carefully across the deck to the two men that he hadn't noticed when he boarded. One had a Remington 870 pump shot gun with a folding stock, rifle barrel and extended magazine. It was a lot like the Ithaca that Costa had except for the folding stock. Frank approached the man and asked to borrow the weapon. The crewman looked up at his captain in the lighted wheel house. Capt. Lowe could not hear what Frank's request to the crewman had been but he knew. Capt. Lowe nodded in the affirmative and the crewman slipped the shotgun off his shoulder and handed it to Frank.

"The safety is in the rear of the trigger guard and it's on safe," the crewman said.

"Thanks," Frank replied dejectedly as he climbed over the side and onto the dock. Frank set the weapon to fire and walked up the boardwalk.

Manson had crawled another ten feet closer to the dock. He heard Frank's footsteps and then Frank came into his view. The pain was incredible but he managed to sound elated and said, "Thanks, Frank. I knew you wouldn't leave me."

Frank ignored Manson and walked by him stepping over his legs. Manson closed his eyes and sobbed. Frank stopped at the end of the boardwalk where the semicircular parking area began. All he could hear was the big engines of *The Other*

Woman. He glanced to his left and knew that the shadowy mass on the ground next to the Manson brother's truck were the bodies of Ronald Manson, John Sikes and Ed Horsley. Frank slowly walked to his right and stopped at the truck he and John had arrived in. He listened again. Still nothing. He opened the door and was startled by the dome light. Frank froze. Nothing happened. Frank pushed the back of the seat forward and pulled out his black leather briefcase. He placed the briefcase on the seat of the truck and thumbed the locks and opened the case. Four hundred thousand dollars in one-hundred-dollar bills. In the pocket of the briefcase was a business-sized envelope stuffed with Frank's in-case-of-an-emergency identification. After tonight there would be no more Frank Silveira. Frank removed the envelope, some of the cash, closed the case and shut the truck door. Frank walked up the line of trucks. He saw Charlie Hancock's body but wasn't sure who it was as it was face down. He could tell it wasn't Anthony. He stepped over Adamson and looked into the next truck. Costigan and Palermo were unrecognizable. He prayed that neither of those bodies were Anthony. Frank couldn't remember the last time he had said a prayer and thought that God probably wouldn't recognize his voice anyway. Frank took ten more steps and stopped. In the dim light of the lantern he saw his little brother, Anthony Silveira, lying on his back. Anthony's eyes were closed and it looked like he was sleeping except that there was no sign of breathing. He checked for a pulse anyway but there was none. Frank knew that Anthony's sleep was now permanent and there was nothing more to do. Frank was relieved, almost grateful, that Anthony's body had not been in the same condition as Costigan's and Palermo's. "Thank you, God." Frank murmured. A viewing at the funeral home would be important to his family. Frank's thoughts flashed to John. Frank knew that the funeral home would be able to clean up John and make him presentable as well. Frank hoped John would be cleaned up before his sister or John's wife were called to make proper identification. "Sorry, Maria," Frank said to himself.

Frank walked briskly back to *The Other Woman*. Manson could hear and feel Frank's footsteps but he did not have the strength to open his eyes or speak. Frank did not slow or pause as he walked by Manson. See you in hell, Manson thought. Real soon too, I hope. Frank set the shotgun to safe, climbed aboard and tossed the shotgun to the crewman who he had borrowed it from.

As Frank entered the bulkhead door he heard, "You're welcome, asshole."

"Screw you," Frank said under his breath. He would be on this tub another ten hours.

Chapter Six

Arnold got back into the truck, forced the shifter into first gear and drove off. He said nothing to his boys but they followed along as he knew they would. Arnold was about a half mile from home when his headlights caught the large shiny eye of a deer standing on the shoulder of the road. Arnold saw the sparkling silver dollar again. It had landed on someone's sleeve. He could see President Kennedy's profile. Something told him he had lost but a voice told him "tails you win." The voice sounded familiar. It sounded like Sam's voice. Arnold left Korea behind but he didn't know it. He could not understand where he had been but he felt it wasn't a good place. He could smell gunpowder. The deer took two steps towards the road and Arnold swerved left. Carl followed his father's maneuver not knowing why until Sam called out, "Deer!" Both vehicles missed the deer. Arnold looked at his watch in disbelief.

They came through the door together with Carl leading the way. He glanced at his mother. The glance was long enough for her to see the bruised and swollen eye on the left side of Carl's face. Oh, Arnold. What did you do? Anne thought but would not say out loud. Carl heard his father say something about getting the car stuck on the Fish Creek Road. It was as good a story as any he thought. "Yep. I told Carl not to stop there," Sam said. Sam lied with such ease that even his father wondered if the story that had just popped into his head as he walked up the steps might be true. Arnold didn't know what was true and he was puzzled by the gunpowder smell. Carl went to the bathroom to check out his face. Nothing he could do to hide that bruise. Carl used a clean wash cloth and warm water and carefully cleaned the back of his head. There was a large bump and some dried blood there. He cleaned the area the best he could but would have to ask Sam to be sure he got it all.

Sam looked at his mother and gave her a weak smile. Sam took his seat at the dinner table that his mother had already set for supper. "Wash your hands first," she said. Sam got up and went into the bathroom. Carl looked at his brother. He didn't know what to say. He couldn't believe what had just happened. He knew if his father hadn't found them, he and Sam would be dead. But what now? What was going to happen to their father? Sam was just looking back at him. Sam wouldn't know the answers to Carl's questions.

"Look at the back of my head," Carl said. "Do you see any blood?"

Sam studied the back of Carl's head. It was wet and he could see the bruise through Carl's short blonde hair. I thought you were dead he thought.

"Nope. Look's good to me," he said in a voice that sounded like he didn't have a care in the world.

Carl looked back at Sam. "Thanks," he said. Carl left the bathroom and went to his room and closed the door. Sam washed his hands as his mother directed him to and went back to the kitchen. His father had hung up his coat in the coat closet and was on his way to the bathroom to wash up when Carl came out of his room. They stood in the narrow hall and looked at each other.

Carl was a younger version of his father. He was about the same height but had different colored hair and was not as heavy. Arnold had weighed fifteen pounds less than his oldest son at the same age. Carl hugged his father. Arnold was overwhelmed. He and Carl had not hugged since he was eight or nine years old.

"Thanks, Dad," he whispered.

"You're welcome," his father whispered back. Arnold wanted to know what happened, or did he. Arnold felt like he should cry but the tears did not come. The two arrived at the dinner table together and sat in the usual places. Anne brought out the reheated chowder and placed the bowl next to the biscuits and butter. Darren was the last at the table. He looked around at his family. Something wasn't the same but he was hungry and he soon forgot about it.

***

Frank stood in the wheel house of *The Other Woman* as they made their way south and passing between Little Spoon Island and Great Spoon Island. He had finished telling Capt. Lowe what had taken place at the off-load site. "Fifteen men killed by one man," Capt. Lowe said not quite believing what he had just heard. The man sounded credible and he had returned with the money. Capt. Lowe had met some very ruthless people in his time but never had met anyone who had murdered his own brothers for such a small amount of money. He decided that he believed Frank and expressed his condolences. Now to the business at hand.

"Where do I get rid of this load now?" he asked.

"When we get in radio range of the Cape I will set things up," Frank answered. "Just make for Provincetown."

***

Carl did not sleep well. He had the same dream three different times. Each time he woke up just as Frank Silveira was about to kill his mother and father while they slept.

***

Frank didn't have a lot of friends left and didn't want to explain what had happened in Maine. He had a friend who owned a tuna boat in Provincetown. With the assistance of the Camden marine telephone operator he was patched through to Stevie Macedo. Frank couldn't go into details but Stevie would understand.

"Stevie, this is Frank," he said with a sense of urgency.

"I'm listening," Stevie replied knowingly. "Two empty bait trucks, two Zodiacs and a car you won't need for a while," he said. "Where?" Stevie asked.

"Airport. Five a.m." Frank said.

"The sun will be coming up then," Stevie reminded Frank.

"I know," Frank replied. Stevie's line went dead. Stevie knew the drill, though this wasn't commonplace. Frank would not have called and given him eight and a half hours to set this up if he wasn't in a bad way. A friend in need is a friend indeed, Stevie thought and smiled. Things were getting boring lately anyhow. He made some calls and had it ready by midnight. Stevie would take a quick nap and set the alarm for three thirty in the morning. As he drifted off his mind thought about money.

***

Arnold was up at four in the morning. He packed his lunch and left a note thanking Anne for mixing up the ham salad. This was the normal routine and nothing had changed. He opened the coat closet to get his heavy insulated denim work coat. He pulled the coat from the hanger and as he closed the door he saw a blood smear on the door. Arnold stared and then looked at the sleeve of his coat. He hadn't seen it before now but there it was. There was dried blood on the coat and now on the door. Arnold was feeling panic. It wasn't his blood or his son's blood. Whose was it? he thought. Arnold went to the kitchen and got a bottle of Lestoil and a cleaning rag. He cleaned the door and wiped down his coat. Arnold picked up his lunch, got in the truck, tossed the rag behind the seat and drove to Stonington.

***

Capt. Lowe was able to bring *The Other Woman* within two hundred yards of the beach at Race Point. He had arrived at four thirty and Stevie and his four-man crew were already there. The conditions were perfect. It would be high tide at 6:57 this morning and the 5:49 sunrise would be diminished by the overcast sky. It took the two Zodiacs eleven trips apiece to get the bales to shore. They all worked together and got the dope off *The Other Woman* and into the two fish trucks by seven. Capt. Lowe even provided some muscle. He wanted out of here more than anyone. He had the most to lose. His home port was Gloucester so he wouldn't look too out of place at the end of Cape Cod. He just wanted to put as much distance between him and Frank as he could and as quickly as he could.

Frank put ten fifty-pound bales in Stevie's truck as payment and Stevie handed Frank the keys to his sister's 1968 light yellow Rambler station wagon.

"She won't report it stolen until tomorrow," Stevie promised.

Frank gave directions to the barn in Stowe, Vermont, where the pot was to be stored. "Here's the key to the barn door lock," Frank said. "There won't be anyone at the barn or house," Frank continued. "It's in the woods and the closest neighbors are over a half mile away. Just unload it and leave."

"What happened?" Stevie asked.

"Watch the news," is all Frank would say as he got into the Rambler and left. Frank was now Alan William Collins. He was born in Fall River, Massachusetts, on September 23, 1942, and died there September 24, 1942. Alan had been resurrected by Frank on January 5, 1970. Alan would now live as long as Frank did.

Chapter Seven

Osnoe Haskell woke with his usual headache and cotton mouth. A bowl of Wheaties with water instead of milk and a twelve ounce bottle of Rheingold beer was his first and sometimes only meal of the day. He finished his breakfast and made his way to his Dodge Dart. The Dart's bumper was against his metal trash can and the trash can was against the house. The trash can was bent where the bumper made contact. Don't remember that, Osnoe thought. He left his home on the Dow Road and made his way to the Walker Estate. Julia had told him that the renters had arrived and she wanted him to make sure everything was in order. Everything in order, he thought with contempt. I'm the caretaker not the butler. He went as she asked. After all, the Walker family paid well and Julia would always recommend him to new home owners in the area. Julia knew about Osnoe's alcoholism but helped him get work in spite of his potential to be unreliable. He should have been appreciative but he actually resented her thoughtfulness. He thought of her getting her Girl Scout merit badge for helping the drunk. He didn't need her but if she wanted to spread the wealth his way he wouldn't turn it down. His reflexes weren't very good and his right headlight and fender hit the chain as he tried to stop. "What the hell!" he yelled at no one. Osnoe saw that the chain was locked. He stepped over the chain and started down the drive. These shit heads were going to have to supply him with a key and Julia was going to pay for the damage to his car. If anyone thought he was going to walk to work they were mistaken. Osnoe noticed Ralph Costa's feet and legs first. He stood staring at the gaping hole in Costa's neck and those open eyes. He threw up on Ralph's legs, staggered backwards three steps and half walked half jogged to his car while wiping beer and Wheaties from his beard and shirt.

***

Frank sat in the yellow Rambler and stared at his sister's house. He didn't want to be the one to tell her about Anthony, John and Ralph. He couldn't sit there forever. He had to leave but couldn't until he talked to Maria. He saw Maria shake her dust mop out the front door. Frank got out of the car, climbed the four steps to the door and walked in without knocking.

"Hey, Frank. What a nice surprise," Maria said without really looking at him. She stood the mop next to the refrigerator and turned to face him. She now saw that Frank had something on his mind and it appeared to be bad.

"What's wrong?" she asked.

"Sit down," he said. They both sat at the small kitchen table together. He looked at the pictures of his two nieces and nephew on the wall next to Anthony's high school graduation picture.

"Anthony, John, Ralph and everyone else that went to Maine with me are dead," he said with no emotion. Maria was stunned. She stared at Frank, trying to absorb what he had said. She didn't know who went to Maine with Frank or the fact that they or anyone went to Maine at all.

"What do you mean 'dead'?" she asked. "What happened?"

Frank explained that they were there to pick up a load of dope from a boat. As soon as Maria heard the word "dope" she began to feel a rage well up inside her.

"How could you take Anthony with you on a deal like that!?" she screamed. "He was a good, smart kid. You and John ruined him."

Frank had expected this and just kept on talking. He told her about the two kids and the crazy man in fisherman's boots that killed everyone and left with the kids. He finished by telling Maria that she couldn't tell anyone he had been here and she couldn't repeat what he had told her. Frank placed fifteen thousand dollars on her table. Capt. Lowe wouldn't miss it, he thought.

"This is to bury the guys," he said. She stared at the money and he walked out the door. Maria recovered from the shock and ran to the door in time to see the Massachusetts registered yellow car drive away. Maria went back inside and cried.

***

Julia had just gotten to the office and was watering her African Violet when Osnoe fell through the door. She could smell him from across the small room. It was hard for her to keep from gagging and her left hand went to her mouth. Osnoe was screaming something about a body in the driveway. Julia managed to calm him a little, gave him a glass of water and listened.

Julia assured the State Police dispatcher that she would be at this number the rest of the day and Mr. Haskell would be available at his home if either were needed. Osnoe did not go straight home. He purchased two bags of Rheingold beer and then went home. "If they want to talk to me they better get here soon," he said to no one. It was twenty minutes later when Trooper Dan Gervais' 1970 Ford LTD police cruiser flew through town and past the high school at about seventy miles per hour with his single revolving blue light on the roof and siren wailing. Carl was in his Algebra II class and Sam was running the mimeograph machine for the librarian, Miss Carter. A State Police car in town was not unusual and most speculated that a car accident had occurred. Carl and Sam knew where the police were going.

"519 Orono. I'm at the scene. The road is chained off. I'll be out on foot," Trooper Gervais informed the radio dispatch.

"10-4 519," responded the dispatcher. Trooper Gervais would be alone but that is the way it was for law enforcement in rural areas. Not much worried him at six foot three inches tall and two hundred and twenty pounds. The call was given to him as a dead body in a driveway. He had been to many calls like this in his four years as a trooper. They were usually heart attacks, drunks dying of hypothermia and the occasional suicide. He found Costa's body quickly. He saw the vomit on his legs first and thought it was a drunk that passed out and died of hypothermia. That thought was short lived when he saw that Costa's throat had been cut nearly ear to ear. Trooper Gervais walked back to his police cruiser and picked up the Motorola radio microphone.

"519 Orono," he said.

"Go ahead 519," the dispatcher replied.

"Confirmed 10-49. Adult male. Start BCI," he informed the dispatcher. Trooper Gervais was calm and confident. Not excited. He used the code 10-49 rather than inform all the civilians listening to police scanners that he was at the scene of a possible homicide. Not that it would make any difference. When the electronics store sells the scanner and the local frequencies you want to monitor they also supply you with the universal Ten Code list. There's a code for everything from homicide, 10-49, to 10-3, a two syllable, two word code that replaces the three syllable two word phrase "Go ahead", though most radio users just say "Go ahead" in spite of the code.

"I'll be back out on foot checking the residence," he continued the radio broadcast.

"10-4, 519. Keep us advised," the dispatcher requested.

Dispatchers are like parents and the police officers they communicate with are like their children. They know you will "keep them advised". The three word phrase is their code for "We're worried about you. Please be careful." He acknowledged their request and hung the microphone in its small chrome cradle on the dashboard. He walked back down the driveway and stopped briefly at Costa's body.

"You look like you didn't see it coming," Gervais said to Costa. Costa didn't answer. Trooper Gervais always talked to dead bodies. He pretended they were alive. It seemed to make the unpleasant job easier. He was about to have several conversations in a very short period of time. He walked, almost strolled down the narrow winding driveway. He came to where the driveway opened into the parking area and saw several Ford trucks with campers that all looked alike with Rhode Island registration plates. The second one from him was still idling and the driver's door was open. Trooper Gervais now became very alert. To his left and at the edge of the trees he saw Vinnie Sliwa's body. He was clearly dead but Gervais could not see any injury. A few feet from Sliwa were Patrick O'Halleron and Anthony Silveira.

"I see what your problem is," he said to O'Halleron, "but you look like you're taking a nap," he said as he moved his gaze to Anthony. O'Halleron's crushed larynx and throat were obvious even to the untrained eye.

Gervais slowly made his way to the idling truck. The radio was on and he could hear the unmistakable voices of Sonny and Cher singing "The Beat Goes On". He saw two bodies on the ground. One on its back with an obvious chest wound, Percy Adamson, and one face down, Charlie Hancock. Trooper Gervais peered into the truck and glanced at the house at the same time. Stay alert. He was thinking to himself. The interior of the truck was covered with blood, skin, bone fragments, pieces of brain and strands of hair. Arthur Costigan and Carmine Palermo had met a large caliber firearm at close range. Gervais noticed three green expended Remington cartridges on the ground.

"There must be another one here. There are four of you and only three expended rounds," he said to the four dead men. "Don't worry, the crime lab crew will find it," he told them.

Gervais continued toward the house between the trucks and the tree line. I bet this is the route the killers took, he thought.

He froze in his tracks. "If I am on the same route as the killers, I'm probably screwing up foot impressions or other evidence," he admonished himself. He looked around but couldn't see anything. He moved more carefully. He noticed a truck parked with the back of the vehicle facing the water. On the boardwalk he saw Donald Manson's body.

"Don't go anywhere. I'll check on you in a minute," Gervais said only loud enough for him to hear.

On the ground next to the last truck in line he saw Edward Horsley, John Sikes and Ronald Manson.

"That's what happens when you wait for the fight to come to you. You made it too easy for 'em," Gervais told the group. He wasn't taunting them. He was just imparting some constructive criticism. Trooper Gervais was getting a feel for who these men were. Gervais wasn't one to stereotype. He had long endured the rude comments about his Franco-American heritage. In his younger days he had corrected some with his intellect and others with his fists. Now he just smiles and remembers. Each of these men was wearing similar style black leather boots associated with bikers. Their hair, beards and the tattoos that were visible also would lead one to believe that they were part of some outlaw motorcycle group. Most of them appeared to have guns but didn't seem to have had the opportunity to use them. His last clue was this location. It was a long way from their Rhode Island "club house" and there may have been some sort of crime going on here. Bikers and crime. That's not much of a stretch of the imagination, he thought. Trooper Gervais had recently investigated several burglaries in the area that involved antiques being stolen from summer homes that had been closed for the winter. He had no suspects but all indications were that organized thieves had targeted those places and the stolen property went out of state. He also knew that the local thieves didn't have the ambition to steal furniture. They would take the booze though. He had been talking to the local real estate agent about some of those burglaries. She had some of them listed for sale and had all the contact information for the owners.

He noticed that they weren't wearing their colors. Usually they wore leather or denim vests with their club name and local chapter emblazoned on the back. Some would have a symbol or initials of the important position they held within the hierarchy of the club on the front of the vest.

"You guys didn't want to attract attention while traveling, did ya?" he said. "Well, you'll soon be the talk of the town now." Trooper Gervais didn't think it took this many people to steal furniture. He also didn't think anyone would kill this many people over furniture.

He walked carefully towards the entrance of the house looking in every direction seemingly at the same time. He could see those now familiar black biker boots near the far side of the boat house. They were pointing straight up. He walked over to investigate. John Silveira's face was covered in blood and his eyes were closed. Gervais saw the Mossberg with the broken stock and guessed that he had been hit in the face with the weapon. Good guess but wrong. Gervais did not want to leave the guns he saw unattended but everyone he had seen so far was incapable of using them now. "Leave 'em like you found 'em," the crime lab detectives would always preach. This could be a dangerous proposition for a trooper working alone in an unsecured and therefore unsafe crime scene. "This is why I work six days a week, on twenty four hour call for $290 every two weeks," he laughed to himself. Law enforcement officers don't do the job for the money. They all have reasons that range from the realists who like the challenges and the occasional excitement that the job brings to the idealists who think they can make a difference in someone's life. Most do it for both reasons but none do it for the money.

Det. Ernie Manset was the first detective to arrive. He parked his unmarked car behind Trooper Gervais' vehicle.

"953 Orono. Off with 519." Det. Manset turned off the ignition before the dispatcher could respond. He wouldn't be able to hear them tell him to get back to them as soon as possible with updated information. He didn't need to. They always asked and they always had to wait. Dispatchers hate not knowing how the call that they received and assigned officers to was unfolding. They had a special affection for the officers that kept them informed even after the crisis or emergency was under control. Det. Manset was not one of those officers.

He was an extremely organized and capable detective. Nothing escaped his attention and he wrote down everything he saw. He recorded the obviously important to the seemingly innocuous. He assigned date and time to each observation in the anal retentive way that prosecutors lived for and defense attorneys dreaded. Manset prided himself on being a good detective and enjoyed proving it on the witness stand.

He surveyed the chained off entrance to the driveway. He noted the rusty chain and the shiny new lock. He was especially interested in the tire impressions. He had learned from experience that they could tell a story. He had to be careful though because they also could lead you down the wrong road. Det. Manset also enjoyed puns but there was no one here to share that one with. He noticed that there were several tire impressions turning right into the driveway and none that appeared to make a left turn entering or a right turn exiting. There actually only appeared to be four exiting vehicles. Or more accurately one and three that had been parked at the gate and had backed out. Two of the vehicles apparently hadn't expected the chain to be there as there were skid marks where someone had applied the brakes in a panic. One didn't stop quickly enough as evidenced by the broken headlight glass and light blue paint smudges on the brown rusty chain. These tire impressions appeared to be the most recent. The disturbed soil was darker than the rest. Det. Manset noted that the only set of tire impressions that appeared to have been made by a vehicle that had been on the other side of the chain and had exited the driveway were very wide like you would find on a race car. The wide tire impressions looked as though they had driven over all the others except the ones that appeared to belong to the vehicle that hit the chain. Det. Manset theorized that the wide tired vehicle had left before the chain was in place or they put it in place when they left. Ultimately he decided that he didn't know what it meant but these observations would fall under the obviously important category. He made sketches of the tire impressions to augment the photos that would be taken. He could hear a siren in the distance. Must be Larry, he thought. He can't go anywhere without that damn siren. Det. Larry Aronson couldn't go anywhere without driving ninety miles an hour so the siren was quite important to him.

Trooper Gervais was now inside the house. He had concluded that James O'Shea had been shot through the window from a long distance. At least seventy-five feet, he thought. He was puzzled by the man, Sammy Sangelo, with his pants down and with a hole in his chest. Gervais really didn't need to know but would have a little better understanding after looking at the bathroom off the kitchen. He could hear the siren of Det. Aronson's police car. "The cavalry is here," he said to Sangelo. "My job will soon be sitting in my car, keeping a log, functioning as a communication center and command post until they find a more permanent location. Well, I had some fun briefly," he said to the dead. Trooper Gervais checked every room and closet in the sprawling home looking for more victims, survivors and those responsible for the carnage. It took him nearly half an hour and he had done it with his Smith & Wesson .38 caliber revolver drawn and ready. He was sure he wouldn't need to use his gun but not that sure.

He exited the same front doorway he entered and followed his same route back by the trucks with the identical campers. He opened the door of the first camper. It was empty. Not just empty but gutted. No beds, no tables or anything one would associate with camping. An empty shell. "I wonder what the cargo was to be," Gervais pondered. He looked down the boardwalk to where Donald Manson's body lay. He didn't check on Manson. He was obviously dead and someone else with more training and more pay could deal with him. Gervais walked by Costigan's and Palermo's truck without looking at them. "Spirit In The Sky" by Norman Greenbaum was playing on their radio. As he passed by the rear of the truck the engine sputtered to a stop. Gervais thought if he could find out where they gassed up last and did the math on gas consumption at idle he could determine how long they had been here. He would mention that to the crime lab guys. He noted the date, time, the color of the truck and the license plate number in his notebook.

By the time he had made his way back up the driveway there were three detectives and their supervisor, Sergeant Robert Brubaker. Brubaker stood there chewing on a wooden match stick watching the detectives photograph and sketch the area around the body of Ralph Costa.

"Where have you been hiding?" he asked Gervais with sarcasm dripping off each word. Gervais had no military service prior to joining the State Police and a fact that Brubaker, a former lance corporal in the United States Marine Corps, liked to point out to all that would listen. Brubaker was five foot ten inches tall with a very physically fit thirty-five-year-old body. He still looked like the fine Marine fighting machine that he had been. Brubaker never mentioned that he enlisted after the Korean War and was discharged long before the Vietnam War started. His entire service to the United States of America involved being a gate guard at various gates around the Charleston Naval Shipyard in Charleston, South Carolina. Information that Gervais would appreciate knowing.

"Semper screw you," Gervais replied. This got Sgt. Brubaker's attention but he let it go. He knew his question and tone warranted the response he received. Gervais was a squared away trooper and would have been a fine Marine in Brubaker's estimation. This was a comparison that Gervais would not have appreciated. He disdained the GI Joe types.

"You're going to need more people and you should have the lab guys here," he calmly said. His voice did not hint at what he had just seen.

"Thanks, Dan, but I think we can handle this OK," Brubaker said somewhat sincerely.

"I'm sure you four can take care of that one guy just fine but there are eight vehicles to process down there along with a mansion that has more rooms than the police academy," Gervais said with authority. "Oh. Did I mention that there are fourteen more bodies scattered all over the place, too?" he said with the same sarcasm that Brubaker had just used on him.

The four detectives all looked at each other and then back at Gervais. "You're screwing with us, right, Dan?" Det. Aronson said.

"Nope," he replied. "You boys have got your hands full today." That was an understatement. It would take them two days to process the scene and another three days to complete the autopsies.

***

It seemed like a police car or some other official looking vehicle went through town every ten minutes. Julia Henderson couldn't imagine what was going on at the Walker Estate and she was going crazy not knowing. She even called the state police dispatcher back to try to get some information. They had said they couldn't release that information. What they didn't tell Julia is that they didn't know much more than she did and they were anxious to find out more themselves. Julia would have to call Caroline Walker and let her know that something dreadful had happened but wanted to wait until she actually knew something. The number and frequency of the police vehicles was also noticed by Carl and Sam. They had no questions and weren't looking forward to being questioned. They seemed like the only two at school that were oblivious to what was happening. Det. Manset would have found their nonchalant attitudes in a sea of tension and wondering as being suspicious had he been at the school that day. No one at school noticed because no one there had the insight as to what goes on in the minds of the guilty like Det. Manset did.

The VHF radio aboard the *Two Boys* chattered with descriptions of death and destruction as the fishermen got word of the police presence on the Sunshine Road. It didn't take long for the word to get out. Information was gleaned from scanners and then rebroadcast on home based VHF radios only with a reconstructed version of what the broadcasters believed was going on. Then the fishermen added their speculation as they talked to each other. Eventually it was concluded that Armageddon had begun and it started on the Sunshine Road in Deer Isle, Maine. This version of the events would not have been disputed by the fifteen dead men and Frank Silveira. It was a version that had evolved from one dead man being found in a driveway by a drunk. It was a version, like all repeated stories, that resulted in bizarre exaggerations of what really had happened. Except this time it had happened nearly the way the electronic gossipers had speculated. Arnold listened with detached interest but deep down he thought he knew what was happening and feared his boys knew more than he did.

Anne was teaching school at the Brooksville Elementary School, a job that was only supposed to be for two weeks and it turned in to a teaching position for the rest of the school year. No police cars roared by the school and there were no scanners or VHF radios located there. Anne was having a good day with her fifth grade students and she had no idea what waited for her at home on Deer Isle.

The phone rang at Osnoe's home. He didn't hear it and he wouldn't hear it for several more hours. The ten bottles of beer that Osnoe drank in the last hour and a half had done their magic. The state police needed to talk to Osnoe but that would have to wait. Julia picked up her phone on the first ring. Julia politely told the state police dispatcher that she would be happy to go to the Walker Estate and meet with Det. Aronson. Julia locked up the office, got into her Maverick and drove to the Walkers'. There were cars parked on both sides of the road making it difficult for the local traffic to get through. She parked in behind a line of police cars and walked towards the driveway entrance. She was greeted by Trooper Gervais.

"Good morning, Julia," he said genuinely glad to see her. "Thank you for coming."

"I'm happy to help, Dan. How bad is it?" she asked though the answer was obvious. She had seen a single trooper handle a three car accident on the Little Deer Isle end of the causeway that had two fatalities. This many police would seem to indicate a tragedy of epic proportions.

"I can't really say," he apologized. "It is real bad. I have never seen or even heard about anything like this."

"You must be Miss Henderson," a pleasant but professional voice behind her spoke. Julia spun on her left heel and faced the man who had addressed her.

"Det. Aronson, I presume," she said with a smile.

"You can call me Larry," he replied. Gervais rolled his eyes and included Julia's name on his scene log and noted the time. Det. Aronson quickly but neatly took notes as Julia described the man who had rented the property.

"I remember he was from Rhode Island," she said. "I have his address and phone number back at my office," she said.

Det. Aronson looked around and saw that his car was blocked in by several other cars. Sensing his predicament Julia volunteered to drive him there. Det. Aronson accepted. As they left Julia turned and waved good bye to Gervais. He smiled and waved back. Julia handled the three speed floor-shifted transmission like a pro. Det. Aronson was impressed and enjoyed watching this woman handle a car like a man.

"Here it is," she said opening the rental file. "Charles Richards, 1153 Church Ave., Warwick, Rhode Island."

Det. Aronson also took note of the phone number. Julia explained that the key was there Monday morning and gone Monday afternoon. She took him back to the Sunshine Road and dropped him off. He thanked her for her help and just like that her involvement in the biggest thing that happened in Deer Isle in her lifetime was over. Over for now. Things have a way of changing and surprising you as years go by. In Julia's case it would be many years.

Chapter Eight

Sgt. Brubaker had six detectives from his section at the scene. Sgt. Camille Martel and his five detectives came down from Aroostook and Washington Counties. The crime lab sent their four detectives from Augusta. Sgt. Brubaker was in charge and Det. Aronson would own the case long after all the extra help was gone. Sgt. Brubaker called in everyone he could get after he realized the magnitude of the situation and the lieutenant suggested the northern section should be called in. The Attorney General and State Police Col. Parker Hennesey made an appearance and offered their support and votes of confidence.

The detectives and lab personnel methodically started at the chain and lock and worked their way to Ralph Costa. Photographs were taken and diagrams drawn along with measurements being recorded. Evidence was collected, numbered and cataloged. Plaster casts were made of tire and foot impressions. The first piece of physical evidence collected was the wrapper that the Master lock came in. Ralph Costa was photographed and his position was measured and triangulated. The purpose, in theory, is to be able to put all evidence, including the body or reasonable artificial likeness of the body, back in their original location for the viewing pleasure of judges, juries and lawyers. It rarely was requested but the detectives always did it. Usually their efforts were transformed into poster size diagrams for court room presentation and that satisfied everyone's needs. Dr. McSweyn did a cursory examination to see if there were any wounds on Costa's body other than the obvious. He also looked for identification. He found none on Costa or any of the deceased. No driver's licenses. No nothing. He did find a shiny new key that fit the Master lock on the chain and a Remington 12-gauge slug.

"This is getting interesting," Det. Aronson said with a hint of mirth in his voice.

"Please don't start, Larry," Brubaker said. "I'm really not in the mood."

"No," Aronson protested. "I'm serious. This guy looks to be the first killed according to Dr. McSweyn and he still has the lock key. He also doesn't have a gun, but he has ammunition."

"We don't know what that means yet so save it until we're done," Brubaker said.

Aronson looked away and continued to take notes. The chain was unlocked, removed and packaged as evidence along with the lock and key. The live slug cartridge was packaged and labeled as evidence.

"Send in the first hearse," Brubaker called out. Dr. McSweyn had tagged Ralph Costa as "John Doe #1". Aronson bagged his hands to preserve any evidence on them and he was placed in a body bag from the medical examiner's office. The funeral home people also put him in a transport bag, placed him on a gurney, strapped him down and loaded him into the back of the hearse. The hearse left for Augusta. Two hours, ten minutes and 97 miles later Costa was in the state morgue.

The investigative team of Dr. McSweyn, Det. Aronson, Det. Manset and the two crime lab detectives moved to the body of Vinnie Sliwa. Sgt. Brubaker set up two more teams. One team would process Donald Manson's body and John Silveira's truck near the dock. The second team would process John Silveira's body. These were isolated scenes in and of themselves and Brubaker wanted to save some time. He also wanted to send some people home. He didn't like the circus feeling and he really didn't like another sergeant looking over his shoulder. The extra crew was the lieutenant's idea and somehow he managed not to show up. Probably kissing someone's ass in Augusta, he thought. The lieutenant would make it to Deer Isle in time to make the news releases. Brubaker had no doubt of that.

"Larry. Stick with the doc," Brubaker said. "You two are going to check every body before it's bagged." Brubaker wanted to make sure at least one detective saw everything. He believed that you retained much more from seeing than you do reading. Det. Larry Aronson would be the one detective.

"This is the second one who still has his eyes open and this guy doesn't even look hurt," Aronson said.

"Except that he's dead, moron," Det. Manset added.

"That will happen sometimes when death is sudden or unexpected," Dr. McSweyn explained thoughtfully.

"I would say both apply to this guy," Manset said. "It appears he was draining Mr. Winkie when his lights went out."

"Mr. Winkie," Aronson laughed. "That's not a very manly name for it."

"Well, look at the little fella," Manset said, trying to act serious. "He can barely see out past the zipper with his little eye."

"He was scared," Aronson defended.

"Jesus! Will you guys give it a rest?" Brubaker said, unable to hide his exasperation. Dr. McSweyn smiled but no one saw it. Dr. McSweyn searched Vinnie's body for some sort of injury that would cause this man's death. McSweyn and Aronson checked Vinnie from head to toe and then turned him over onto the body bag that Manset had unzipped and laid out. Vinnie's coat pockets were empty except for a box of Luden's cough drops. Aronson pulled up the back of the coat to access his pants pockets.

"Well now, Mr. Doe," Aronson said. "That's some gun your packing." A .357 caliber Colt Python revolver was in a pancake holster pushed down the back of his pants at the small of his back. Aronson removed the weapon and holster. Vinnie wasn't wearing a belt and that was as good a place as any to put a gun that you weren't planning on using. Dr. McSweyn continued to examine Vinnie, focusing on the spine. Aronson removed the revolver from the holster.

"Six inch barrel," Aronson said as he released the cylinder. "Loaded with hollow points."

"I guess he needed to have that six inch stuffed down his pants to make up for Mr. Winkie," Manset said with a grin.

"What the hell is wrong with you, Ernie?" Brubaker barked. "You seem to have some cock fixation."

"Are you a homo or something?" Manset looked at Brubaker and appeared stunned. Nothing was said for about five seconds.

"Sorry, Sarge," he said clearly humbled. "Just trying to lighten things up."

That was awkward, Aronson thought. Brubaker walked across the parking area towards Sgt. Martel and his crew who were processing John Silveira's body. I knew Ernie was a homo, Brubaker thought. Det. Ernie Manset didn't seem to have a sense of humor the rest of the day.

"I think I found the problem," Dr. McSweyn said. "There's a small abrasion at the base of his skull and feels like the skull may have separated from the spine."

"That would do the trick," Aronson said.

"It would indeed," Dr. McSweyn agreed.

"How?" Manset asked in a sullen subdued voice. Geez. I wonder what's eating him, Aronson thought.

"Blunt trauma with extreme force," Dr. McSweyn said. "As for the weapon, your guess is as good as mine right now." Dr. McSweyn bagged his hands, tagged Vinnie Sliwa as "John Doe # 2" and zipped up the body bag. He was face down. Det. Manset walked back up the drive and called out to Trooper Gervais to send down the next hearse in line. Twenty minutes later Vinnie started his trip to the morgue.

The group moved the few feet to the body of Patrick O'Halleron.

"Another obvious one, right Doc?" Aronson half said, half asked.

"Yes," Dr. McSweyn said patiently. "His larynx has been crushed and it would appear with way more force than necessary."

"Is there such a thing as too much force if you're trying to kill someone?" Aronson asked sarcastically.

"I was implying that there may have been a certain amount of anger or rage involved," Dr. McSweyn replied indignantly.

"Yeah. Maybe," Aronson said very seriously. "Or, that's how he was trained to do it."

Dr. McSweyn didn't respond. "There are some distinctive marks on his throat," Dr. McSweyn said. "I'll be able to tell better when we do the autopsy. It may help you identify the weapon used."

Aronson took more notes. They found no other injuries but they did find a Colt Gold Cup National Match .45 caliber pistol stuffed down the front of his pants and a spare clip in his left pocket.

"These guns have to be stolen," Brubaker said. He had returned to the group unnoticed.

"What was your first clue, Dick Tracy?" Manset said with a venomous tone. Det. Manset was still reeling from Sgt. Brubaker's verbal assault against his manhood and he couldn't hide his anger. "Could it be the missing serial numbers?"

Brubaker didn't know the serial numbers had been ground off. His conclusion was that the last two weapons were very nice and very expensive firearms and these guys looked like shit birds.

"Screw you, Ernie," Brubaker said dryly.

"His hands have some abrasions and the index finger on his right hand has a freshly broken and split fingernail," Dr. McSweyn said in a monotone.

"He fought for his life," Aronson said.

"Not enough," Brubaker said.

***

Frank was traveling south on Interstate 95 going by the Kimberly Avenue exit in West Haven, Connecticut. He glanced in his rear view mirror and saw a Connecticut State Police cruiser with its emergency lights flashing coming up behind him. Frank looked at the speedometer and he was doing eighty five miles per hour. "Shit." Frank said out loud. Frank started to pull over on the very narrow shoulder. The trooper sped by without giving Frank a second look. Frank admonished himself and concentrated on driving the seventy miles per hour speed limit. The six cylinder Rambler would appreciate it, too.

***

Carl and Sam walked up King's Row across from the high school where Carl's car was parked. It was lunch time and they wanted to get something to eat at Walker Pickering's store. It would have been a short walk to the store but they wanted to go for a ride. Potato chips, root beer and Slim Jims would be lunch today. Carl drove the Roadrunner down by the Mill Dam and parked on the side of the road.

"What do you think is gonna happen?" Sam asked.

"I don't know," Carl said, staring out the windshield. Carl was lost in thought. He was hit pretty hard last night but he remembered punching the bastard that was squeezing his nuts. He also realized that the guy was now dead and that he had probably killed him. Carl's hand was swollen but he didn't think it was broken.

"Why is Dad acting like nothing happened?" Sam asked.

"I don't know," Carl replied. "It was as if he kills people every day."

"No," Sam said. "I mean it's like he doesn't *know* anything happened."

"Is that possible?" Sam asked. Carl thought for a while.

"I suppose it's possible," Carl said. "I know war screws people up. Maybe that's what happened to him. Maybe he just snapped."

"Dad wasn't in a war," Sam said confidently.

"Yeah, he was, Sam," Carl said with equal confidence. "He was a war hero."

"What do you mean?" Sam asked. "I found his medals in the bottom drawer of Mom's jewelry box," Carl said.

"Medals!?" Sam said excitedly. "You mean like the Medal of Honor?" Sam asked in disbelief.

"No," Carl said, "but close. Two of them were Silver Stars."

"Is a Silver Star a big deal?" Sam asked.

"They only give those to heroes, Sam," Carl said with pride.

"Wow," Sam said. "Why were you in Mom's jewelry box?"

Carl looked at his brother.

"Never mind," he said, "I was just snooping."

Carl was looking for money but he wouldn't tell Sam that. "Do you think the state police will know we were there?" Sam asked.

"If they talk to that drunk, Osnoe Haskell, they will," Carl said.

"Who's that?" Sam asked.

"He's the guy that almost ran into Dad's truck last night," Carl said.

"Oh yeah, but did you see him?" Sam said. "He looked like a zombie."

"Let's hope he didn't recognize us," Carl said.

"Or remembers at all," Sam replied. "Carl?" Sam said, with fear in his voice.

"What now?" Carl asked.

"I think your Celtics hat is still there," Sam said.

***

Dr. McSweyn and Aronson bagged O'Halleron's hands and rolled him onto the body bag and zipped it up. He was now "John Doe # 3".

"Larry. You and doc need to go over to Sgt. Martel's scene so they can bag the guy and get him out of here," Brubaker said.

"Yeah sure, Sarge," Aronson said as he walked away. Brubaker and Manset just stared at each other for a few seconds.

"Go up and tell them to send down another hearse," Brubaker said.

Manset turned away and walked up the driveway. Manset was about thirty feet away when Brubaker called out, "Tell them to send down two hearses."

Manset just raised his right hand in acknowledgement.

"Must have hit a nerve," Brubaker thought.

***

"Anne's fish chowder is great," Neil said.

"Thanks. It is good. I almost ate it all but I remembered my promise," Arnold said. I can remember that, Arnold thought, why can't I remember finding Carl and Sam?

"I was wondering why you were eating ham salad," Neil said with a laugh.

"Anne made this too and it's better than you can get at Miller's in Bangor," Arnold said. The boat was relatively quiet as the two men sat and ate. Just the melodic idle of the 455 Buick and the nearly calm water lapping against the hull. The VHF radio blared.

"Two hearses have already left and Vern said two more just went down," the unidentified voice said. Arnold and Neil looked at each other both with their own thoughts but their thoughts were entirely different.

"Do you suppose it was locals?" Neil asked not really expecting an informative answer. Arnold didn't respond. He was watching that twirling and sparkling Kennedy half dollar again. This time it landed in gravel in front of a truck with Rhode Island plates. "Arnold," Neil repeated.

"What?" his word stumbled out as he came out of his daydream. "Oh. I doubt it," Arnold said. "If it were locals we would have known by now."

"I suppose you're right," Neil agreed. "That Henderson girl will rent those summer homes to anyone who has the money."

"That's a fact," Arnold said. "And anyone who wanted a vacation here this time of year can't be all that stable either."

Neil laughed, got up and put the *Two Boys* in gear as Arnold prepared the drag for another pass across the ocean bottom. They're from Rhode Island, Arnold thought but didn't know why. Another scallop dragger approached the *Two Boys* from the west.

***

"You left it there?!" Carl said dumbfounded. Sam was scared now. He felt the fear building and tears trying to force their way out.

"I didn't mean to," he said trying to remain calm. "That guy that pulled me out of the car grabbed it when it fell off my head and threw it at me in the house," Sam continued. "I didn't dare pick it up and everything happened so fast when we left."

"We're screwed now," Carl said with the voice of resignation.

"It's not like your name is on it," Sam reassured Carl.

"My initials are under the sweatband in the hat," he calmly explained. "All they have to do is pull the edge down and it's right there for all the world to see. CP."

"Maybe they won't see it," Sam said.

"They're state troopers, Sam," Carl said. "Of course they'll find it."

***

"What have we here?" Aronson asked while trying to sound like Sherlock Holmes.

Sgt. Martel looked at Dr. McSweyn and asked, "How do you put up with this guy?" Martel's French accent wasn't thick but it was noticeable. It was a surreal moment for Dr. McSweyn. He had been a linguist for the Army Intelligence during World War II and he found it quite amusing that he was standing between two men, one American trying to sound English and another with a French-Canadian heritage trying to sound American.

"It makes the day go by quicker," McSweyn said with a smile. Sgt. Martel shrugged his shoulders and explained that "John Doe #4" had severe injury to his face but no other obvious wounds. There was a loaded Mossberg 12-gauge shotgun with a broken stock found near the body and a loaded .380 caliber Walther pistol in his right coat pocket. Sgt. Martel pointed to the tire impressions in the grass to the left of the body and said, "Very wide tires and here not that long ago. The grass is still compressed." "We have photographed, measured and documented everything," he continued. "We haven't packaged the shotgun yet. It's over there in front of the boathouse," Sgt. Martel said while gesturing to a location behind Aronson.

"It's unloaded now." Dr. McSweyn did a cursory survey of John Silveira's body and agreed with Sgt. Martel's assessment. A complete autopsy would be more revealing. Dr. McSweyn located a loaded Colt .45 caliber pistol pushed down the back of his pants with no holster.

"This guy had at least two weapons maybe three and he still didn't stand a chance," Sgt. Martel said.

"Whoever did this knew what they were doing," Brubaker said. "And he was invisible to them."

"You thinking supernatural, Sarge?" Aronson asked, sounding deadly serious. Brubaker did not respond. Dr. McSweyn smiled again. Silveira's face was very bloody and the injury was hard to see. Dr. McSweyn examined the shotgun stock. There was no visible blood but that wasn't always conclusive. A facial injury involving the nose usually caused instant blood flow at the time of impact. He guessed by the extent of the damage to the gun's stock that it must have hit a much harder surface than this man's face. He kept his guesses to himself though. He didn't want the detectives to think he didn't have all the answers. The answers would come after a thorough autopsy of the body and a laboratory examination of the shotgun. John Silveira was tagged and the body bag zipped. The detectives carried the body to the hearse rather than take a chance that the hearse would destroy any evidence that might still lay undiscovered on the lawn. Silveira's hearse and O'Halleron's hearse left at the same time.

"Four down and eleven to go," Aronson said in a fake cheery voice. Brubaker threw him a cold stare but didn't bother to say anything. Aronson and Dr. McSweyn left for the body on the boardwalk. Aronson started whistling the tune, "Hi ho, Hi ho, It's off to work we go." Brubaker followed them and just looked at the ground as he walked. I should send him to Kittery to work the truck scales but he's such a good detective, Brubaker thought with a sigh.

Det. Larry Aronson was the best Brubaker had seen in a long time. He was a natural and gifted investigator that saw everything and had a knack for obtaining confessions. He actually got more confessions after the Supreme Court's 1966 *Miranda* decision. He would read a suspect his "rights" as it's now called—the constitutional rights that all citizens are guaranteed but it seemed only a select group ever needed. That group would be the law breakers. They were the same people who usually didn't know why they had rights or where the rights came from. All they knew was that the cops had to read their rights to them when they were arrested. If they didn't, the cops screwed up and the criminal would get away with whatever law they had broken. At least that is what they thought. The *Miranda* decision only said that a law enforcement officer had to read a suspect his rights if they questioned the person while in police custody. The *Miranda* decision resulted in having the police try to talk a suspect out of talking to the police. This would seem to be counterproductive to anyone of average intelligence. Larry had a way of reading a suspect his rights so that when he was done they would insist on talking to him. He didn't leave anything out and he didn't add anything. Larry would just do it in a way that made the suspect feel that Larry was really looking out for him and that Larry didn't care what he had to say because Larry already had the crime and the suspect's involvement figured out. They were magical moments that Brubaker never tired of watching. He did get very tired of his childish jokes and irreverent observations at death scenes. Brubaker resigned himself to the fact that the investigative magician came with a junior high school sense of humor.

Brubaker noticed the Ithaca 12-gauge shotgun lying on the hood of one of the trucks.

"What's the story with that gun?" Brubaker directed to no one in particular.

"That weapon could probably tell quite a story," Sgt. Martel responded.

"That's where it was when I got here and it's empty. We already photographed it, and the serial number has been filed off. The other two firearms we found were missing serial numbers," Brubaker said. "They'll be hard to trace."

Sgt. Martel had three detectives working on Donald Manson and the truck parked near him. They appeared to be finished and were waiting for the medical examiner. Aronson looked at the three bodies lying on the ground next to one of the trucks. They were so close to each other that it looked like someone had just tossed one onto the other. The blood trail from this group to Manson was hard to miss. It was evident that he had crawled about fifty feet down the boardwalk and had stopped three times. There were also foot impressions in the blood. These impressions indicated that someone had walked from the house to the dock, returned to a truck and then back to the dock where they just disappeared at the end. The foot impressions had no tread, just smooth leather, like the boots the dead men were wearing.

"You know that some cold-blooded bastard walked by this guy at least three times and probably didn't even look at him," Brubaker said.

"Probably one of the killers," Sgt. Martel responded.

"Why do you think there was more than one?" Dr. McSweyn asked.

"You think one person could do all this?" Sgt. Martel said incredulously.

"Why not?" Dr. McSweyn asked, like a college professor trying to inspire a debate among his students. Sgt. Martel ignored the offer.

"There is nothing to indicate that more than one person is responsible for all this but there seems to be sufficient evidence to show that at least two people survived this," Aronson said.

"You'll get no argument from me," Dr. McSweyn said with a smile.

"At least one left by sea and possibly another by land," Aronson added.

"Thank you very much, Paul Revere," Sgt. Martel said. Everyone laughed. Finally, Aronson thought. Aronson believed that a loose detective worked better and accomplished more than a stressed out, up-tight detective. Aronson believed it was his secondary mission to loosen people up so they could all perform their primary mission better.

"Is his wound where I think it is Doc?" Brubaker asked.

"Yes, if you're referring to his genitals," Dr. McSweyn said.

"Jesus," was all Brubaker said as he walked away.

"All I can say now is that he lived a while," Dr. McSweyn said. "I'll tell you more after the autopsy." Donald Manson was tagged as "John Doe # 5" and placed in a body bag.

"What about the truck?" Aronson asked.

"Above the driver's side visor was a Rhode Island driver's license issued to a John Silveira of Warwick," Sgt. Martel said. "And above the passenger side visor was a Rhode Island license issued to a Charles Richards of Warwick. The gutted camper had roller ramps and several extension cords in it. They match the lights, cords and roller ramps on the dock."

"You know, Sarge," Aronson said. "I've only read about this but it looks like a marijuana smuggling operation."

"I've never heard of that happening north of Florida," Sgt. Martel said.

"Oh sure, Sarge," Aronson said. "The feds have made busts of small boats like sailboats and fishing boats all the way up as far as Boston."

"Any end up like this?" Sgt. Martel asked.

"No," Aronson said using all his will power to keep from telling Sgt. Martel what an incredibly stupid question that was. Sgt. Martel got the message though.

"My guys and I are done," Sgt. Martel said. "You want me to send another hearse down when I leave?"

"Uh ... I ... uh, no," Aronson stammered. "He's not going anywhere and there's a lot of evidence between him and the driveway."

"OK. Good luck," Sgt. Martel said as he and his five detectives left.

"Hey, Ernie," Sgt. Brubaker said. "There's a guy down there with his cock shot off."

Det. Manset didn't turn around or acknowledge the statement. He continued to diagram and photograph the body of Anthony Silveira. Even with the thin beard he looked like a boy barely fifteen. He didn't look dead and he couldn't see any obvious injury. He looked like he was asleep. He had no identification and he was carrying a Smith & Wesson Chief's Special five shot, two inch barreled revolver.

"If they're done, I could use Aronson and the Doc up here," Manset said.

"I'll check," Brubaker said. Sgt. Brubaker met Sgt. Martel and his crew on their way out. "Thanks, Camille," Brubaker said. "You guys were a big help."

"Are you sure you don't need us anymore?" Sgt. Martel asked.

"I don't think so," Brubaker said. "Besides Fort Kent is a long way away and you should get back before the shit hits the fan in the County," Brubaker added.

"Yeah, I guess you're right," Sgt. Martel said as he walked towards the driveway. "See ya, Ernie," Sgt. Martel said.

Det. Manset turned around. "Thanks, guys," he said. "Watch out for the moose."

"Looks like smugglers, Sarge." Aronson said. "But something obviously went to shit."

"You mean drug smugglers?" Brubaker asked.

"That would be my guess," Aronson said. "This equipment on the dock was for a boat they were expecting. The boat clearly arrived or "bloody boot guy" jumped into the ocean."

"I can see that as an option considering what his other choice was," Brubaker said. Aronson smiled. "Ernie wants you two at his body," Brubaker added.

"Oh yeah. I almost forgot," Aronson said. "Martel's crew found an ID that matches the name of the guy that the real estate lady rented this place to."

"Make sure whatever IDs we find are documented as to location they were found and in which vehicle," Brubaker said. "When you are sure that's been done, package them and give them to the doc."

"None of these guys have had identification on them so far and we may find them in the trucks they came in," Brubaker added.

"10-4, Sarge," Aronson said.

"Watcha got, Ernie?" a light hearted Aronson asked.

"I don't know why this guy is dead," Manset said.

Dr. McSweyn kneeled down and opened his left eye lid. "See those red specks on the whites of his eyes?" Dr. McSweyn asked. Both men bent over for a closer look.

"Petechiae," Manset said.

"Asphyxiation," Aronson chimed in.

"I've taught you boys well," Dr. McSweyn said with a smile.

"I guess I'm the only one that doesn't know what's going on," Brubaker said.

"When someone is being choked and suffocated the blood vessels in the eyes will burst causing these little red specks," Aronson eagerly explained.

Sgt. Brubaker looked at Dr. McSweyn for confirmation.

"That's it in a nutshell," Dr. McSweyn said.

"I don't see any bruising or damage like that other guy, John Doe # 3," Aronson said.

"I'll be able to tell you better once I open him up," Dr. McSweyn said.

"That's what you always say, Doc," Aronson quipped.

"Well, Larry, because that's the way it is."

Det. Manset had already searched, photographed and documented Anthony Silveira's body and the relatively small area, far from his Rhode Island home, where he took his last breath. Only four of the sixteen men at the Walker Estate even had any idea why they were being killed and only one of them survived. The rest didn't know why and never would. Dr. McSweyn made the process final. He tagged Anthony as "John Doe # 6" and zipped the body bag.

***

Ronnie Grover's 36-foot Webber Cove fiberglass lobster boat was new last summer and even with its scallop gear it was a handsome boat. Ronnie had named it *Dream Girl* and everyone thought the name was a pet name for his wife Judy. Even Judy thought so. Only two people actually knew who it was named for, Ronnie and his girlfriend, who happened to be married, and she wasn't going to tell anyone. *Dream Girl* pulled up alongside the *Two Boys* just as Arnold and Neil had dumped its drag on the cleaning table.

"Hey Ronnie," Neil said. "What's up?"

"Have you guys been listening to the VHF?" Ronnie's stern man, Billy Wallace, asked.

"Yeah," Neil answered. "I wonder who they are."

"Isn't that where your boys were supposed to be last night?" Ronnie asked now, looking at Arnold.

"That's where they were supposed to meet your son," Arnold said with a hint of annoyance in his voice. "But it was chained off just like Gary said," Arnold added.

"Well, where were they?" Ronnie asked, sounding like Perry Mason. Neil and Billy watched the exchange and had no idea where it was going but it didn't sound good to either man. Arnold got his composure. Why is Ronnie questioning me? Arnold thought. My boys had nothing to do with what happened at the Walker Estate. Arnold told Ronnie that he had driven down to Sunshine and Stinson's Neck and then headed back to check the beach at Oak Point when he found the boys stuck on the soft shoulder on the Fish Creek Road. Arnold knew that this story was not true and he couldn't explain to himself or anybody else why he felt compelled to tell it. Ronnie accepted Arnold's story and the four men talked about scalloping and then went their separate ways.

"That was queer," Neil said.

"That's Ronnie," Arnold said.

***

Aronson looked at Brubaker to get his attention and then walked up the driveway and stopped near where "John Doe # 2" was found. This was Aronson's signal that he needed to talk about something he probably screwed up. Brubaker was very familiar with this signal.

"What now?" Brubaker asked as he approached Aronson.

"I think I pissed off Sgt. Martel," Arnold said.

"Go on," Brubaker said impatiently.

"Well, Sarge. I was explaining my theory about drug smugglers and he asked some questions that maybe I thought might have been, you know, stupid," Aronson explained.

"What did you say to Martel?" a now worried Brubaker asked.

Martel was a lot tighter with the lieutenant than Brubaker was and he didn't need any extra grief. Brubaker could create plenty of grief on his own.

"I didn't say anything bad," Aronson said. "It just may have been the way I said it. Well anyway. As soon as the discussion was over he said he and his guys were leaving."

"Is that it?" Brubaker asked expecting much worse.

"Yeah," he said. "I had already told Sgt. Martel that after they finished with the guy on the dock that I was cutting his crew loose," Brubaker said, clearly relieved.

"Oh, great. That's a relief," Aronson said sincerely.

"But," Brubaker said in a very serious tone. "Watch your frigging attitude from now on."

"Yes sir," Aronson said sheepishly.

Det. Manset had heard the last part of the conversation between Brubaker and Aronson and when Aronson joined him he asked, "What was that about?"

"My mouth," he said.

"Surprise! Surprise!" Manset laughed. "Let's process this truck and get it out of here so we can get to the two headless horsemen," Manset said.

"Right behind you," Aronson said already in a better mood. Aronson liked just about everything, but he liked working the best.

Det. Aronson and Det. Manset went from bumper to bumper when they searched the truck. The camper looked new and the interior was completely gutted like the rest. Above the driver's side visor was a Rhode Island license issued to Vinnie Sliwa of Fiskeville, Rhode Island, and one hundred fifty three dollars rolled up and held together with a rubber band. Above the passenger side visor was a Rhode Island license issued to Patrick O'Halleron of West Warwick, Rhode Island. There were cigarette butts and roaches in the ash tray and the key was in the ignition. This truck only had 1,257 miles showing on the odometer. You could barely notice the new vehicle smell through the cigarette and pot smoke. All the trucks were registered to Narragansett Drywall and Paint of Warwick, Rhode Island.

"Did you notice that some of these guys are Irish, some are Portuguese and others are Italian?" Aronson asked.

"Yeah. So?" Manset responded.

"Well I don't know about Rhode Island but in Boston the Irish and Italians don't actually get along," Aronson said.

"I don't think these guys are a crime family," Manset said. "They all probably grew up in the same neighborhood and have been friends and outlaws together since," Manset continued. "I'm sure we'll find brothers and cousins in this group too."

"I wouldn't want to be the one that has to give the death message if we're talking multiple deaths from one family," Aronson said.

"If these guys are bikers they'll have one hell of a funeral," Manset said. "The only gang that does it better are the police."

"Amen to that," Aronson said.

The crime lab detectives dusted for prints after Aronson and Manset completed their search. The driver's licenses would be helpful in the identification of the victims if they weren't fakes but fingerprints would be conclusive.

"Hey, Sarge," Aronson called out. "We're ready for the first tow truck."

They didn't have to wait long. The closest tow truck was about two miles away at the Porter Brothers Mobil station and garage. They had heard Trooper Gervais call for their tow truck on the police scanner in the office and were ready to go when the dispatcher called on the phone. They couldn't decide who was going to go if the call came in and the call always came in. They were the best and most reliable tow truck service on the island. They knew they would get the call. They both would go of course. They finally decided to close the place down for the time it took to get whatever vehicle that needed towing hooked up and on its way to who knows where. Probably the state police barracks in Orono or maybe even the state police headquarters in Augusta. They both could go to the Walker Estate but one would have to stay behind while the other made the longer trip. They would flip a coin to decide who stayed at the garage and who would drive the tow truck. Bruce won the coin toss and David would stay behind. Trooper Gervais waved them through and noted their arrival on the scene log. Bruce and David Porter felt like the privileged few that get invited to movie premiers or boat launches. Actually they were the first civilians to be allowed in to the scene since Osnoe Haskell discovered Ralph Costa's body. The brothers took it all in. The detectives, the crime lab investigators and the seven, no David pointed, eight trucks with campers. These were nice, brand new heavy duty Ford pickups just like their two tow trucks.

"Is that a body bag near the eighth truck?" Bruce asked.

"It sure looks like it," David replied.

"My God!" Bruce exclaimed. "They've already had five hearses in and out of here and there's still another body."

Bruce carefully backed the F300 four wheel drive Ford truck with its Holmes tow truck body around to the first truck and camper in line. The two men got out and went about the business of hooking up the truck. They would barely look at the detectives that were watching them work but they were memorizing every little detail they saw. Bruce noted that the four wheel drive front wheel hubs were in the free position and he asked Det. Aronson to make sure the four wheel drive selection lever was in neutral. Bruce knew from previous experiences with the state police that you didn't enter, touch or adjust anything on a vehicle without permission.

"Take it to the Orono barracks, please," Sgt. Brubaker requested. "They'll be expecting you and will show you where to park it."

"Yes sir," Bruce replied as if he were speaking to a military boot camp drill instructor.

"Oh," Brubaker added. "I would appreciate it if you didn't discuss what you've seen here with anyone."

This time Bruce and David said "yes sir" and in unison. They both lied of course. Bruce and David would take turns calling friends, relatives and anyone else that would listen to what they had seen at the Walker Estate. Everyone on the island knew that but the state police evidently didn't. Trooper Gervais knew it too and warned Sgt. Brubaker but Brubaker called the Porter brothers anyway. The tow truck easily pulled out of the driveway with a load that was bigger than itself. Bruce made the slow left turn onto the Sunshine Road being careful not to hit any of the police vehicles. Trooper Gervais helped guide them out. David looked out the passenger window and smiled at the news reporters with their cameras. Bruce would be upset the next day when it was David's smiling toothy grin on the front page of the Bangor Daily News and not his. He was happy that their business name and phone number showed up clearly on the door. All of eastern Maine would know who they were. Thanks to the AP wire service all of North America would know who to call for a tow truck if they needed a vehicle removed from the scene of a mass murder. David's mother thought his smile was inappropriate considering the circumstances and told him so.

Chapter Nine

"Where do you want to start?" Manset said as he peered into the truck where the remains of Palermo and Costigan sat in a bloody cocoon that used to be a new and clean cab of a Ford pickup.

"May I make a suggestion?" Det. Stan Sawyer from the crime lab asked.

"Sure Stan. What do ya think?" Aronson asked.

"Why don't we seal the cab with a tarp and take the whole vehicle to Augusta, bodies and all?" Sawyer said. "The medical examiner and the crime lab guys can work on it together in a controlled indoor environment."

"Just what I was about to suggest," Lieutenant Paul Sampson said. Lt Sampson had come out of nowhere. He had a terrible habit of just walking up without being seen. He would usually just stand there and listen before making some profound statement or taking credit for someone's idea he had overheard, as he did on this occasion. Fortunately he did not come at a time when his name was used in the same sentence as asshole or moron—which was often the case. Lt Sampson was a 23-year State Police veteran. He could have retired three years ago and most were wondering why he hadn't. He had served in Germany in the final months of the fighting as a Second Lieutenant in the Army. He was what soldiers called a 90-day wonder. A 90-day wonder was created when you took a college graduate fresh from boot camp, put him through officer's school in 90 days and sent him into a war zone to lead seasoned war veterans. It is rumored that this actually had good results on occasion but no one can verify it. Most if not all of these 90-day wonders are as green as an early spring blade of grass but think they are General George S. Patton. Lt. Sampson fit the mold perfectly. He was 5 foot 9 with the physique and ego of Barney Fife. He did see combat in

Germany and was nearly killed. He wasn't wounded. It was just that three men in his unit had plotted his murder. They would have been successful if not for another soldier overhearing the plot. The soldier sympathized with the three conspirators—he just didn't think murder was the way to go about things. The three soldiers served time in Leavenworth, the whistle blower was killed in combat on the last official day of hostilities in Europe, and Sampson was transferred to the Pentagon as an aide to a one star general. Sampson didn't re-enlist as he was encouraged not to. In return the one star wrote a glowing recommendation for Sampson to be presented to whoever Sampson went to for employment in the civilian world. The chief of the Maine State Police, Col. Robert Marx, had no reason to doubt the sincerity of the Army general's letter and accepted Sampson as a recruit for the State Police Academy. This same letter was alluded to during promotion interviews. Sgt. Brubaker now had the most incompetent, pompous and overbearing supervisor that any reasonable man would dread to have for a supervisor. Thanks to that one star Army general and his letter of lies. If Sgt. Brubaker knew any of this he would be even more depressed than he already was.

"Make it happen, Sgt. Brubaker," Lt Sampson said in a tone that would have made Julius Caesar proud. He then turned and walked back the way he had come to address the media and inform them how his investigation was going.

"I've got an idea, Sarge," Aronson said. "Just give me a few minutes."

Sgt. Brubaker just looked at Aronson and nodded his approval. He didn't care what Aronson's idea was. Sgt. Brubaker was just thinking how nice Sampson would look in one of these body bags. Aronson jogged by the sauntering Sampson, talked briefly with Trooper Gervais and then drove to the Porter brothers' garage.

"Hello, detective," David said. "What can I do for you?"

"Trooper Gervais told me that you have a car trailer you use for your antique car," Aronson said.

"Yes. That's right," David replied.

"Can you bring it up to the Walker Estate with your other tow truck?"

"Certainly!" was David's enthusiastic reply. "But I'll have to get my younger brother, Cecil, to run the station while I'm gone."

"How long will that take?" Aronson asked.

"I'll be there with the trailer in thirty minutes," David promised. Aronson drove into town and stopped at the Barter Lumber Company and purchased a tarp, some rope and duct tape. Forty five minutes later the truck and its passengers were loaded and on their way to Augusta. The tarp protected the evidence and bodies and it also kept Joe Citizen from being traumatized by the condition of the two men. Trooper Gervais guided David Porter and his load along with Crime Lab Detective Stan Sawyer out of the driveway and onto the Sunshine Road. David Porter got his smiling face on television this time as his mini parade served as the back drop for Lt. Sampson's interview by the television news. Bruce Porter would be beside himself for missing this one. David's smile would be short lived. The tarp had partially blown off while traveling on Route 1 in Searsport. Det. Sawyer had to use his police siren to get David to stop so they could cover the cab of the truck back up. David had not been prepared for the grizzly sight and nearly fainted. He ran back to the relative safety of his tow truck as Det. Sawyer secured the tarp. The rest of the trip was uneventful. Neither David nor Det. Sawyer knew that they had attracted some attention while Det. Sawyer was trying to get David to stop. There were a handful of motorists and pedestrians in Searsport who had witnessed the event. One of them was a prominent member of the Maine House of Representatives. He was not happy about what he had witnessed in the cab of the truck and told the governor so. The governor was less impressed and expressed his dismay to the chief of the state police. The state police chief, contacted the captain in charge of the Bureau of Criminal Investigations who contacted the Orono barracks and requested that Lt. Sampson call him immediately. Trooper Gervais got the radio call and informed Sampson. Trooper Gervais suggested that he might be able to use the phone at the Porter brothers' garage. Sampson made the phone call in front of seventeen-year-old Cecil Porter. He managed only a few "yes sirs" but mainly listened to his Captain's tirade. Sampson returned shaken and red faced and stomped down the driveway and confronted Sgt. Brubaker. The initial confrontation was as far as Sampson got. Sgt. Brubaker politely and skillfully stopped the lieutenant from berating him in front of the detectives and with the skills of corporate negotiator turned the tables on Sampson. Sgt. Brubaker pointed out to Sampson that he had concurred with Det. Stanley's suggestion and was about to suggest it himself. He reminded Lt. Sampson that he watched and supervised the covering and sealing of the cab and at no time did he point out any deficiencies during the process. Finally, Sgt Brubaker told Sampson that he did not ask for Sgt. Brubaker's input during the decision-making process and simply told him to make it happen. Sgt. Brubaker did all this without raising his voice or using any disrespectful words or phrases. Sgt. Brubaker finished by saying, "The buck stops with you, Lieutenant. You left me out of this when it was being decided and you can leave me out of it now."

Lt. Sampson was even more red faced than when he started but there was nothing in what Sgt. Brubaker said he could dispute nor was there anything in the way he said it that would suggest any kind of disrespect. Sampson left. No one spoke until at least two minutes after Sampson was out of sight. They just stood there and watched him walk away. Sgt. Brubaker wished he smoked. This seemed like such a good time for a cigarette. Aronson was the first to speak but all he could say was, "Holy shit."

Brubaker's response was for them all to get back to work. Even Manset was impressed but he still loathed Brubaker. This had all taken place before the truck and the two bodies arrived at their destination. Shit rolls downhill fast in state government and even faster in the State Police. Sgt. Brubaker's detectives were very appreciative that none of the shit got on them.

Chapter Ten

The last class of the day was over and Sam waited at the front steps of the school for Carl. Carl came out the door with Belinda Graham. Belinda was a classmate of Carl's and every guy in school would have been happy just to talk with her let alone date her. Carl and Belinda weren't a couple but when Belinda decided she needed a male companion Carl was her choice. Carl would not listen to anyone who said he had wasted the last three years since she moved here from Colorado by waiting for her to make the next step to a relationship. She wasn't going to make that step with anyone who was a Maine native. It was common knowledge that as soon as she graduated from high school it was back to Colorado where her father still lived. It wasn't that she didn't like her stepfather and she got along very well with her mother. The problem was that Colorado was her home and she missed her father. Carl's problem was that he was a gentleman and treated her as special as she thought she was. She was a straight A student and got all the lead roles in Drama Club and it looked like she was going to be the valedictorian. It was too close to call between her and Eugene Stinson and it might even get down to the last day of school to see who would be first and who would finish second. It wasn't her brain that first caught Carl's and every other male's eye. She was 5-7, 120 pounds. She had black hair, a Snow White complexion and sparkling blue eyes. Her 120 pounds was distributed so well that girls would watch her walk by and a few male school teachers couldn't keep their eyes to themselves. She wasn't using Carl, as some thought. She liked him and in another place, Colorado, and another time they would certainly have been an item. She never asked for anything from Carl but friendship and a date for the prom. He was always happy to oblige. Except for today. Belinda had asked for a ride home and a ride home meant driving by the

Walker Estate while the police were still there. Carl wanted to say no. He couldn't come up with an excuse. He probably could have but didn't really try. Carl and Belinda walked up King Row to Carl's car with Sam tagging along behind. "Get in back, Sam," Carl said. Sam looked at Carl as if there was any place else he would be allowed to sit. Carl tried to engage Belinda in conversation about graduation as they approached the Walker Estate in hopes of just driving by without much fanfare. Carl would experience no such luck. Trooper Gervais was in the road stopping traffic which only consisted of Carl's car and a fuel truck coming from the other direction. As Carl brought his car to a stop a hearse pulled out of the Walker Estate driveway.

"This is so unbelievable," Belinda said.

"I know," Carl said.

"It is so scary to think there might be a murderer around here," she said.

"It might not be murder," Carl said weakly.

"What else could it be?" she asked.

"I don't know," Carl said. "It could be a lot of things. You know like carbon monoxide poisoning."

"Carl. Let's go," Sam said.

Carl took his gaze from Belinda and saw Trooper Gervais waving him forward. Det. Manset was standing by the road as Carl released the clutch and drove forward. Manset watched the car as it drove by and stared at the passengers. He was especially interested in the rear tires of Carl's Roadrunner. Manset scribbled the plate number of Carl's car in his notebook as it drove out of sight.

"Did you see the tires on that car?" Det. Manset asked Trooper Gervais.

"Yeah. What about 'em?" Trooper Gervais asked.

"They look the same size as tire impressions here and down there in the grass," Det. Manset said.

114

"Ernie. Nearly every car and truck owned by someone under the age of thirty on this island has tires just like those," Trooper Gervais said dismissively.

"Yeah. Maybe so but that's the first one I've seen," Det. Manset said.

"When things wind down you can come down here with me and we'll hold a road check," Trooper Gervais said. "You'll fill a notebook with plate numbers."

"I'll take you up on that, Dan," Det. Manset said as he walked back down the driveway.

Percy Adamson had just left in the hearse. He was known as "John Doe # 7". The detectives, Dr. McSweyn and the remaining crime lab detectives methodically processed the rest of the bodies under the watchful eye of Sgt. Brubaker. The day was getting long but they carefully examined each body and the surrounding area. Charlie Hancock, Ronald Manson, Ed Horsley and John Sikes. They each left in separate hearses with their new John Doe designations. Donald Manson wasn't forgotten and was carried out to a waiting hearse as a beautiful red-orange sun was setting. Sgt. Brubaker had decided to finish the bodies in the house and the evidence in their immediate area and then shut down for the evening. Everyone would be fresh tomorrow to search the rest of the trucks. The Assistant Attorney General stated that the detectives would need a search warrant for the house after the medical examiner removed the bodies because it was still rented until the end of the month. He also stated that there were no exigent circumstances that would allow the search of the vehicles without a warrant. He said that they should be okay on the vehicles they had already searched but the detectives should attempt to obtain warrants for each of the vehicles including the ones they already searched. The truck with the two bodies was the medical examiner's until the bodies were removed and they would need a warrant for that vehicle too. It appeared that the trucks were all registered to the same company and officers of that company were certainly going to be suspects. Sgt. Brubaker informed the group of the prosecutor's requests. Det. Manset started to question why they needed warrants for the vehicles when the Carroll Doctrine clearly allowed for warrantless searches of vehicles because they were mobile and easily concealed.

Sgt. Brubaker stopped him with a look and said, "I'm sure the AAG is aware of a Supreme Court decision as old as that one, Ernie, and he still wants us to do it his way. And why is that? Everyone," Brubaker said while raising his arms like an orchestra conductor. "Because we investigate and they prosecute," they all said in unison.

"They don't tell us how to investigate and we don't tell them how to prosecute," they all finished together.

"Very good, class," Brubaker said with a smile.

"Asshole," Ernie said only loud enough for himself to hear. This was good news for the detectives but it was bad news for Trooper Gervais. Trooper Gervais' work week was six days on and two off and he was on call 24 hours a day. The scene needed overnight security and it would be Trooper Gervais' assignment to perform that security. Sgt. Brubaker gave him the bad news.

"Run into town and call your wife," Brubaker said.

"I'd rather face the guy who killed those men than make that call," Gervais said wistfully.

"Is there a problem, Dan?" Brubaker asked sincerely.

"No. No problem yet," Gervais said. "Elaine's mom and dad are coming over for supper and she wanted me there."

"Sorry, Dan," Brubaker said.

"Don't be," Gervais responded. "I was thinking about shooting myself so I wouldn't have to go," Gervais said with a smile. "But this is almost as good."

"Give me the scene log," Brubaker said. "I'll take care of scene security until you get back."

Trooper Gervais drove to the Porter brothers' garage to use the phone but Cecil had closed early. He continued into town and saw Julia Henderson's car was still at her office. Trooper Gervais stopped and went in. Julia was just about to turn off the lights to leave when he walked through the door.

"Hi, handsome," Julia said with her usual flirty smile. "What can I do for you?"

"Hi Julia. I need to use your phone if you don't mind," he said.

"Of course. Go right ahead," Julia said. "Is it police business?" she asked. "Should I leave you alone?"

"No. Not police business," he said. "Much worse. I have to call my wife."

Julia laughed and Trooper Gervais dialed the phone. "Hi," he said. "Yep .... nope ... but ... I'm sorry ... yes, ... I know .... yes dear ... I don't know ... probably tomorrow, too." Elaine hung up the phone with such force that Julia could hear the phone hit the receiver.

"I love you too," Gervais said sarcastically after the line went dead.

"I didn't mean to eavesdrop but I take it from your side of the conversation that you won't be home for supper," Julia said.

"You could be a detective," Gervais said wryly.

"I know," Julia said with indignant confidence and then broke into a laugh. "I'm making a macaroni and cheese casserole for supper," she said. "I'll bring you some and some coffee later."

"You don't have to but I won't turn it down," Gervais said.

"Good then," she said. "I'll see you around 6:30."

"Thanks a million, Julia," Gervais said.

"I've got to get back." "Bye Dan," Julia said sweetly.

"See ya," Gervais said as he went out the door.

"How'd your wife take the news, Dan?" Brubaker asked, already knowing the answer.

"Actually she took it a lot worse than I thought she would," Gervais responded with a laugh.

"Sorry," Brubaker said.

"Don't be," Gervais said cheerfully. "The lovely Miss Henderson is bringing me supper this evening," Gervais said with a smile. "Coffee too."

"No dessert Gervais," Brubaker said in a very stern voice. "Understand?"

"Whatever do you mean Sarge?" Gervais said with a sly smile.

"You know exactly what I mean," Brubaker barked. "You will not get your horn scraped while guarding my homicide scene."

"Sarge. I have no such intention. She's bringing me supper. Nothing more," Gervais said with sincere honesty.

"That better be all that goes on," a calmer Brubaker said. Brubaker knew that some troopers strayed on occasion but he was reasonably confident that Gervais wouldn't risk screwing up a case of this magnitude. It was just that if Julia Henderson was willing it would be hard for any man to say no.

"I know what you're thinking, Sarge," Gervais said reassuringly. "She's not a slut. She's just a flirt."

"The two sometimes go together, Dan," Brubaker said. "Watch yourself."

***

Carl stayed at Belinda's as long as he could. Sam was even invited in. The two boys left and this time Sam was back in front.

"What's going to happen Carl?" Sam asked.

"I – Don't – Know!" Carl yelled. The outburst was so loud and so unexpected that it startled Sam into silence. Carl was as lost as Sam was and he had no answers. Carl was also dealing with the fear of being arrested for killing that man. He knew it was self-defense but he was still scared. Trooper Gervais waved as they drove by and the hearse carrying James O'Shea pulled out behind them. Carl stopped the Roadrunner at the stop sign and waited for a granite truck to go by. He looked in the rear view mirror and gazed at the black Cadillac hearse. He could see the glass shatter, heard the shot gun blast and saw the man the others called "Pig" stagger to the floor, curl into a ball and die. He wondered if the hearse behind him carried James "Pig" O'Shea. The hearse sounded the horn once and Carl turned right onto Route 15. The hearse pulled out behind them just as Arnold was coming by the Settler's Cemetery. Arnold caught up with the hearse by the Congregational Church and the three vehicles traveled together for the next three miles. Carl turned into his driveway and O'Shea continued by in his black Cadillac hearse. Arnold pulled in behind his boys. Carl was scared, Sam was confused and Arnold had a good day scalloping and he wondered what Ronnie's problem was today. Arnold also wondered what the half dollar spinning in front of his mind's eye was all about.

***

"So. I see we saved the best for last," Brubaker said. Sammy Sangelo was lying on his back on the dining room floor. He looked like he was floating in a giant congealed pool of blood. He had an obvious chest wound. There was a sawed off 16 gauge shotgun on the floor a few feet from the man. The pool of blood didn't quite make it to the gun.

"Why are his pants down?" Aronson asked no one.

"Gervais said it looked like someone had the shits real bad in the bathroom off the kitchen," Manset said.

"He must have been in the bathroom when the shooting started," Brubaker surmised.

"Either the shooting didn't take long or this guy had to go real bad," Manset said.

"He had to go real bad," Aronson said walking back into the room. "There's shit on the bowl, the seat and the floor."

"Let's get this done," Brubaker said. "Let's do it by the numbers like the rest of them. I know you're tired so take your time," Brubaker added.

Sammy Sangelo received the same thoughtful attention and methodical detective work the rest of them did. Brubaker was very proud of his crew. They were irreverent, to be sure, but the dark humor they engaged in was a survival tactic, no different than emergency room nurses and doctors. It was what they did and said to get through the day and keep their sanity from teetering over the edge. Sangelo was the last of the fifteen to leave and Det. Aronson was the last detective to leave. Det. Aronson had several more hours of work ahead of him preparing the affidavits for the search warrants. Sgt. Brubaker wanted to meet back at the Walker Estate by 9:30 a.m. It was 6:15 p.m. and Trooper Gervais was in his cruiser at the head of the driveway waiting for supper.

***

The Petersons sat down to Anne's homemade spaghetti and meatballs. Anne had worked all day at school, came home and prepared a meal every bit as good as what you could pay for at an Italian restaurant. She had made the sauce on Monday afternoon. It simmered to perfection. They were going to have it Tuesday but the surprise haddock had to be cooked first. This was Carl's favorite meal but he barely touched it. Carl twirled the limp strands of spaghetti without purpose. He pushed a meatball from one side of the plate to the other as the rest of his family ate as if it were their last meal. Carl nibbled on a butter soaked piece of garlic bread. Darren was saying something to Sam but he couldn't hear what was being said. All Carl could hear were shotgun blasts and screams of wounded dying men. He saw the blood gush from "ball squeezer's" nose. He saw the blood ooze through the clothing of the man who had been shot through the window. He saw the vacant but alert look in his father's eyes as they met in the foyer of the Walker Estate. He heard that last deafening shotgun blast as he and Sam scrambled down the steps and walked through the shadows as their father had instructed. He wondered at the time who shot who. Was that what was troubling him, he thought? Was he more worried about losing his father than what his father had done? What he had done for Carl and Sam? It wasn't really fair to include Sam in this guilt. That was it, he realized. Carl felt guilty for the whole turn of events. If he hadn't wanted to buy pot from Gary they would not have been at the Walker Estate. Sam wouldn't have had to come along and their father would not have had to rescue them and those men could have done what they came to do and left with their lives. Guilt. It was his fault, Carl thought. Without realizing it Carl had hoisted a whole meatball above his dinner plate. The meatball tumbled from the fork and landed in the middle of the spaghetti and sauce. The impact caused sauce to splatter outwards in several directions at once. Thick crimson drops of sauce landed on the yellow-white garlic bread. Several drops landed on Sam's bare forearm but the majority of the splatter hit Carl squarely in the center of his white T-shirt. Darren snickered. Carl's mother jumped from the table to get a wet cloth to clean the mess. Sam began to wipe the spots from his arm with a white paper napkin. Arnold was staring at Carl's T-shirt without speaking. Arnold was now looking at that twirling, sparkling Kennedy half dollar as gravity slowly brought it down. Down to its place of rest for all to see. To see what the decision would be. Win or lose. It landed in the mass of blood and human tissue that used to be Arthur Costigan's head. The image jolted Arnold back to reality. But that seemed so real Arnold thought.

"That goes in your mouth, son," Arnold said with humor. "Not everywhere else."

"Sorry, Dad," Carl said with way too much emotion. The words were like silver threads in his mind trying to line his terrible dark cloud. Carl meant them with all his heart. Sorry, Dad, he thought over and over. There didn't seem to be enough silver thread to line the growing dark cloud.

Chapter Eleven

Arnold was wondering why, after all these years, his combat flashbacks were coming back. They weren't the same as the flashbacks he had in the three years that followed his return home from Korea. Those, he recalled, always involved hand to hand combat with Korean and sometimes Chinese soldiers. They all ended with a North Korean soldier thrusting a bayonet so deep into his chest that he felt it pierce the muscle and skin of his back as it came out the other side. This is when he always sat straight up in bed with Anne trying to comfort him. When he would regain his senses he could see smoke, he could smell decaying bodies and he could hear men screaming and distant gunfire. Then as quickly as it came over him it was gone. The only indication of what had happened was perspiration leaking from every pore of his body and a frightened and comforting wife.

"The same nightmare?" Anne would ask in a soft soothing voice as she held Arnold close.

"Yep," was always his reply. "I'm okay now. Sorry I scared you."

Arnold never told her the details of the nightmare. He rarely went back to sleep afterwards—he just stared at the ceiling and listened to Anne's soft breathing as she slept.

Arnold just realized something. His combat flashbacks always occurred when he slept. He had them anywhere and anytime now and that half dollar was always there. The only thing Arnold smelled during these new flashbacks was the familiar smells of the ocean and gunpowder. He heard nothing and the images were snapshots rather than complete scenes. They seemed so real he thought. Arnold was troubled most about his missing hour that night and what his boys knew about that missing hour. Arnold looked at Sam and he seemed like the same Sam. Carefree and curious to a fault. He looked at

Carl. He had become somewhat distant the last year or so but now he looked totally lost and even scared. Arnold was now becoming scared of what he didn't know and what he knew Carl did know.

***

Frank Silveira was driving somewhere south of Rocky Mount and north of Elm City in North Carolina. He was very tired and had stopped in New Jersey to take a nap. He hadn't been there thirty minutes when a New Jersey trooper tapped his night stick on his window. His new identification worked and Frank "Alan W. Collins" Silveira was sent on his way with a caution against resting in a rest area. Interstate 95 came and went. The further south Frank traveled the more time he spent on Route 301. Frank laughed to himself as he passed billboards on Route 301 informing him that he was entering Klan country. The signs were in disrepair but they were still legible for all the free world to see. Frank was a criminal, a chauvinist and a murderer but he didn't consider himself a racist. He would do business with blacks. Their money was green just like his. He didn't like the idea of his niece dating a black boy in high school last year and against his sister's wishes he explained his dismay to the young man. Frank's justification was to keep the family's Portuguese heritage pure. He would have felt the same way had she been dating an Italian, an Irishman or a Jew he had later said. Frank didn't think of himself as a racist but his actions and words indicated that he was—with no exceptions. If Oscar Washington thinks it's hard to get a drywall contract in Warwick he ought to try to run a business down here, Frank thought. These damn signs are probably the reason that the old neighborhood is filling up with blacks, Frank thought angrily. Frank would add the Klan to his mental list of groups to hate. Frank's attention was drawn to the road ahead. He had just crested over a slight rise in the road. He blinked and then focused on two sets of headlights. A tractor trailer rig was in his lane passing a Greyhound bus. Frank slammed on the brakes of his borrowed Rambler.

***

"Sorry I'm late," Julia said with a pretty smile as she slid into the passenger seat. She was wearing tight black corduroy slacks and a heavy white sweater. She cradled the aluminum foil covered dish in her hands as she wiggled her butt across the seat. "The news saved this story for last and I wanted to see you on TV," she said as she shut the car door.

"Was I on?" Trooper Gervais asked.

"Yeah. You were," Julia informed him. "They had your name spelled correctly too."

"Great," he said. "That should help my kids remember they have a dad and what I look like."

"It's not that bad," Julia said with a laugh. "Is it?" she added.

"No, but it seems like it sometimes," he said.

Julia handed him the covered dish, "I hope you like it," she said.

"I'd eat the asshole out of a dead skunk right about now," Trooper Gervais said sincerely. "I'm sure I'll love it."

"Jesus! Gross!" Julia squealed. Trooper Gervais smiled and started eating. He didn't say another word until the macaroni and cheese, the apple sauce and the slice of homemade bread with butter was gone. Julia filled him in on what the news had to say and expressed her curiosity about whether or not Mr. Richards was among the dead.

"This was great," he said.

"Thank you." Julia took the plate and utensils from Trooper Gervais and reached for the door handle.

"Just like that. Feed me and run?" he asked.

"No silly," she said. "I left the coffee thermos in my car.

"Oh," he smiled.

Julia returned with the coffee and poured Trooper Gervais a cup full of hot coffee that was already sweetened, with whole milk added.

"How did you know how I liked it?" he lied. Trooper Gervais liked his coffee black but this would do.

"I didn't," she said. "That's the way I like it."

They both laughed and for the next fifteen minutes they discussed everything from real estate prices to the dead men from Rhode Island.

"I've got to go," Julia said. "I hope the night goes by fast for you."

"Thanks again, Julia," Trooper Gervais said.

"You're welcome, Dan. Good night," she said as she got out of Trooper Gervais' police cruiser. Trooper Gervais was not ashamed of what he was thinking. Sgt. Brubaker was right to worry, Trooper Gervais thought. Julia Henderson could make a man forget about what was right and moral. Well, not forget, more like not care, he laughed to himself. Just then Trooper Gervais was jumped from his carnal thoughts by the sound of Julia's Maverick lighting up the rear drive wheel in a cloud of blue smoke and high pitched squeal. She sounded her horn as she sped past. Trooper Gervais just smiled as her tail lights disappeared quickly from view.

***

The Greyhound bus driver looked in his mirror just in time to see the tail lights of Frank's car bounce back on to the road from the narrow shoulder of Route 301. Frank let off the brakes and steered for the shoulder as the bus driver hit his brakes. The truck driver, who hadn't slept since he left Austin, Texas, swerved back in front of the bus, missing it by inches. The rear corner of the trailer knocked the driver's side mirror from Frank's Rambler as they passed each other. Frank spent the next couple of miles plotting the death of the unknown trucker. Frank probably wouldn't consider the fact that the truck driver was living off amphetamines to make his delivery on time as a reasonable excuse. After all, the Slayers manufactured and sold amphetamines to anyone who would buy them, including truck drivers. If anyone would mention this irony to Frank he would explain that was different. He wouldn't be able to explain why it was different and people didn't argue with Frank often.

The night was long for Frank, Trooper Gervais and Carl. Frank got back on I-95 in Kenly, North Carolina, and drove a little more than two hours and stopped in Florence, South Carolina. Frank needed a bed and checked into a motel. He kicked off his boots and was asleep a moment after his head hit the pillow. Frank dreamed but he wouldn't remember them in the morning. Carl also had dreams during his restless sleep. Carl's dream would be the same as the one he had the night before and would continue to have for the next six months. Carl's dream always woke him up and he remembered every detail. Trooper Gervais didn't sleep thanks to Julia Henderson's sweet hot coffee. He didn't dream but he had vivid and explicit thoughts about Julia that turned into a fantasy that he reenacted over and over again until the sun came up.

Sgt. Brubaker and his crew arrived at 9:30 a.m. and Det. Aronson showed up with the approved search warrants at 10:05 a.m. It took most of the day to process the trucks and campers. The detectives seized all the papers and identification they found in each truck. Lifts of latent prints were taken, photographs taken and hair and blood samples removed. The trucks were all towed to the barracks in Orono. The Porter brothers didn't get all the trips but got the majority of them. Bruce told his mother they had made a killing off the murders. She scolded him for being so thoughtless and greedy. The following Sunday she had him stand up in front of the entire congregation and beg Jesus for forgiveness.

Stevie Macedo's sister's car was found in long-term parking at the Miami International Airport on June 27, 1970. Frank had wiped down the entire car trying to eliminate any of his fingerprints. It didn't matter. The insurance company had settled and Macedo's sister actually got more for it than she had paid. The local police showed up, confirmed it was stolen and called a tow truck. Frank had left two one hundred dollar bills in the registration envelope to pay for the damage to the door and mirror. That would turn out to be a bonus for the towing company. Frank Silveira aka Charles Richards aka Alan Collins disappeared. His brothers, his cousin Ralph and his twelve friends had their funerals and were buried after the largest motorcycle mourning ride in the history of the United States. It rivaled a similar funeral held for a New York City police officer a few weeks later. Maria cursed Frank on a daily basis for a long time.

Det. Larry Aronson typed, cataloged, filed and stored reports, photographs and evidence. Det. Aronson and Det. Manset made several trips to Warwick, Rhode Island. The cooperation they received from friends and family of the dead men was minimal. The families wanted to help but they knew very little. The friends wanted the deaths avenged but had an aversion to helping the police no matter what the reason. They did learn that Frank Silveira had gone on the doomed trip but had not returned. That was the only piece of credible information they received on the Rhode Island trips and they already knew about Frank before they left Maine. Sgt. Brubaker was not impressed. Sgt. Brubaker was less impressed with the fact they had accounted for sixteen men but had evidence of at least seventeen men having been at the Walker Estate. "Who belonged to the unidentified set of prints on the *Ithaca* and where was that person now?" That was the question asked at every meeting on the case. The question asker always was greeted with blank expressions and shrugging shoulders.

Frank Silveira was indicted on fifteen counts of felony murder and several firearms violations by a Hancock County Grand Jury thanks to Julia Henderson's identification of Charlie Richards and fingerprints in the truck and on the *Ithaca*. The Bureau of Narcotics and Dangerous Drugs didn't doubt that the Walker Estate was supposed to be an off-load site but they had no evidence that would sustain an indictment. Maria planned to tell the detectives what Frank had told her but she didn't. As angry as she was with Frank right now he was the only brother she had left and maybe someday he could come home. She knew that was probably not true but a sister can hope.

Det. Manset and Trooper Gervais held three road checks over a two week period in April. A road check usually consists of two police officers setting up a road block on a safe stretch of roadway. The purpose is to check every car that travels the road. The most common use for the road check is to inspect vehicles for safety defects. This road check was to identify and document vehicles with wide tires. Det. Manset's intent was to find the same vehicle that had been at the Walker Estate at the time of the murders and Trooper Gervais was intent on showing Det. Manset that it was going to be like finding a needle in a haystack. They documented thirty six cars and trucks with similar width tires as the tire impressions that were found at the Walker Estate. Carl's Roadrunner was among them. Det. Manset's report was thorough. Every car was photographed, tires measured, registration and Vehicle Identification Numbers recorded. Det. Manset noted names, dates of births, and addresses of each person in each car. Det. Manset was pleased with their efforts and as an added bonus Trooper Gervais cited three unlicensed drivers and arrested one man for an outstanding warrant for failing to pay a traffic fine. The problem was that they had found the needle but they just didn't know it.

All the firearms recovered at the Walker Estate were identified as being stolen on August 10, 1969 from a gun dealer in West Haven, Connecticut. Unfortunately the dealer could not have them back as they were evidence. A Maine Superior Court judge ruled against the gun dealer's petition to have his firearms returned and allow the State of Maine to use photographs of the firearms instead. West Haven PD didn't care who retained possession of the firearms. They didn't have any suspects and the case was closed. The gun dealer now has better insurance.

All the detectives agreed that Frank did not kill his crew but they were no closer to finding out who did than they were on the morning of March 18, 1970. Det. Manset was unwavering in his belief that his "wide tire" report held the answer to all their questions. Det. Manset interviewed the forty-seven people whose names were in his report and got nothing. Not even a hint of a suspect. Sam's interview was short. Det. Manset noted in his report that Samuel Peterson was an open and honest young man. He also noted that Carl Peterson appeared nervous and evasive but attributed that to possible marijuana use. Det. Manset knew he had talked to an eye witness. Maybe even the killer, he thought, but he doubted that.

Eventually the case file was put on a shelf and it gathered dust. Det. Aronson would pull it out occasionally and read excerpts to see if anything jumped out at him. He used the crime scene searches as examples of proper evidence collection and preservation when he taught classes for the current group of troopers at the State Police Academy. The case became folk lore to the troopers who listened to Det. Aronson's lectures. Most thought it was no big deal that these criminals came to an untimely and violent end. Det. Aronson was dismayed at this attitude. To him and to any true homicide investigator it made no difference who the victim was. What was important was solving and ultimately proving the case. An unsolved homicide was like a scarlet letter to Det. Aronson and his fellow investigators.

Arnold Peterson's flashbacks subsided and eventually stopped around the same time as Carl's nightmares. Neither knew that the other's torment had occurred or that it had stopped around the same time. Carl's baseball team was eliminated in the second round of the playoffs and his graduation was a few days later. True to her word, Belinda Graham left Deer Isle a week after she received her diploma. Belinda said good-bye to her friend and Carl said good-bye to the love of his life. Carl worked on his father's boat until Thanksgiving. Everything happened very quickly. Carl turned 18 in July and registered for the draft as was required by law. In October he received his notice to report to the United States Army. The next day he drove to the recruiting office in Bangor and enlisted in the Navy. He spent Christmas and New Year's in boot camp and the next three and a half years in Iceland. It wasn't the Hawaiian paradise he hoped for but it also wasn't South Vietnam.

Sam Peterson and his younger brother Darren seemed to live normal Deer Isle, Maine, lives. Arnold continued to fish. Lobsters mostly and occasionally he would rig for scalloping but not full time. Anna's teaching degree allowed Arnold to take winters off to work on gear for the next season and dig clams on the good days. Darren went off to college and Sam had one girlfriend in high school. They conceived a child and were married a month after graduation. Sam was content to stay on Deer Isle and make a living from the ocean. His wife, Sharon, wanted more.

Chapter Twelve

Sam had an epiphany one sunny June afternoon in 1977. He had been digging clams in the hot sun and managed to dig four bushels of clams in three hours. That figured out to eighty-eight dollars for his effort. The noon sun was heating the dark mud and the rising tide was chasing him back to the high water mark. The water was warmed by the mud and provided Sam with his own heated swimming pool. He carried his clams to the high water mark and took off his boots. He walked a few yards back to the edge of the slowly creeping water and sat in the mud, clothes and all and lay on his back. The warm water slowly began to surround him like a soothing bath. He had his eyes closed to shield them from the sun. As he lay there with his mind nearly void of thoughts he noticed that the light was not as bright and his opening eyes discovered that a cloud, one lone cloud, covered the sun. What remained was a vivid blue sky and this one cloud with its own bright halo. Sam thought that as nice as this was, there had to be more. At that moment his wet meditation was interrupted by a loud and painful wail. Sam sat up and leaned on his elbows. As the water drained from his ears he heard the unmistakable sound of a police siren and it was getting louder as it got closer. That would be an interesting life Sam thought.

It was a rare moment in Sam and Sharon's three years of marriage. Sam actually had an idea for their future that she approved of. She was thinking job security, benefit package and prestige. Sam was thinking of high speed chases and stakeouts. Both thought it would be something good. Sam applied with enthusiasm but somewhere in the part of his mind where reality was king he didn't think he would be hired. All the troopers he had met or just seen doing their jobs seemed larger than life and he had never thought of himself that way.

He was hired after a yearlong hiring process but not without jumping what should have been an insurmountable hurdle. During the polygraph phase Sam was asked a question about knowledge of serious and unsolved crimes. The examiner went back to this question twice and explained that Sam was having a problem with it. Sam feigned disbelief and couldn't explain why it should react that way. The evening of 3-17-70 was now more vivid than it had ever been. Eight years had passed and this was the first time he had replayed the night in his mind in detail. He was breathing hard, his heart was racing and he was sweating. The examiner turned the machine off, removed the attachments and calmly asked Sam to explain what was wrong. Sam hung his head, sighed and explained that he and his brother Carl shot two deer the fall of 1974 while Carl was home on leave. The examiner said, "So. What's wrong with that?" Sam explained that Carl didn't have a license so Sam tagged one deer and that Carl's friend Gary Grover tagged the other. The examiner laughed and stated, "What's the problem? They both got tagged, didn't they?"

Normally the examiner would have hitched him back up and asked the question, "Except for the incident we have just discussed, do you have knowledge of or were you involved in a serious crime that has gone undetected?" But he didn't. He had built a rapport with Sam and liked him and believed his story. A mistake he had never made before. Sam had such an honest and disarming way about him. He appeared incapable of lying. Actually just the opposite was true, but only Sam knew that. For the last eight years he had lived a lie every day. Wondering when his father would be taken to jail. Wondering how his mother would react. Wondering when the friends of the dead men would kill Sam and his family. It hadn't happened but it surely would. The papers had said one man survived and got away and was now a fugitive. Maybe that one man was as scared of Sam's father as Sam was of the one man that got away.

Sam's career in the Maine State Police went surprisingly well. He was making a name for himself for solving burglaries and was pulled off the road to assist with homicide investigations in his patrol area. He was promoted to detective in 1986 and assigned to the Organized Crime Unit/Anti-Smuggling Task Force. He was part of an established and elite six-man unit that was attached to the DEA office in Portland. The group he joined was so successful that their names were known in Bogotá, Columbia, and not thought of fondly there.

With this job came access to the Drug Enforcement Administration's database. It was a slow day in January of 1987 and he was the first back to the DEA office after breaking for lunch from their annual "What will we accomplish this year?" meeting. This is as good a time as any, Sam thought. He found the file he was looking for in the "Closed Cases - Intelligence" section. It was originally a BNDD (Bureau of Narcotics and Dangerous Drugs) case. Since 1927 the responsibility of enforcing drug laws fell to the IRS and the Department of Treasury. President Johnson created the BNDD in 1968 to provide more uniform and consistent enforcement of the expanding illegal drug trade. President Nixon took that idea one step further with what was called the Reorganization Plan No. 2. It brought several competing agencies together and put them under the Department of Justice. The DEA was born in 1973 and its goal was to stem the tide of illegal drugs into the United States. It would achieve its goal by bringing agencies together rather than their being rivals. An admirable plan but as Sam was about to read it didn't always work that way.

The report he wanted was filed under Frank Silveira. It contained excerpts of state police reports and a few select photos that some federal agent thought important enough to create this file. There was no independent information generated by BNDD. The pictures that figured most prominent were of the equipment on the dock, the trucks and the gutted campers. There was an interview of Julia Henderson, the real estate agent, detailing her contact with Silveira/Richards and it had a red stamp on the top of the page reading "High Priority". BNDD and the DEA used what they learned from Henderson's interview to profile how and why the smugglers selected certain off-load sites. The picture of Silveira in the file was the same picture that was in the Bangor Daily News when he was indicted for the 15 murders. It was a mug shot from Boston PD after he had put a St. Louis Cardinals fan in intensive care at Mass General after the seventh game of the 1967 World Series. The Cardinals fan had made some remark about the Yaz that hadn't set well with a very drunk and angry Silveira.

There was another out of focus picture alleged to be Silveira that was taken in 1980 on the island of St. Kitts off the coast of Venezuela. It was a surveillance of a Miami man being investigated by the US Treasury Department for counterfeiting. Frank had the unfortunate luck of walking through the picture as it was being taken. No one took notice until 1982 when a former Warwick, Rhode Island, police officer now working for the Treasury Department thought he recognized Frank while reviewing the file. After careful examination they decided it was him. According to this report he had not been seen since. The only report included with the picture outlined date, time and location the photograph was taken.

Sam reviewed the file and was mesmerized by the photos. The song "Love Me Two Times" quietly crept into his thoughts. He read and relived that fateful evening. In a picture labeled "#53 of 240 - Dining room from hall doorway." It was dated 3-18-70 and had the detectives initials "LA" —Det. Lawrence "Larry" Aronson. Det. Aronson taught at Sam's academy and though he did discuss the "Biker Massacre" in Deer Isle he couldn't go into detail because it was still an open case. He described the methodical way the crime scene was processed and how the evidence recovered led to the indictment of Frank. Det. Aronson even pointed out to the rest of his training troop that Sam was from Deer Isle and lived only three miles from the scene. How in the hell did he know that? Sam thought. Fortunately there were enough egos going on in the class that no one was impressed with that revelation and therefore no one asked Sam about it. Sam looked closely at the picture and there on the floor next to a dining room chair was Carl's Boston Celtics hat. Sam continued reading the report and when he reached the evidence log he noticed item number 157 – Boston Celtics ball cap – 3-18-70 1743 hrs, Det. Cpl. Ernest Manset. Carl's hat was taken as evidence and is now likely stored in some cardboard box somewhere waiting to reveal what it knows. "That can't be a good thing," Sam said to himself. He found the corresponding crime lab report that described the process of examining the hat and its findings. "Reasonably new hat. Minimal sweat stains. Two blonde human hairs approximately 8 inches long. Letters C P in blue ink located under flap of interior sweat band." In the Conclusions and Recommendations section Sam learned that the hairs were preserved for future comparison to a known sample. Sam involuntarily ran his hand through his short, now light brown, hair. "Jesus," he said quietly. "It's definitely not a good thing." The author of the lab report speculated that the hairs were from a female based on the length but would not rule out male ownership. The letters "C P" were likely the initials of the hat's owner. If the BNDD thought this was important enough to include in their report, Sam thought, sure as hell the state police thought it was a big deal too.

Sam noticed a presence behind him. It was Gavin Faulkner, the Senior Agent in Charge of the Portland DEA Office.

"Are you memorizing that case file or what?" Gavin joked.

Sam felt like a kid with his hand caught in the cookie jar but managed a "No Gavin. I'm just curious. This happened in my home town when I was 14," Sam said with a matter-of-fact tone.

"No problem," Gavin replied. "Just put the file back where you got it when you're done and be sure to sign the log."

He had forgotten about the log. Any one removing files had to sign them out and back in again. Sam had thought that rule was for when reports left the office, not within the office too. Oh well. Sam finished the report and filled out the log. One good thing had happened though. Sam learned that the feds were no closer to finding Frank or charging him with smuggling than they were in 1970.

The last page of the report was dated 11-24-82 and all it said was "Cross file with CE-82-X035." This was a State Police /DEA task force case number he realized. Sam put the Silveira report away. The case was closed and the statute of limitations on the potential drug charges had long since expired. He wasn't very concerned that anyone ever accessed this report. He found the X035 file and took it to his desk. It was an intelligence report on a suspected smuggle at Cape Cod, Massachusetts, on the morning of March 18, 1970. It was a debriefing of Hector Ramirez of Lynn, Massachusetts. He had been arrested on November 5, 1982, by a Cumberland County Deputy for possession of heroin. Ramirez was stopped for a stop sign violation and he allowed the deputy to search his car. Hector had 534 one-gram packages of heroin hidden in two tennis ball containers. After spending three days in jail he decided to trade information for leniency. This is how it works in drug enforcement. You keep flipping the small guy until you get the big guy. Sam read on wondering what could have been bigger than seizing over a pound of heroin. Sam could not believe what he was reading. Special Agent Donald Speer of the Portland Office took Ramirez's statement. It was a very detailed account of an off-load on Race Point at the end of Cape Cod. Ramirez supplied the agent with the captain of the vessel's name, the name of the vessel and the names of the other three crew members. Nothing here meant anything to Sam. They were names he had never heard. He turned the next page. Sam read on with wide eyes and a pounding heart. Ramirez talked about going to a place on Deer Isle, Maine. It was the intended off-load site. They picked up a man that Ramirez only knew as Frank and he told a story about a man in fisherman's boots killing his off-load crew. Frank made arrangements for a new crew to meet the vessel on Cape Cod where they off-loaded 10,000 pounds of marijuana. Ramirez detailed four other marijuana smuggles between October of 1969 and April 1971. Ramirez got his bail reduced to a manageable amount for supplying the information and he was out of jail two days later. The last paragraph of Special Agent Speer's report outlined an action plan that involved coordinating with the Maine State Police to share only the information that pertained to unsolved multiple homicides that occurred on 3-17-70. Sam's hands were shaking. He couldn't understand how or why this information had gone no further than this report. He couldn't bring it to anyone's attention and he didn't know a way to get rid of it. Even if he kept the report he could do nothing about the copies that went to Boston and Washington, DC. The interview was done on 11-15-82 and the report written and filed on 11-24-82. There was an updated report filed on 2-17-83 that explained that Ramirez had failed to appear for his arraignment on the heroin charges and a warrant was issued. Sam was relieved that this hadn't gone any further but wondered how law enforcement could ever solve crimes when this is how they shared information. This report never made it back to the file cabinet. Nowhere on this report was there a designation that referenced it back to the original BNDD report. Likely an oversight, Sam thought. The odds were very good that they weren't filed together in the Boston or DC offices. The main worry was if someone queried any of the names in the report on the DEA's computer database as part of another investigation. The officer asking would be directed to contact the Portland office and then the file would be pulled to see what if any information could be released. Sam hated relying on chance but it was chance that led him to this report. He returned to the original BNDD report and removed the last page and made sure he got the little corner that the staple had refused to give up with the rest of the page.

In the spring of 1987, after the formation of Maine's new Bureau of Inter-governmental Drug Enforcement, or BIDE, it was decided that there was no more smuggling in Maine and the unit was dissolved. The rest of the Organized Crime Unit was dissolved as well and its detectives scattered throughout the Maine State Police.

BIDE was a result of a scandal involving a few state police officers. It was a bad situation to be sure but not worthy of dissolving an entire division that included auto theft, arson, gaming and drug enforcement. The US Attorney and the Maine Chief's Association along with the Maine Sheriff's Association had been lobbying hard to take away state police control of drug enforcement in Maine and put it under a multi-jurisdictional control. This scandal gave them the leverage and the governor made it so.

The detectives from the smuggling unit went their separate ways. Wes and Andy went to CID I, Bill went to CID II. Stan went to Troop C and Robbie went to the Intelligence Unit, the only unit that survived the dissolution of the Organized Crime Unit. Sam went to CID III. That division included his home town of Deer Isle. That was the division that was responsible for the "Biker Massacre". Det. Cpl. Daniel Gervais was now responsible for the case and made it his mission to bring Sam up to speed on the case. Det. Gervais had plans and none of them included working the case any longer.

Sam knew the technical and legal aspects of the case better than most from his time studying what the DEA had for reports. He knew what had happened because he was there. If he were called to be a witness all he could testify to was seeing O'Shea crumple to the floor after a gunshot from outside and hearing several other gunshots. He could testify that he had seen his father with a shotgun and that was about it. That was still way more than anyone other than his brother and father knew. What he knew alone was enough to get his father convicted. Don't forget Frank Silveira, Sam thought.

He pretended, very convincingly, to have only a cursory knowledge of the case and became Gervais' student of the case. Sam was relieved to learn that Det. Gervais did not have the Hector Ramirez information from the DEA files but there was other information in the report that worried him even more. After three hours of going over the reports in the case file Det. Gervais got out his notes that weren't included in the case file. As if the report wasn't bad enough, he thought.

Det. Gervais read out loud. "I met with the CI "GG" on 7-19-83. GG related that he had heard that the murders were committed by a local man who was rescuing his sons from drug smugglers. GG did not supply names or his sources. GG was under indictment for burglary and wanted a deal. He insisted that this was all he knew." Det Gervais informed Sam of a fact that Sam was already aware. The informant, Gary Grover, was killed in a motorcycle accident in Weir, NH, during bike week in 1984. Sam was reeling on the inside, calm and cool on the outside. Who else had Carl told about that night? How could he talk about this? Of course he must have been high or drunk at the time.

Sam managed to ask Det. Gervais, "Any more leads to back up his story?" Nope was the reply. Gervais added, "But if it's true and Grover knew about it, you can be sure others know about it too. I'm counting on your local connections to solve this," Gervais added.

"You can count on me," Sam replied.

Sam was now dedicating all his professional and personal skills to finding out who else knew what Grover knew. He just didn't know how and what he was going to do with the information. Certainly no one he knew or grew up with was going to tell him what they knew he already knew. Sam was the authority now. He was a state trooper and he was keeping this secret. Sam certainly couldn't be trusted by the people that knew.

"This isn't going to be easy," Sam said out loud without realizing it.

Det. Gervais responded, "Maybe not but you have the best chance of getting into that community and winning their trust."

Sam was back in the real world now. The world he needed to stay in if he were to survive this unexpected twist of fate.

"Yeah. You're right. I just meant that if this was in fact a man protecting his sons from bad people, real bad people, it's going to be difficult to find anyone, even an enemy, to give him up," Sam said thoughtfully and with a certain insight reserved for people who had actually been confronted with that situation. I did cover up a very serious crime once, he thought.

Chapter Thirteen

Sam had investigated the assault of a 53-year-old man named Walter Stokes. He was retired from the Coast Guard, his wife had died several years ago from breast cancer, and he was currently the janitor at the elementary school. He would make snowmen to greet the kids when they arrived at school and nearly every day he would show up at lunch time and carry trays for the younger students when they had finished their meals. Everyone liked him. Teachers described him as helpful and friendly and the children called him Uncle Wally. Stokes was in a coma in ICU at Eastern Maine Medical Center in Bangor when Sam first saw him. The neurologist explained to Sam that along with the broken ribs and ruptured spleen, Stokes had three skull fractures. One fracture resulted in two pieces of skull penetrating his brain. Surgery to reduce the brain swelling had been completed and once he was stabilized and the swelling went down they would repair the skull. They would repair the skull as long as Stokes didn't die first.

Police work involves a lot of luck, though Sam had been told by Col. Mac Dow that a hard working trooper makes his own luck. Whether he made his own luck or not Sam always applied the basics to solving a crime. Sam believed if you treated every crime as if it were a homicide your solve rate would be better than average. The basics meant going through the neighborhood of the crime and interviewing potential witnesses. This also meant working the area at the time of the crime. Walter Stokes was attacked as he exited his Ford Escort in the school parking lot at a little after 4:00 a.m. Sam knew the time because a local clam digger recalled seeing Walter leave his home at 3:50 a.m. and it was an eight-mile drive from Walter's home to the school. Your average witness doesn't remember exact times. Only people needing an alibi remembered exact times. Charlie Greene, 32, and a clam digger since the age of 12 didn't need an alibi. He lived his life by the time of the tides and the weather. He always knew what time it was and how long it took him to get to where he had to be. Besides, Walter made a wide turn as he entered the road and Charlie had to swerve to miss colliding with Walter. Those are the types of events people remember the time of, but you have to find them quickly. In this case Charlie called Sam to let him know what he had seen and hoped that it would help. Sam lived for people like Charlie. It made his job easier and it made him look good. Sam liked catching the bad guy but not for a righteous reason—you know, that "truth, justice, and the American way" thing. It was more of a competition thing for Sam. The bad guys commit crimes and try to get away with it and the good guys, the police, people like Sam, are charged with catching them. A high stakes game to be sure. At least it was for the criminal. There was literally nothing at stake for the police. They did what they could and hoped for the best. The ones with the competitive streak did better than the report takers. The report takers politely interviewed the victims, spread some fingerprint dust around or interviewed the witnesses that hung around. They submitted the report and closed it with the famous line: "All investigative leads were exhausted. Recommend case be closed until new evidence arises." Evidence rarely arises. You have to look for it. The report takers could look for it but they like traffic work better. Sam had nothing against traffic enforcement. He knew traffic enforcement was important and actually fun, but how do you explain to the home owner you just ticketed for 74 mph in a 55 mph zone that running radar was more important than getting his two hunting rifles back that were stolen from his home two weeks ago. That's a hard one to explain. At least it was for Sam, and he actually did exhaust all investigative leads and usually was successful for doing so. It was nice that people appreciated his efforts but Sam did it because it was fun to show the bad guys he was smarter than they were.

Sam parked the unmarked Chevrolet Caprice across from the school at 3:30 a.m. and watched. The Caprice was what they referred to as a stealth car that was used for traffic enforcement. Sam was surprised it fooled anyone. It didn't have lights on the roof and it was painted green. A Subaru color, Sam thought. It still had dual antennas on the trunk. One antenna was for the police radio and the other for the Citizen Band (CB) radio so the police could monitor Channel 9 for emergencies. It had blue lights on the rear window ledge and one on the dashboard. It had dog dish hub caps, larger wheels and tires and dual exhaust. The hole left from the window frame mounted spotlight was filled with some kind of black rubber putty stuff. The car looked obvious to Sam but it seemed to fool the rest of the motoring public.

At 4:15 a.m. a red AMC Pacer slowed to a stop in front of the school. It stopped on the wrong side of the road and the headlights illuminated the school parking area. The driver placed a folded newspaper in the green *Bangor Daily News* box that was mounted on the same post as the school's rural delivery mail box. "This looks promising," Sam said to himself. Talking to oneself out loud is not necessarily a sign of mental illness. At least Sam hoped it wasn't.

Sam pulled in behind the departing car and activated the stealth car's blue lights and the Pacer immediately pulled over. This was a routine stop. No danger, no fear and no suspicion. That being said, Sam still checked the rear hatchback to make sure it was secure. He pressed his bare fingers on the glass that would leave his own fingerprints. He returned his right arm to his side so his wrist rubbed against his State Police issued 9mm Berretta. Sam stopped just short of the driver's door as he held the six-cell Kel-Lite on his left shoulder and shined the light into the driver's compartment. The light on the shoulder looks normal enough but it is actually a defensive posture that prepared the trained police officer to instantly bring a severe blow to whoever needed it with little or no warning. Of course

Risk Management preferred you didn't use your flashlight as a club but that is how Sam and his fellow officers were trained. Sam had never used the flashlight as a club and he had never shot at anyone. Sam was trained to approach vehicles this way and it was second nature now.

"License and registration please," Sam said in his monotone robot voice. As the driver passed them out the window Sam recognized Artie Barbaro from the True Value Hardware Store in Harrington. Artie was like a lot of people in rural Maine. You need two or three jobs to make ends meet. Artie left home at 2:00 a.m., picked up his papers at the Feed and Seed Store on Route 1, folded them and on bad weather days put them in plastic bags. His route covered two towns and fifty miles. Artie would get home by 6:30 a.m. He had just enough time to have some breakfast with his wife, make sure the kids were ready for the 6:50 a.m. school bus, put on his True Value Hardware shirt and get to work by 7:30 a.m. The store opened at 8:00 a.m. Artie worked until 3:00 p.m., drove home and usually gassed the car up on the way so his wife would not have to on her way home from the blueberry factory at 11:00 p.m. Then Artie started all over again at 2:00 a.m. Sundays were very important to the Barbaros.

"Hi, Artie," Sam said but this time his voice had some personality and a friendly tone.

Artie responded, "Mornin', Sam. What's wrong?"

Artie addressing Sam by his first name was another sign that Sam was doing things right as he enforced the laws of Maine in his assigned area. The people he protected and served were comfortable with him and trusted him. He was the Trooper but he was also a neighbor and to some a friend.

"Nothing's wrong with you, Artie. Walter Stokes was attacked here yesterday morning and I was wondering what you saw when you delivered the paper yesterday," Sam explained.

Artie pondered a moment. You always see things when you perform your routine duties day in and day out. The unusual stands out but the usual is rarely if ever noted or stored for future recollection. Artie turned towards Sam who was now standing at Artie's window and the beam of the flashlight was no longer shining into the car.

"You know, Sam, I do remember that Walter's driver's door was still open and there was a white Dodge pickup idling around the corner of the gym parked by the monkey bars. I didn't see Walter but I thought he must have been carrying tools or something into the school and wasn't finished yet. I didn't give the truck much thought but it was an odd place and time to be parked," Artie said.

This is good, Sam thought. "Were you here the same time as this morning?" Sam asked.

"Yeah. Give or take a minute or two," Artie said. "Do you think that Dodge had something to do with Walter being attacked?" Artie asked.

"I don't know," Sam replied. Sam was sure that the truck was owned or at least being used by Walter's attacker but the police were not allowed to rush to judgment. A phrase that defense attorneys loved to use when addressing juries. The police are almost always portrayed as semi-intelligent, well meaning but poorly trained public servants that are always looking for the easy way out rather than the truth. The sad thing is that a lot of the public actually believe this and the public is where juries come from.

"Did you notice what the registration plate number was?" Sam asked with a hopeful lilt in his voice.

Artie pondered again. Sam liked it when witnesses took the time to think about what they did or didn't see. That meant that they were exploring that part of their brain that actually registered the events. The witnesses that answered quickly usually were telling you what they thought you wanted to hear or what they thought they should have heard or seen.

Artie finally responded, "I can only say that it was one of those lobster plates. That lobster glows red when your headlights hit it." Artie added, "It looked a lot like Joe Keifer's truck. You know that ugly white 1970 Dodge with the big round headlights. Man those are ugly trucks."

Sam laughed and agreed with Artie. A 1970 Dodge pickup truck had to be the homeliest vehicle made in America since the Edsel. Sam did know the vehicle. Joe had backed into the school bus after a basketball game a few months ago and Sam did the report of the accident. Joe had two daughters that attended the school. One 9-year-old with dark brown hair and huge puppy dog brown eyes. Sam couldn't remember her name but remembered that she could melt ice with those sweet sad eyes. She had her mother's Native American features. Joe's other daughter was 13 and blossoming the way 13-year-old girls do. Her name was Jessica and she, only in the seventh grade, was every bit as good a basketball player as any of the varsity girls at Narraguagus or Sumner High School. Sam was sure that coaches for both teams would be hoping Jessica would attend their respective schools. Families in towns without their own high school usually had a choice and Narraguagus and Sumner were Jessica Keifer's choices. Jessica looked more like her dad with strong Eastern European features, tall for her age, athletic with blonde, almost white, shoulder-length hair and bright blue eyes. Sam asked Artie if he had seen anything else unusual that morning.

Artie didn't ponder this time. His voice elevated at least two octaves. "That damn Smithson boy and his '64 Chevelle nearly killed me again yesterday morning. He came over that rise on the Kansas Road all four wheels off the ground."

Artie's voice was still rising and began to sound a little feminine. Sam was holding back a smile.

"He must have been doing 80 miles an hour. I was just about to pull across the road to deliver Stan Rooney's paper but I saw the glow of the headlights on the power lines and waited.

Damn good thing too because you would have had an awful mess to clean up."

Sam waited for what he knew was coming next.

"You should be out after him in the morning. He's gonna kill someone one of these days, probably me," Artie said as he was winding back down to a normal tone.

Sam assured Artie that after he got done with Walter's case he would make a project out of Steve Smithson and his '64 Chevelle. Sam thanked Artie for his help and sent Artie on his way. Artie had a tight schedule.

Sam was rushing to judgment again. If Joe Keifer was Walter's assailant he must have had a good reason. Joe drove a dump truck for a local construction company, was on the school board and taught a Sunday School class at the Congregational Church. What kind of reason would a person like that need to beat someone to death? Sam knew the answer. The same reason Sam could beat someone to death. The same reason Sam's father killed 15 men with no remorse whatsoever. To protect his children from harm. Or worse, to avenge harm done to his children.

Sam got home at 5:00 a.m., read the paper that Artie delivered, and got his two sons out of bed to get them ready for school. Sam's wife Sharon followed the boys downstairs. Sharon and Sam had been married for what, nine years, it seemed like ninety years. He wished Meatloaf had released "Paradise by the Dashboard Lights" prior to 1974. Maybe he would have reconsidered his decision that May evening in the seat of his father's Ford pickup truck. At least he had two wonderful healthy sons who thought the sun rose and set on their father. Sam mused that for every silver lining there had to be a dark cloud and Sharon was Sam's dark cloud.

Sam's thoughts drifted back to Joe Keifer as Sam's sons, Todd, 8, and Mike, 5, ate their Apple Jacks. Sam looked at his boys and knew he could do the same thing for them that his father had for him and his brother that March evening in 1970.

The same year Dodge built the ugliest truck ever manufactured by an American auto maker.

Sam brushed his teeth for the second time this morning. He told the boys to get into the green police car and said "See you later" to Sharon without looking at her.

Mike laughed and said, "Police cars aren't green, Daddy. They are blue."

Todd corrected his little brother in the tone and manner of a much superior being. "This car is an undercover car that Dad uses when he has to do detective work."

"Oh," was Mike's only reply. Todd was always right and Daddy didn't correct Todd so it must be true, Mike thought. It was an ugly green though.

Sam dropped the boys off at school and went back to work. He parked in a turnout on Route 1 and waited. Within fifteen minutes a red Mack with the Downeast Construction logo drove by Sam. He looked closely at the driver. It was Eddie Horton. Horton was still in view when Sam's CB radio began to broadcast. "Smokey on the side in a plain brown wrapper. Just east of the bridge." Eddie loved that trucker CB lingo. Sam monitored channel 19 and set channel 9 as a priority override channel in case of an actual emergency. A different voice chimed in.

"For Christ sakes Ed. That's Sam in a *green* car not a brown one."

Sam was laughing out loud now.

"He doesn't have portable scales and these trucks don't go fast enough to attract any attention."

Charlie Johnson also drove for Downeast Construction and he had seen Sam earlier at the school. Eddie did not respond. Twenty minutes later the truck that Sam was waiting for went by. Sam pulled out to follow, activated the blue lights and followed Joe Keifer's truck until Joe pulled over.

Sam calmly walked to the driver's side of Joe's truck, stepped up on the running board and told Joe politely but with an unmistakable authoritative voice to turn off the truck and come back to Sam's car. Joe didn't ask why and did what he was told. Once they were both seated, Sam looked directly at Joe and said, "You know why I have you here, right?" Joe stared at the back of his truck and mumbled something that Sam could not hear over the police radio. Sam turned off the radio. The radio is a police officer's life line in an emergency. Sam was not worried. He had done this a number of times but it still was not a good idea. As good as Sam was at reading people and his surroundings, human nature was unpredictable.

Sam knew he had the right person just based on Joe's body language. Sam said to Joe, "You know I didn't stop you for a traffic violation because you know you weren't doing anything wrong. You know that you were seen at the school yesterday morning because the headlights lit up your truck when the red Pacer drove by. I know why you tried to beat Walter to death." Sam let that last statement hang there and waited for Joe to say something.

Joe, with a half-hearted attempt at indignation, said, "You seem to know everything. So what do you need me for?"

Sam calmly stated, "I don't know which of your daughters Walter hurt."

Sam saw Joe begin to stiffen. Sam could see Joe's left temple pulsate with a steady but fast rhythm. Sam also saw those huge hands, hands like his father's, clench into huge battering ram-sized fists. Sam's thoughts now went quickly from getting a confession to how he was going to survive being beaten to death in this car.

Almost as soon as the rage began, a calm came over Joe and he looked at Sam and asked, "What would you have done if it was one of your boys that excuse for a human molested?"

God, I love this job Sam thought to himself.

"Well for starters I would have hidden my vehicle in a better place."

Joe looked at Sam as if he were crazy. Sam was a cop. Not just a cop, a state trooper. They were like the Mounties. They always got their man and they showed favoritism to no one. Is Sam telling me he would actually have done the same thing? Joe thought. Sam's voice interrupted Joe's thoughts. Sam's voice sounded honest, open and compassionate. Sam's voice sounded like he actually understood the grief and rage Joe felt when Mary, Joe's beautiful brown-eyed nine-year-old girl, told Joe the most horrible story a parent could hear.

"And I certainly would not have left him alive. Dead men tell no tales, Joe."

Those words hit Sam like a ton of bricks. Sam's own words. That's right. Dead men don't tell tales. Dead men can't be witnesses. Sam's father didn't get them all. Not that those 15 dead men were not enough but the one that got away could tell tales. Though it didn't seem as he had, yet.

"Is this some kind of cop trick?" an incredulous Joe responded.

"Sort of," Sam said in a matter of fact tone. "I've been trying to figure out how I was going to resolve this problem ever since I figured out what happened to Walter," Sam said more to himself than to Joe.

"What the hell do you mean *resolve* this!" Joe was almost yelling and spittle was spraying from his mouth when he spoke. Sam reached to the center of the dash. The State Police had finally ordered police cars with AM/FM/cassette players installed in them. Not for the troopers, mind you. No, they couldn't do something nice like that. They ordered the radios, and "order" is the word that Sgt. Booker used, to make it look like he did something nice for his fellow troopers. If the truth should be known it cost more to have them deleted than to have them installed. But the reason they were there was to improve resale value. Yeah. Thanks, Sarge.

Sam had a cassette tape in place for just such occasions. It was at the right spot so all he had to do was push it in and the

152

music did the rest. The tape was *Eat A Peach* by the Allman Brothers Band. The song was "Mountain Jam". A live instrumental that lasted over 30 minutes. For some reason when this song was played just loud enough in the background it seemed to soothe the nervous and calm down the agitated. Joe didn't even notice Sam push the tape in but its effect was almost immediate. Joe began to relax which meant he would understand what Sam was about to propose.

Sam began, "The most important thing is that Mary receives the proper counseling and medical attention if necessary."

Joe's wife is a registered nurse and against everything she was ever taught but with the detached professionalism of a gynecologist she performed a sexual abuse medical exam on her own child in the comfort and privacy of their small master bathroom.

"Physically she's fine. Samantha checked her out," Joe interjected.

"Good. Good, Joe. That's a big help because doctors are mandatory child abuse reporters and there would be no way to accomplish what I am proposing if she had to have medical attention," Sam said with a little nervousness in his voice. Sam hoped Joe hadn't noticed. Evidently Jaimo's and Butch's melodic drumming was doing the job.

"I'm listening," Joe said with the sound of unexpected hope in his voice.

Sam asked, "What did Mary tell you?"

Joe took a breath and then sighed, "He told Mary that he had a treat for her. He told Mary to follow him to the janitor's closet." Joe's voice began to waver and Sam saw a tear form at the corner of Joe's left eye. Just then Duane Allman's lead guitar sang out and Joe refocused his thoughts. "He let Mary have a taste of some canned white cake frosting from his finger. He then convinced Mary she could have as much as she wanted if she would taste it from his frosting spreader."

153

Joe stopped abruptly and stared once again at the back of his truck. Sam waited a moment and said in his most sincere and compassionate voice, "The frosting spreader was his penis. Right, Joe?"

Joe nodded his head in the affirmative and began to sob. His chest heaving and head bobbing to the rhythm of the music. Joe explained, "Mary didn't know it was wrong but now she does and she won't speak to anyone."

Sam explained to Joe that is where the counseling comes in. Counselors are mandatory reporters of child abuse also but Sam knew a woman who, with assurances from Sam, would bend the rules for Joe. Sam didn't explain that the woman had helped Sam forget about his dark cloud at home on more than one occasion.

Joe told Sam that the morning after Mary's revelation he went to the school, waited for Walter and sucker punched him from behind. Walter went down like he had been shot. Joe stated that he had his steel toed boots on and kept kicking Walter until his leg got tired. Joe was sure Walter was dead and that was his intention. Joe walked back to his truck, started it and sat there for a few minutes while he contemplated what he had just done. While sitting there the news delivery person drove by and Joe figured it would be all over soon.

Joe asked, "How can you not arrest me?"

Sam responded with an unsure tone, "I don't know, Joe. I've never done this before. I know you can use deadly force to protect yourself or a third party but that law wouldn't apply in this situation. The other problem is that Walter is still alive. I don't know what he is going to say or will be able to say if and when he recovers."

Sam perked up a bit and said, "What I do know is that I had you come to my vehicle which is considered in my custody in this state. I questioned you without advising you of your rights. A rookie mistake because I was so upset at how badly Walter had been beaten. That means if this doesn't work and you are charged, what you just told me can't be used against you. It's nothing illegal," Sam continued. "It'll just look like I made a mistake. You aren't going to say anything different are you, Joe?"

Joe was getting it. Joe smiled and said, "No." Sam told Joe to take care of his daughter and promised that he would hear from his counselor friend in a day or two. Sam assured Joe that he would take care of the rest. Sam thought, this feels right but it is so terribly wrong. Sam wondered if his father had the same thoughts on that cold and cloudy evening so long ago.

Sam turned his police radio back on.

"Orono 914," the radio blared.

Sam picked up the microphone, "Go ahead Orono."

"Orono 914, we received a motorist report of a white older model Chevrolet traveling west on Route 1 at a high rate of speed. Last seen in Harrington village two minutes ago."

"10-4 Orono. I'll keep an eye out."

Sam calculated that if Steve Smithson was doing 80 mph, by the time Sam turned the car to face east so the radar antenna would be aimed at vehicles traveling west the car should be just coming over the crest of the hill and a quarter mile away from Sam. Sam held the radar control in his hand and watched the road. Five seconds later the white car came into view and was clearly traveling at high speed. Sam's visual estimation was 95 mph. Sam didn't get speeds like that often but this car was going at least that fast. Sam pressed the button that transmitted the Doppler Radar radio waves. In an instant the speed indicator on the Kustom Signals KR-11 radar indicated and locked on to 102 mph. Sam released it and checked again. This time it was 103mph. Sam left it locked on, turned on the blue lights and Steve Smithson pulled to a stop just beyond where Sam was parked. The cassette tape just cycled through to the beginning and "Ain't Wasting Time No More" began. What a great day Sam thought.

"914 Orono, I have the vehicle stopped. 103 mph," Sam said.

"10-4 914," the dispatcher responded.

Walter "Uncle Wally" Stokes came out of his coma three weeks later. His last recollection was four days before the attack when he was sweeping the gym floor. Walter wanted to help Trooper Peterson catch whoever did this to him. Walter had no idea why anyone would do this to him unless it was some drug crazed hippie looking for drugs. Yeah right. Capt. MacDonald in North Carolina already tried that one, Sam thought to himself or did he say it out loud. He looked to Stokes for a reaction but didn't get one. I guess not, Sam thought.

Sam finished his report on the assault of Walter Stokes. On the recommendation line he typed, "All investigative leads were exhausted. Recommend case be closed until new evidence arises."

"There," Sam said to himself out loud. "That wasn't so bad."

If I could do that for someone I barely knew I certainly can protect my father. One big difference, Sam thought. Dad killed 15 men just doing their job. Yeah, it was an illegal job but if Carl and I had not been there, nothing would have happened. Who's to say that they wouldn't have let us go when they finished unloading the dope and left? Well, we will never know. Besides, Joe only beat up a child molester.

Chapter Fourteen

"What about the notes that aren't included in the report yet?" Sam asked.

"I'll have Brenda type them up before I retire," Det. Gervais said.

"Retire?" Sam asked.

"Yeah. June 28th is my last day but it's not official until August 1st," Det. Gervais said. "You seem surprised," Det. Gervais said with a smile.

"I didn't know. I didn't think you'd ever retire. That's only two months away," Sam stammered.

"What? You don't think thirty-two years is long enough?" Det. Gervais laughed. "Why in hell do you think I was going over the "Biker Massacre" case with you?"

"I thought you wanted my help," Sam said still in shock.

"No, lad. It's all yours now," Det. Gervais said. "And it has Sgt. Cohen's blessing." "It's kind of funny, too," Det. Gervais mused. "Your name and Carl's name are in the report."

"Yeah, funny," Sam said lost in thought.

"This case file is the CID III copy but I'll make another one for you," Det. Gervais said.

"Dan," Sam said. "I'm sure you've got better things to do your last two months. I can copy a new file."

Det. Gervais thought a moment, "Sure. OK. But you have to get it back to Brenda soon or she'll have your ass."

Sam was the new guy and only knew Brenda as the CID III secretary. She had been there about four years and if you thought of the Criminal Division as a ship she would be the first mate. She always seemed to know where everyone was and what cases they were working on. She knew every detective's birthday and she usually had a card or note for them. She knew the names of the wives and the girlfriends and called them by their first names when she had to phone the detectives at home. She was very careful not to refer to a wife by the girlfriend's name. Of course most people thought of the Criminal Division as a den and Brenda was the fox. Brenda was twenty-something plus and in a world of wrinkled suits she stood out. Brenda always dressed as if she were doing something special for the day that required her to look her best. Her best was, by most heterosexual male standards, incredible. She was a striking brunette with the eyes, lips and cheekbones of a model. She had a tomboy attitude and seemed not to know how attractive she was to others. Even the gentlemen that preferred blondes would rethink their idea of perfection after seeing her. Brenda had no problem working in a male dominated environment. CID III was her home and the detectives were her family. No hidden agenda. No sexual tension. She just did the best job she could and everything else was "bullshit" as she was fond of saying.

"I'll type up your notes," Sam said with a smile. "I would imagine she wouldn't be quite so hungry for my ass if I saved her some work."

"It's your ass, lad," Det. Gervais said with a warning tone. "I don't care how many reports you type for her, she'll be pissed if she has to look for that case file."

"But she will remember the good deed," he added.

Sam copied the file in less than two hours and delivered the original to Brenda the next day.

"You solve it already?" Brenda asked with a smile.

"No. I just copied it," Sam replied. "Dan told me you collected the asses of delinquent report returners."

"Oh. Did he?" Brenda asked with mocked dismay.

"Yeah, he was quite clear on that," Sam said. "It's not much but I would fall out of my chair without it."

Brenda laughed and directed Sam to have a seat. "Now that I've got you here I need you to fill out this personnel form," she said. "The LT needs to know everything from the serial number on your handcuffs to your kids' birthdays."

Sam looked the form over and then he looked up at Brenda. "Why my kids' birthdays?" he asked.

"Damned if I know," she said in a matter of fact tone. "I've never seen him send cards to anyone."

No wonder everyone likes you, Sam thought.

"What the LT wants the LT gets," Sam said in a sing-song voice.

"You're learning," she replied. Sam filled out the form and passed it across the desk to Brenda.

"Thanks," she said as Sam got up to leave.

"Any time," he replied. Sam turned to go out the door.

"It looks just fine," she said with a sly tone.

"What?" Sam asked.

"Your ass," she said. "It will look nice in my collection. Try not to sit on it too much."

"I'll do my best," Sam said. As Sam walked down the hall of the barracks he heard Brenda pick up the phone on the first ring. "Criminal Division" she said, still laughing. Sam stuck his head in the dispatch door and said good-bye to the two that were on duty that day.

Sam got back into his unmarked cruiser and drove out of the barracks parking area. On the seat next to him were Det. Gervais' three notebooks. Each marked BC-70-0106. No other copies existed.

"Orono any units on I-95 north of the Hogan Road," Sam's radio blared. Sam hesitated about five seconds. The tone of the dispatcher did not reveal what kind of an emergency it was. Police Communication Officer Wood was a seasoned veteran and nothing rattled her. She could be requesting help in apprehending a speeder or managing a three-car five-person fatality. Her voice gave no hint. No uniformed units in the area Sam thought so I guess I'm the closest.

"1251 Orono," Sam said into the microphone. "I'm on the Kelly Road."

"10-4 1251. Attempt to locate a red late-seventies Dodge pickup. Unknown New Brunswick reg. Involved in an armed robbery at the Exxon on Hammond Street," PCO Wood broadcasted with no emotion. "Two 10-49s. 10-32 handgun. Last seen getting on I-95 northbound."

"10-4 Orono," Sam acknowledged. "I'll set up on the Kelly Road on-ramp."

Two murder victims and the suspect is armed with a handgun. Sam thought. He looked at the dashboard clock. I'm going to be late for supper again. Sam looked up just as the red Dodge raced pass.

"Shit! He's flying," Sam said out loud. There I go talking to myself again, he thought—or maybe said—he wasn't always sure. "1251 Orono," Sam said just as cool as PCO Wood. "I have the vehicle northbound at Kelly Road. He's traveling at a high rate of speed. I'll advise when I catch up to him."

"10-4 1251," PCO Wood said. "I have 531, 534 and 503 coming your way." "Be careful Sam," PCO Wood added without keying the microphone.

The red Dodge was half a mile ahead of Sam before he got on the interstate. Sam was not in a pursuit vehicle. It was in a brown 1987 Chevrolet Celebrity four-door with a V-6 motor. It didn't look like much but it would go 125 mph. It didn't handle well at that speed but Sam still took the Chevy to its limits every chance he could. Sam caught up with the red Dodge just north of the Stillwater exit. The truck was doing 95 mph and Sam settled in about five car lengths behind. Way too close. Sam had his blue dashboard-mounted light activated, the wig-wag head lights and the siren that only he could hear at these speeds.

"1251 Orono," Sam said. "New Brunswick passenger car 2-3-6-A, Adam-G, George-K, King. Two people in the truck. Still northbound, 95 mph, not stopping."

"10-4 1251," PCO Wood acknowledged. "503 and 531 have a 10-77 at the crossover in Argyle. 534 will divert traffic at Stillwater."

"10-4 Orono," Sam said. This will be over in three miles, Sam thought. Unless they get by the road block. Sam moved within two car lengths of the truck without realizing it. They're slowing down, he thought. Just then the passenger smashed out the rear window of the truck and started shooting at Sam. The first shot smashed through the windshield and the rearview mirror exploded. Sam was sprayed with flying glass and chunks of plastic. The second shot buried itself into the hood of the car near the right headlight. Sam did not slow down. Instinctively he reached for his Beretta 9mm and accelerated. The third shot hit the windshield without stopping, nicked the steering wheel at the one o'clock position, tore a hole in Sam's sport coat and grazed the inside of his bicep as he was drawing his weapon. He didn't notice the burn. The slug continued through the seat and lodged into Sam's freshly copied case file on the back seat.

"Orono 1251. 10-20?" PCO Wood asked. She received no answer. "Orono 1251. What's your 20?"

Sam couldn't answer with a gun in one hand and the steering wheel in the other. PCO Wood's second location request showed a little hint of concern. God she's cool, Sam thought. Sam gripped the wheel with his gun hand and activated the passenger power window button and it went down. The rush of air at 100 mph was deafening and actually made the car handle different. The passenger shot three more times from his Smith & Wesson .44 Magnum revolver. All three shots hit the Chevy. One through the rear passenger door, one into the trunk lid and into the spare tire and one sliced into the right rear tire. The tire did not blow immediately but the air was coming out fast. Sam had not felt the tire going down yet. As Sam pulled alongside the truck he started squeezing the trigger and did not stop until the slide locked back indicating that it was empty. Sam had fired eleven shots in less than six seconds. Every 9mm round hit the truck with four striking the driver in the left knee, left thigh, left wrist and one into his chest lodging in his heart. The other seven impacted on various solid parts inside the door without entering the passenger compartment. The passenger was reloading the .44 Magnum. He wouldn't finish. Both vehicles were traveling about 90 mph. Sam's rear flat tire caused him to swerve right and the other driver's injuries and pain caused him to swerve left. Sam's Chevy struck the truck square on the left rear wheel. The truck was already in a skid and the impact caused the truck to spin 180 degrees. The truck traveled a very short distance backwards and then it violently spun back 90 degrees and began to barrel roll. The driver was ejected during the second roll. He hit the pavement head first at about 70 mph and an instant before being run over by Sam's Chevy. Sam had locked the brakes but the impact with the truck caused him to spin out of control. The Chevy was just completing its first 360 degree spin when it impacted the tumbling body of the driver. In the middle of the second spin the Chevy skidded into the grassy median backwards. The rear bumper plowed into the soft sod and dug in catapulting the Chevy into an end for end roll into the dark green fir trees. The Chevy rolled one last time and came to rest on its roof. The nimble ten-foot fir trees sprang back into place as if to swallow the Chevy. The only indication of where Sam and his car rested was a telltale plume of steam. Sam was still strapped in his seat but unconscious. The truck had rolled over eight times and the passenger was ejected during the sixth roll. His body was launched over forty feet in the air and he landed in the tall grass on the right side of the highway. The ground was soft where he landed but he still suffered a broken left femur and broken right arm. He was stunned but conscious and now unarmed. He tried to get up but the pain pushed him back down. Sgt. Carter and Trooper

Packard were over a half mile away but saw the hideous crash as it happened. They sped to the scene in separate cruisers.

"503 Orono. 1251 involved in a 10-50 with the suspect. Start a 10-57 and notify the OD," he barked.

"10-4," a very subdued PCO Wood responded. "Status of 1251?" she asked.

"Unknown," Sgt. Carter responded. "I don't see his vehicle."

"10-4 503. 10-57 en route," PCO Wood said. PCO Wood was very fond of Sam. He had worked the desk at the Orono barracks while waiting for the academy to start. They had become very good friends. She had never had a brother and he didn't have a sister. They both filled a need that they didn't know they had and both were the better for it. Except for today.

"Is he OK?" Brenda asked as she walked into the dispatch area. Brenda had heard the events unfold on the police scanner in her office. PCO Wood looked up from her console and said,

"I don't know."

"And if he is all right, that jerk Carter won't tell us," she added.

Sam was not all right and PCO Wood got the news from Sgt. Carter on channel six. Channel six was a short range radio channel used for informal police conversations between cars. Most civilians with scanners didn't have the frequency and the range was only ten miles. Sgt. Carter was within that range and requested that PCO Wood send a trooper to Sam's home and pick up his wife and boys and bring them to Eastern Maine Medical Center in Bangor. He also requested a fire truck for the now burning Dodge pickup. PCO Wood made the calls and advised Sgt. Carter the status of each request he had made. She made her log entries and fought back the tears that were now welling up. She was losing the fight. Brenda walked back to her office in a daze and called the lieutenant and Sgt. Cohen.

"You better not die you little shit," she said to herself as she hung up the phone. "My ass collection isn't complete."

Sgt. Carter returned to Sam's car and talked to him. Sam was breathing but it was labored and Carter did not dare to release him from the seatbelt for fear of causing more injuries. So he just talked to him. Sgt. Carter was not an outwardly emotional man but now he was holding Sam's hand and telling him how proud he was as if he were talking to his son. He did not say one negative word. His voice was calm and his words were smooth. Sgt. Carter was afraid Sam would die and he didn't want Sam to be scared. Sam heard and felt nothing. As Sgt. Carter kneeled beside the car he noticed Sam's 9mm lying on the headliner of the car. He saw the slide locked back and noticed several empty casings. He had been in a gun fight just before the crash he thought. Oh shit.

The ambulance crew was quick and efficient. They opened the driver's side of the car with the Jaws of Life and gently lowered him to a backboard after cutting the seatbelt. Sam's breathing immediately improved.

"Check him for bullet holes," Sgt. Carter instructed. The EMT began cutting off his clothes. By the time he got to the ambulance Sam was only wearing a pair of white Fruit of the Loom undershorts.

"He has no holes," the EMT said, "but he's got a suspicious burn on the inside of this right bicep and there is a hole in his sport coat and shirt that looks like a bullet hole."

Sam was rushed to the emergency room and diagnosed with a "closed head injury" with brain swelling. An emergency surgery was performed to reduce the swelling and the doctors put Sam into a drug-induced coma as the brain healed. The surgeon advised Sharon to prepare for the worst. They couldn't tell Sharon if Sam was going recover fully or even if he would survive at all. Todd and Mike just stood by their father's bed and stared.

"I'm pregnant," Sharon said. Sharon had not found out herself until a few hours ago and she had told no one until now. The surgeon said nothing, looked at the nurse and instructed her to call if Sam's condition changed. The nurse did not have to ask if he meant for the better or for the worse. Doctors only worried about the worse.

The section of Interstate 95 was blocked for several hours while investigators from the Attorney General's Office investigated the officer-involved shooting. When a police officer uses deadly force in the line of duty the Attorney General of the State of Maine is the unbiased investigator. They examine evidence and interview witnesses then make a determination as to whether or not the officer was justified in using deadly force. They then wait about a month and make their findings public. The month is so the public will think they spent many hours investigating before making a decision. The decision was usually made within the first few hours of the investigation. They had never ruled against a police officer. The lead investigator had often commented that Maine police officers actually wait too long before using deadly force. "Better to be tried by twelve than carried by six," was his motto. He had been one of the six on too many occasions. The decision on this case could take a little longer. The surviving passenger, Wilbur Yeager, of Fredericton, New Brunswick, told the investigator that as soon as his friend Anthony Tomah, of Big Cove, New Brunswick, saw the blue lights he activated his turn signal and started to pull over. Yeager said the next thing he knew there were bullets hitting the truck and Anthony. Yeager said he returned fire in self-defense. The AG investigator politely listened and wrote "frigging liar" in his notes. AG Investigator Barry Masters had no doubt about what happened but wanted Sam's version before he closed the case. He especially wanted Sam to be able to give his version of the events.

The autopsy on what was left of Tomah's body revealed four gunshot wounds with the one to the thigh being fatal as it severed the femoral artery and the one to the heart also being a fatal wound. The medical examiner, Dr. McSweyn, had been retired for three years but came in on a part-time basis to help out and to "stay in the game" he would say.

He stated that the heart wound would win out over the leg wound as being the main factor in the unfortunate man's death. The heart wound would have won out if not for the 70 mph impact of his head into the pavement and then being nearly severed in two when run over by Sam's car. Dr. McSweyn wrote in his notes, Cause of death multiple trauma to vital organs due to gunshot wound and car crash. Manner of death, homicide. He would write similar notes two more times today as he examined the twenty-three-year-old female store clerk and the fifty-seven-year-old male gas pump attendant that were shot by Yeager. Susie Smith received one gunshot wound just above the right eye. The .44 Magnum did not make a forgiving wound. Richard Albee received three wounds to his chest. His family would be able to have an open casket service.

It was 3:05 a.m. Sharon had left with Todd and Mike around midnight. Sgt. Cohen was sitting with Sam, half dozing. It was long after visiting hours but Sgt. Cohen's wife was the nurse in charge of ICU. Sgt. Ephram Robert Cohen, Bobby to his friends, was jolted from his semi-sleep to the sounds of frantic nurses working on Sam. Sgt. Cohen looked up and saw that the body functions monitor showed no vital signs and the usual squiggly lines were now flat.

Chapter Fifteen

Arnold and Anne Peterson were on their first Caribbean vacation. They had done the cruise thing several times and friends had recommended the Island of St. Kitts for a quiet and laid back vacation. They gathered their bags at the baggage claim conveyor and walked to the waiting taxis. The first in line was a very well maintained pale yellow 1976 Mercedes 300D. The driver was a forty something man with a dark complexion. His medium length hair was thick and dark except for the streaks of gray at the temples. He wore a long-sleeved white shirt which seemed out of place in the 84 degree sun. The taxi driver loaded the Petersons' bags into the trunk, held the door open for Anne as Arnold got in on the other side. It was a short ride to the hotel and Alan Collins engaged in the usual small talk with his fare.

"Where are you from?" Collins said with a distinctive southern New England accent.

"Maine," Anne said.

"You?" Collins hesitated. In the fifteen years he had been driving a cab on this island no one had ever asked where he was from. His first three years on the island he was a hotel maintenance worker.

"New London, Connecticut," he lied.

"Really," Anne said. "I would have guessed Massachusetts or Rhode Island."

Collins looked at her in the rear view mirror, studying her face. Who was she? How did she know? Anne noticed his puzzled stare.

"I'm an English teacher and I have an interest in diverse American dialects," Anne said quite proudly.

Arnold looked out his window and smiled. "Oh," Collins said. "I grew up in Fall River before my family moved to New London when I was twelve."

He hoped that shut her up.

"I knew it," she said with a satisfied smile. "We're from Deer Isle," Anne said. "Ever hear of it?"

"Nope," Collins said as he felt a heavy weight form in the pit of his stomach. Every day he tried to put that night behind him. Time had not healed the festering wound and the memories of that night clung to his thoughts like a creeping invasive vine. Collins knew there was no reason to look but he adjusted the mirror anyway. Arnold looked up. Collins nearly ran over an old man on a bicycle while he was staring at Arnold's blue eyes. He knew those eyes. They were older now but they were the same eyes he saw on March 17, 1970.

"That was close," Anne shrieked.

Collins regained his composure, apologized and continued to the hotel without looking back. Collins carried the Petersons' bags to the front desk and Arnold gave him a generous tip. Collins looked him in the eyes and thanked him. He was positive now. Collins lingered by the newspaper rack long enough to hear their names, the room number, their check out date and then he left. Alan Collins had walked into the hotel but Frank Silveira walked out.

Frank could not believe his good fortune. Seventeen years of wondering who had killed his friends and brothers. Seventeen years of guilt for not avenging their deaths. That would all end soon Frank thought. Frank was at this hotel seven or eight times a day and night. Room 18 was on the first floor and it had a patio. The room was easy to get into and easy to get out of. He already had a plan and he would be as fast and brutal as Arnold Peterson had been.

***

Sgt. Cohen stood and backed out of the way and stood by the window that overlooked the Penobscot River. One nurse was manually forcing air into Sam's lungs, another injected some drug into one of his IV lines and another was preparing the defibrillator as yet another nurse readied Sam for the violent shock his heart was going to experience. The nurse with the defibrillator paddles called out. "Clear!" as the on-call doctor rushed into the room. She placed one paddle on the left side of Sam's chest and the other directly on his left breast. Sam's body jumped as if someone was under the bed and had kicked him violently in the back. They all looked at the monitor. Three seconds later Sgt. Cohen saw the flat line turn squiggly again and numbers followed by letters appeared on the monitor. The nurses looked relieved and the doctor started barking orders.

"Is he going to be okay?" Sgt. Cohen asked.

The doctor hadn't noticed him and was about to expel him from the room when he noticed it was Nurse Elaine Cohen's husband.

"Well, Bobby," Dr. Crawford said. "Not only is he not out of the woods yet, he's not even on the trail."

Sgt. Cohen looked at Sam and then back to Dr. Crawford.

"He's breathing on his own and his heart is pumping," Dr. Crawford said, "We're going to try to keep it that way, Bobby."

"Thanks, doc," Sgt. Cohen said as he looked at Sam's closed eyes.

"You should go home," Dr. Crawford said. "He's not going to wake up until we stop the medication that's keeping him in a coma."

"And maybe not then," he added.

"Sam's wife would not go home unless I promised her that someone would be here with him," Sgt. Cohen explained. "My replacement will be here at four."

Forty-five minutes later Brenda walked through the door to Sam's room. Sgt. Cohen was wide awake and marveled at how nice Brenda looked at this early hour and wondered if it took her long to achieve her current state of beauty. Everything looked normal to Brenda but looks can be deceiving as she was about to find out. Sgt. Cohen filled her in on what had happened less than an hour ago. Brenda was glad she wasn't here for that.

"I'll be at the office as soon as Sharon arrives," Brenda said.

"Thanks," he said. "I'm sure Sharon appreciates this."

He gave her a hug and walked out the door. He felt like he had run a marathon. Brenda leaned over Sam, squeezed his left hand with hers and kissed him on the forehead. She stood back up looking at him as if waiting for something.

"That only works in the movies," the nurse in the doorway said.

Brenda smiled. "I know," she said. "And I've watched every one of them."

The two women talked to each other about everything except Sam but they didn't take their eyes off him or his monitors.

Sharon walked in at eight thirty looking as worn out as when she left the night before. She saw Brenda sitting next to her husband's bed and immediately felt that jealous burn she had felt since they first dated. She hated the thought of Sam receiving attention from women and she wouldn't tolerate Sam reciprocating. It didn't matter if the woman was attractive or not. She just couldn't handle it and it was out of her control she always told Sam. Brenda did not know how Sharon felt and stood up and greeted her with a hug. Sharon let her arms hang limp at her side. Brenda released her embrace and now she felt uncomfortable.

"Were you here all night?" Sharon asked in a monotone.

"No," Brenda said. "Bobby was here 'til four and I came in so he could get some sleep."

What secrets do you and my husband share, Sharon thought. "Thanks," Sharon said. "You must be late for work."

Brenda glanced at her watch for effect and said, "Yeah. I guess I am."

"Don't hesitate to call if you need anything," Brenda said sincerely. I'm not calling you for anything Sharon thought.

"Thanks. I will," Sharon said. Brenda left and Sharon sat in the seat that still held the warmth from Brenda's body. She would have sat somewhere else if there had been another chair.

***

Frank waited until two in the morning. He parked his Mercedes cab in the shadows away from the street lights. He removed a cement block and a hatchet from the trunk. It was about one hundred and fifty feet to the sliding glass patio door of room 18. He walked purposefully at first and in the last thirty feet he broke into a run like a marathoner's final kick to the finish. He threw the cement block at the sliding glass door and followed it through the cascading glass. The panels of the vertical blinds ripped from their anchors, as he ran through them, and they fell to the floor. Two steps inside and he was at the bed. He raised the hatchet above his head and chopped violently over and over at the head of the bed. The white feathers sparkled like oversized snowflakes in the narrow shafts of light that penetrated the dark room. Frank stopped. He was soaked in sweat and the only blood he saw was from the superficial cuts he had received as he ran through the falling glass. Frank made his way to the bathroom and turned on the light. He allowed only a narrow band of light through the door to illuminate the bed. The bed and the room were empty. No luggage, no clothes and no Petersons. The room was cleaned and ready for the next occupant. Frank turned off the light and opened the door to the hall. He looked at the door. Room 18.

Frank made his way back to his cab. He put the cement block and hatchet back in the trunk, got in and drove home. He had no idea where they were or why they were gone. Later that morning he drove to the hotel and walked casually to the front desk.

"Good morning Alan," the clerk said. "What's up?"

"I'm picking up the Petersons," he said. "I promised them a tour today."

"Sorry," she said. "They checked out last night. Something about a family emergency."

"Oh," he said. "Sorry to hear it."

Very sorry to hear it, he thought. Frank hoped that whatever the emergency was, it caused the Petersons much grief and pain. He had been so close.

"Do you have a fare for me?" Frank asked.

"Yeah," the clerk said. "They'll be down in fifteen minutes if you want to wait."

"Where are they going?" Frank asked.

"Airport," she replied.

"I'll wait," Frank said.

Frank dropped the young couple from Eastham, Massachusetts, at the airport, helped them with their luggage and watched them walk through the doors of the terminal. I've been on this island long enough, Frank thought as he drove back to the hotel with his new fare.

Chapter Sixteen

Dr. Dave Edwards, the neurologist assigned to Sam, was not necessarily surprised with Sam's recovery. He had seen it before. Dr. Edwards had been preparing the family for the probability of a long and arduous recovery period where his motor skills may or may not improve and his memory may be permanently or just partially lost. He left no doubt that there would be negative medical issues associated with the injury and the six-day coma. He had seen this much more often.

When Sam opened his eyes he didn't need to look around to see who was there. He had been conscious for the last ten minutes and listened like an eavesdropper as he got his wits about himself. His last recollection was when he felt his car skid from pavement to grass and dirt. He could hear his father and Carl talking about lobster fishing. He heard Darren joking with Todd and Mike. He could hear his mother and Sharon talking with a male voice he didn't recognize but he figured it was a doctor. He heard that he had been in a coma for six days and his recovery would be slow. He tried to speak but his mouth was so dry and his throat hurt.

He managed to croak, "Can I go home now?"

All eyes turned towards Sam and Dr. Edwards was the first to speak.

"Not yet, trooper," he said with a smile. "You haven't paid your bill yet."

Dr. Edwards administered a ten minute barrage of pokes and prods, pricks and tickles all the while asking cognitive-style questions.

"Well, doc?" Sam asked.

"You won't be here long it seems," Dr. Edwards said. "Relax and enjoy the food."

Sam and his family talked about everything and nothing for about a half hour. Then, almost as an aside, Sharon informed Sam that she was pregnant.

"I guess that means a bigger house is in the future," Sam said as tears welled in his eyes.

Everyone laughed. Sam's father suggested that everyone leave and to get some lunch and Sam encouraged them to do the same. Carl was the last to walk out the door and he returned a couple of minutes later.

"Pass me the phone," Sam said. Carl walked over and placed the phone on Sam's lap. "Thanks," he said.

Carl didn't speak. "What do I dial to get an outside line!" Sam yelled hoarsely at the open doorway.

"Nine," was the disembodied reply from somewhere outside the door. Carl started to smile but stopped. He had thought he was going to lose his little brother. He rarely if ever said anything about how he felt about Sam and he was trying to find the words now. Sam dialed the phone and after the first ring he heard, "Criminal Division".

"Hi, Brenda," Sam said like nothing had happened. "Would you call Barry Masters for me and tell him I'm available."

"Sam!" Brenda squealed. "This better be Sam and not some frigging joke."

Her tone had changed in an instant. She quickly decided it was not Sam and more likely it was Det. Brian Curtis messing with her.

"Calm down," Sam said laughing. "It's me."

"You little shit," she said. "You could have warned me first."

"Sorry," Sam said. "I just need to know what's going on and I thought Masters would fill me in."

"So you remember everything?" Brenda asked cautiously.

"You mean do I remember being shot at and emptying my 9mm into the driver's door of the truck," Sam said. "Well, yeah. I remember everything then."

"Holy shit," Brenda said. "I'll call Masters right now and I'll be over after work."

"Thanks, Brenda," he said. "Bye."

"Bye," she replied.

Sam placed the receiver back in the cradle and looked at Carl. "How ya' doing?" Sam asked.

"OK," Carl replied. "I was worried about you."

"Thanks," Sam said. Carl searched but couldn't find the words he needed to use to tell Sam how much he loved him. Sam broke the silence.

"I've been assigned the murder investigation at the Walker Estate," Sam said.

"Is that a good thing or a bad thing?" Carl asked.

"I thought it was a good thing," Sam said, "until I went over the case with Dan Gervais. He interviewed Gary a year before he got killed." Sam paused. Carl's expression did not change. "Gary told him about how and why those men were killed in some very uncanny detail," Sam said.

"If that's true, why aren't you, Dad and I in jail?" Carl asked defiantly.

"Because Gary wanted a deal on his charges and wouldn't give any names until he got a written guarantee from the DA," Sam said. "Lucky for us the DA didn't believe him and neither did his attorney for that matter."

"So why are you telling me this?" Carl asked.

"Who else did you tell?" Sam asked. Carl got up and left.

Sam spent four more days in the hospital and a week later he was cleared to return to work except he wouldn't be allowed to work for another two weeks because of the shooting investigation. Barry Masters had made a determination before Sam came out of his coma and nothing Sam told him changed his decision. Most editorials in the local and regional newspapers hailed Sam as a hero. There was the usual ten percent of the public that called for Sam's resignation for endangering the innocent lives of the motoring public by pursuing the alleged criminals. The murder victims' families and the detectives at Bangor PD were appreciative of his efforts and made it publicly known. It was the ten percent that the attorney general seemed to worry about. The obligatory month usually coincided with the end of the negative editorials and impassioned phone calls to the governor. It worked that way in Sam's case and just over a month later Sam was back to work.

"What did you do on your vacation?" Sgt. Cohen quipped.

"I painted the house," Sam said.

"You poor man," Sgt. Cohen laughed. "The colonel wants you on light duty for a while longer," Sgt. Cohen stated with a serious tone. "He's concerned, and I am too, that you might do something to injure your brain again."

"It's nice to know he thinks I have one," Sam said with a smile. "What did you have in mind?" Sam asked.

Sgt. Cohen handed him a large white binder. "Work on this," he said.

Sam opened the binder and saw it was the "Biker Massacre" case.

"What happened to my copy?" Sam asked. "I thought I had put it in a blue binder." Sgt. Cohen handed him the tattered blue binder with the bullet hole that had penetrated three quarters the way through the pages.

"Yours wasn't in very good shape," Sgt. Cohen said. "The rest of your reports and gear are still in the car," Sgt. Cohen said. "We gathered up as much as we could find and put it back in the car."

"Thanks," he said. Sam got a welcome back hug from Brenda and handshakes from the rest of the guys.

Sam searched his car as if it were a crime scene. He removed everything and carefully packaged it in cardboard boxes. He filled three before he emptied the car of his belongings. He marveled at the damage and the bullet holes. The damage the rescue crew did with the Jaws of Life made the car look much worse than it had been. It still sent a chill through Sam. I don't want to repeat that ordeal anytime soon, Sam thought. Dan Gervais' notebooks weren't there. Sam placed his boxes in his new unmarked car and drove north on the interstate. The location of the crash was easy to find. The black marks from the tires were beginning to fade but you couldn't miss the large black area in the highway where the red Dodge burned. Sam followed the divots his car had made as it rolled into the fir trees. He saw broken glass and pieces of metal that had been cut away from his car. Sam noticed a rubber floor mat and picked it up. Beneath it were the three notebooks, still held together by a large rubber band. They were just as Det. Gervais had given them to him. The notebooks were water soaked and insects and rodents had been chewing on them but they were pretty much intact. They were lost in the crash if anyone asked. Sam and Det. Gervais were the only two that knew of their existence and Gervais was about to start his terminal leave. His official retirement was only a few weeks away. He was practically a civilian now.

It was two fifteen in the morning when the phone on Sam's night stand rang. Sam was used to calls at this early hour. It came with the job, but he was on light duty and Sarge probably wouldn't have him called out unless it was really bad. Sam picked up the phone in the middle of the second ring. Sharon didn't wake up.

"Sam," Carl drawled, obviously drunk.

"What's up, Carl?" Sam asked. This didn't happen often but often enough that Sam relaxed and listened.

"I only told Gary and Belinda," Carl replied. "Belinda didn't believe me," he added.

Believe him or not, it was still one more person who knew, Sam thought. Belinda was a long way away and had only been back to Deer Isle twice in seventeen years.

"OK," Sam said and let it hang there as he suspected there would be more to this call.

"I don't know who Gary might have told," Carl said, sounding a little more sober.

"Thanks, Carl," Sam said sincerely. "We don't need to worry about it now. We'll talk later."

"Sorry," Carl said.

"No problem," Sam said. "Good night, Carl."

"Night," Carl responded and hung up the phone.

"What did he want?" a sleepy Sharon asked.

"Nothing," Sam lied. "He was just drunk."

"Jesus," Sharon said as she rolled back over.

Sam did not fall back asleep until after four.

Chapter Seventeen

Frank circled the block three times. He wasn't even sure if Maria lived there anymore. There was a fairly new green Ford Taurus in the driveway and the house was now white with black shutters. It was a traditional-looking New England home. A lot had changed in Warwick but the old neighborhood was pretty much the same. Frank was driving very slow looking at the house when a single blast of a siren sounded behind him. Frank remained calm, activated his turn signal and pulled over. It's been a long time, Frank thought. No one would recognize me let alone remember me. He hoped his international driver's license would satisfy the cop. Frank watched the officer call in his registration number before approaching Frank's vehicle. No worries there, Frank thought. It was an airport rental and he rented it as Alan Collins. The officer opened his door, got out and approached Frank's car with practiced caution. The officer was reaching for the trunk lid when he stopped and reached for the microphone clipped to his shoulder strap. The officer paused for a moment, looked at Frank in the car mirror and then turned and walked briskly back to his cruiser. The officer activated his siren and waved to Frank as he sped by on an emergency call somewhere in the city. Frank thanked no one in particular and breathed a little easier. He was stopped in front of Maria's house and the activity had attracted her attention. Frank looked up and recognized his sister standing in the window. Her hair was short now and with the passing of time she looked almost a twin of their mother. Maria turned and walked away from the window. Frank got out of his rental car and walked to the front door and knocked. A young man answered the door. He was about twenty-five years old and he looked a lot like Frank.

"Who are you?" was how he greeted Frank.

"I'm Frank." I need to talk to Maria."

"Ma. There's some guy here says he needs to talk to you," Paul Santos said.

This punk doesn't even recognize his own uncle, Frank thought. Maria came to the door as Paul disappeared in the house. She just stared for a moment. Her first urge was to hit him.

"Are you gonna let me in?" he asked.

"Where's your cop friend?" she asked. "You gonna bring him in too?"

"Listen Maria," Frank said. "I know it's been a long time and what I left you with was bad but I'm back now and I need some place to stay."

"You mean some place to hide," she snapped. "Last I knew you still had warrants for fifteen counts of murder."

"Are you gonna let me in or what?" he said losing his patience.

Maria turned and walked away. Frank followed her into the house. The house was as he remembered. The hardwood floor in the dining area still creaked in the same places it did when he was a boy. Maria had replaced the giant flower wallpaper in the living room with smaller flowered wallpaper. The kitchen and dining area was actually one big room but the hardwood floor and the linoleum kitchen floor provided the subliminal boundary that made it seem like two rooms. The avocado kitchen appliances had long since been replaced with white ones. Maria had kept the Silveira family home in nice shape. He joined her at the one hundred and ten year old oak table that had made the trip across the Atlantic with the first Silveira's to come to the United States. The chairs weren't the same as Frank remembered but nothing lasts forever.

"How's Ed?" Frank asked.

Edmundo Santos was Maria's husband. He had worked for Frank's drywall business and then went out on his own as a house painter. Ed didn't like the criminal element associated with Frank's business but they parted on good terms.

"He's dead," Maria said flatly.

It had been sixteen years and she had put the daily pain and grief behind her.

"I'm sorry, Maria," he said and meant it.

"You should be," Maria said with venom in her voice. "That was your fault, too."

"What do you mean?" he asked not really wanting to know.

"You remember that '66 Panhead you were so proud of?" Maria asked.

It was a rhetorical question. Of course he would remember the Harley Davidson motorcycle that he spoke of as if it were a living breathing woman. To Frank it had been better than a woman. He could ride her anytime he wanted and she never complained. He always felt and looked better when he was on her. Best of all, he never had to worry about her running off with some other guy.

"Yeah," he said with a worried voice.

"Well, when your drywall business went tits up, you still had some outstanding bills from your drywall supplier and they were looking to get their money," Maria explained. "They started putting liens on everything. Ed had me drive him over to the shop and he was going to drive your bike back here and store it in the garage."

Maria started to tremble and Frank could see her anger change to grief. "That frigging thing was so loud Ed didn't hear a City of Warwick fire truck as it went through the Church Avenue intersection at 60 mph."

Maria paused and just watched Frank's eyes. She wondered what bothered him more, Ed dying or that precious motorcycle dying.

"He was killed instantly and so was that damn bike of yours."

"I'm sor ..." Frank started to apologize again but Maria ignored him. She was on a roll now. She had wanted to vent this for sixteen years and she was not going to be denied.

"You know what the best part was, Frank?" her voice rising. "You want to know?" she repeated.

Frank just looked at her. Get it over with, he thought.

"I got to watch the whole frigging thing!" Maria yelled.

Paul walked back in the room and did the "don't blink first" routine with Frank. Paul lost. Maria told Paul to leave the house for a few minutes.

"Go park Uncle Frank's car in the driveway," she said a little calmer.

"The keys are in it," Frank said.

Paul went out the door. Holy shit, Paul thought. Ma told me he was dead. Frank had been dead to Maria and his resurrection was not going to improve her life.

"It was quite a show," she continued. "Ed and your bike looked like that stupid cartoon coyote splattered against the front of the truck. He kind of hung there for a second and then fell off and under the truck," Maria said with an evil smile. The rage was coming back again. Frank just watched and listened. Nothing he could say would make any difference.

"Ed and your bike came out the back in pieces," Maria said very calmly. "Other than that I'd say he's OK," she added.

Maria got up and poured them both a cup of coffee. Paul walked back through, tossed Frank's keys on the table and went upstairs. Maria just watched the steam rise from her coffee as Frank tested the temperature with a sip.

"I know you blame me, Maria," he said. "But I found the guy."

Maria looked up at Frank. "The man you told me about the morning you left?" she asked.

"Yeah," he said.

"Is he dead now?" she asked. Maria wouldn't have talked this way before Ed was killed but she was a bitter, angry woman now.

"Almost," Frank said with obvious disappointment in his voice. "But I know who he is," he added. "Ed would still be alive if not for this guy," Frank said.

"That's bullshit," Maria snapped. "You did all this with your little drug run."

"Maria," Frank continued. "It was all planned out. It was in an out-of-the-way place and only the landlord knew I was there. Those kids weren't supposed to be there." Frank was grasping at straws but he had to win Maria over. He needed her help.

"Don't give me that shit," she said. "You could have just given them money and told them to get lost." Frank knew she was right and that's what he would have done if John and Jimmy hadn't gotten carried away.

"You're right, Maria," he said. "But one of those kids killed John with a lucky punch. How could I know that their father was a lunatic murderer?"

"With the crowd you ran with you should have expected trouble everywhere you went," she said.

"I can't argue with you, Maria," he said. "I didn't have a plan for what might happen."

"Nobody ever does," she said.

"I have a plan to finish this," Frank said. "And I need your help." Frank told Maria about his last seventeen years and how he almost had Arnold Peterson.

Maria gave Frank a sardonic smile. "I know why they went home early," she said.

"You do?" a puzzled Frank said.

"He was a national news event," she said. "Evidently your guy's son is Maine State Police Detective Samuel Peterson," she explained. "He got in a high speed shoot-out with two armed robbers. The idiot took himself out and the armed robbers," she snorted with disgust. "He was in a coma for a week and now he's a hero."

"You think Peterson's son is a trooper?" he asked.

"What? You think they'd cancel their vacation for someone else's kid?" Maria asked.

"You're probably right," he said, already thinking of his next move. One of those punks is now a trooper, he thought. Probably the one that killed John. He couldn't imagine that girlish-looking boy being a trooper. It had to be the one that killed John. Frank planned on enjoying his revenge.

Chapter Eighteen

Sam left his home at seven thirty, dropped Todd and Mike off at school and drove to Deer Isle. It was a beautiful June morning and the sun glistened on the water as he drove across the causeway that connects Little Deer Isle with North Deer Isle. The winding ribbon of asphalt followed the natural sand bar and was lined with large serpentine boulders that were quarried from Pine Hill on Little Deer Isle. The boulders served as guard rails but most cars that crashed on the causeway ended up in the ocean. If not for the boulders you had the feeling of being in a boat rather than a car. Sam loved Deer Isle and never got used to the spectacular ocean views. He arrived at his parents' home two minutes before Carl. He signed off with Orono and advised them he would be on his pager. His mother was at school and his father was lobstering. He figured Carl would be hung over and not working so he called him back at six in the morning. Sam enjoyed waking Carl up. Payback, he thought. Carl was driving a Mazda pickup when he arrived.

"Mornin'," Carl said.

"Is she still here?" Sam asked with the anticipation of a kid at Christmas.

Carl perked up. "Yeah," he said. "You want to see her?"

Sam never missed an opportunity to spend time with the most beautiful and powerful creature he ever had known. Well, creature was stretching it, he thought. They both walked into their father's garage, Carl pulled off the cover and there she was. It was like a time capsule to Sam. Good memories mostly and that one bad memory. He'd get to that in a minute. In this moment he wanted to enjoy Carl's 1969 Roadrunner.

"I haven't started it in two months," Carl said.

"Go ahead. The keys are in it." Sam jumped in and the 383 sprang to life after a few seconds.

Carl had fallen onto some hard times after he was discharged from the Navy. Arnold offered to buy the car so Carl could get back on his feet. Carl could buy it back when he could afford it. In the meantime it stayed in Arnold's garage. It hadn't been registered or inspected since 1976 but Arnold still drove it in every Fourth of July parade. The local police looked the other way on that one day each year. Carl had the money on and off over the years but never bought it back. He followed the automotive trade magazines and noticed that the Roadrunner's value was going up every year. Carl also knew his weakness for alcohol and speed and figured the car was better off in his dad's garage. Sam turned off the ignition switch and got out with a smile. Carl opened the hood, checked the oil and closed it back up.

"Let's go in the house," Sam said.

The two men sat at the dining table that as boys they would race through their meals to be the first one to get dessert. Carl looked at Sam and wondered how the roles got reversed. Carl was the one who showed Sam the path from childhood to adulthood. Now it was Sam that seemed to lead the way. Was he going to lead them onto the right path, he wondered?

"How's your head?" Carl asked.

"The hair is growing back fast but it itches a little," Sam said.

It was an awkward moment. Sam was going to have to interrogate his brother. Carl's freedom was not at stake but it was still going to be hard to get information from his older brother.

"What did Belinda say when you told her?" Sam asked.

"She just laughed at me," he said. "She said it was a ridiculous story and asked me if I was trying to scare her."

"What did you say to that?" Sam asked.

"I got mad," Carl said. "I told her every word was true."

"And then what?" Sam asked.

"She started to cry and made me apologize for making up the story," Carl said.

"Did you?" Sam asked.

Carl averted his eyes toward the table and said, "Yeah."

Carl was ashamed that he had told someone about what happened and even more ashamed that he didn't have the strength of will and conviction to stand by what he said. He had let Belinda back him down from the truth. Sam was having trouble reading his brother but he did know that Carl had worshiped Belinda and probably did just what she asked, especially when she cried.

"Why did you tell her?" Sam asked.

"I needed to tell someone," Carl said. "The nightmares were awful and I thought if I told someone it would get better."

Plausible, Sam thought. "Why did you tell Gary?" Sam asked.

Carl looked at the table again.

"We were drinking and Gary was bragging that he knew the bikers that had come up from Rockland who did the killings at the Walker Estate," Carl said. "He said they killed them for moving in on their territory. I know it's no excuse but I was pretty drunk when I told him," he added.

"You must have been fairly sober," Sam challenged. "What Gary told Dan Gervais was right on the money."

"I'm sorry, Sam," Carl said looking for sympathy.

"It's nothing to me," Sam said. "I didn't kill anyone."

"What's your problem then?" Carl snapped. "If it's nothing to you then why are we talking?"

"Because the case has been assigned to me," Sam said. "And I have to figure out a way to cover up the information you spread and look like I'm working and making progress at the same time." Carl didn't look at Sam. "If you hadn't run your mouth I could have worked the case until I retired and got no closer than Dan did because the only witnesses were family and family usually doesn't talk."

187

"What about the guy that got away?" Carl asked.

"He's only been seen once in seventeen years and the federal agent that saw him didn't see fit to share that information with the state police," Sam said.

"Why not?" Carl said.

"It's a problem in the law enforcement world," Sam explained. "It wasn't his problem. He did a report, filed it within his agency and if the state police wanted to know about it, then they should ask."

"How would they know to ask?" Carl asked.

"There you go," Sam laughed.

"So the only reason we're not in jail is because of apathy?" Carl said with disbelief.

"I'm afraid so," Sam said. "And quit saying we, Carl," Sam added. "What you did was self-defense and Dad is likely to get off on the same basis. I'll probably be the one going to jail for subverting a homicide investigation."

"What are you going to do?" Carl asked.

Sam paused.

"I'm going to find everyone Gary told and kill them, Belinda too," Sam said without emotion.

Carl just stared at his brother.

"I'm just joking, you moron," Sam said with a laugh.

"Screw you," Carl said. "What are you really going to do?"

"I don't know, Carl," Sam said. "I have to figure out a way to find the people that Gary might have told and convince them that it's OK to talk to me and then convince my boss they didn't know anything," Sam said. "Doesn't sound very likely, does it?" he added.

"We're screwed," Carl said.

"No, Carl, I'm the one that's screwed," Sam said dejectedly.

"Maybe killing them all is the best way to go," Carl said with a smile.

"It's in the blood," Sam agreed.

Carl looked at Sam thoughtfully. He wanted to help but didn't have a clue of how or what he could do.

"How did you find out about the guy that had been seen?" Carl asked.

"I had access to DEA reports," Sam said. "And apathy had nothing to do with why I didn't pass the information along," Sam said with a sly grin.

"Is this all a joke to you?" Carl asked accusingly.

"No it's not," Sam said. "The humor is just a cop thing. I'm sorry," Sam said.

Sam did have an idea of what he was going to do. He was going to investigate as if he didn't know a thing and see what kind of local talk that started. Eventually someone would tell Sam what was being said. They wouldn't believe the truth. They would be outraged that some low life was disparaging the good name of the state police. They would tell Sam and be the voice of reason that would quell the storm of gossip. Sam knew that there was always a "they". He just didn't know who it was yet. He knew where he would start though. You always start at the beginning he thought.

Sam walked through the door of Over The Rainbow Realty and was greeted by a woman with a phone wedged between her head and shoulder, one hand writing feverishly and the other hand raised with the index finger pointing up indicating "just a minute". She managed a smile. Sam walked around the office and looked at the wall of nautical charts. Some looked new and others looked like they had been there for years. The charts had about thirty push pins with numbers on them stuck in various locations. Sam noticed that the area of the Walker Estate had several telltale holes but no current pin. This chart had been there a long time and it showed. I wonder why she hadn't replaced this one he thought.

"What can I do for you?" Julia Henderson asked.

Sam turned around and looked into the green eyes of a very attractive woman. He recognized her immediately. The pony tail had given way to a business-like short hairstyle. The hair was still auburn but he couldn't tell if it had been dyed or not. She was forty-five years old now and could easily pass for ten years younger. She still liked the shorter-style skirts and with those legs why not he thought. Sam wasn't good at the quick glance at a woman's breasts. He either stared or didn't look at all. He employed the latter on this occasion.

"I'm Detective Peterson with the state police," Sam said as he showed her his identification and badge.

"I didn't do it," she said with a coy smile.

"Well, I guess my work is done here," he said with a similar smile.

Julia extended her hand. "I'm Julia Henderson," she said.

"I know," Sam said. "We've met before."

Julia studied Sam's face and then her face began to turn red with embarrassment.

"You're Arnold's and Anne's son," she stammered.

Sam was enjoying this more than he thought he would. She actually remembered him.

"Yeah," he said. "But when we met the first time you thought I was their daughter."

Julia placed her right hand on her chest to emphasize her heartfelt apology.

"I owe you two apologies," she said sincerely.

"Two?" Sam mocked.

"Yes," she said seriously. "One for being so stupid to think such a handsome young man was a girl and the other for not apologizing to you sooner."

"I got over it," he said. "And you weren't the first to make that mistake and you weren't the last."

Julia was relieved that Sam was so gracious. She noticed that the features that had made him look like a girl all those years ago now made for a very handsome man.

"What brings you here?" she asked.

"Charles Richards," Sam said.

He threw the name out like a dagger just to see what reaction he would get. Julia's demeanor changed just for an instant. She wasn't expecting to hear that name but she recovered quickly.

"Why is his name coming up now?" she asked.

"Nothing new," Sam reassured. "I've been assigned the case and I want to talk to as many people as possible who were involved in the original investigation."

"I see," she said cautiously. "What do you think I have to offer?"

"You were the only person on the island that actually saw him and spoke to him," he said. "That makes you a key witness in my book."

"That's what I'm afraid of," she said. "What's to stop him from killing me?" she asked.

"Me," Sam said with a smile on his face.

"Are you planning on being my personal body guard?" she asked.

"Actually no," Sam said. "I plan on putting Charles, I mean Frank Silveira, in prison before he gets anywhere near you."

"I certainly hope so," she said.

"But the body guard job sounds like it might be a good gig," Sam added with a grin.

Sam had always been attracted to Julia and now he was feeling something more than just lust. He wondered how she felt about him. Immediately Sharon's shrill voice burst into his thoughts and derailed the fantasy that was forming in his mind. Julia smiled at Sam and sat at her desk.

"Have a seat and ask me what you will," she said.

Sam sat down in the chair next to her desk and got out his notebook. Julia went over the events of February 2nd, 1970, as if it had been yesterday. She left nothing out.

"You seem to have made a memorable impression on him," Sam said.

"Unfortunately," she said. "I'm sure I came across as a tease and that pissed him off to put it bluntly."

"What do you think upset him? That you were teasing or that you weren't?" Sam asked.

"I'm pretty sure he was upset that I was teasing," she said. "I don't think renting the Walker Estate was all he had on his mind that day," she added.

"Do you think you'd remember him if you saw him again?" Sam asked. He had decided that he should change the subject. He didn't want to upset Julia and he didn't want to go any further with the thoughts his vivid imagination was coming up with.

"I'll never forget his eyes," she said. "He had eyes that spoke more than his words did and I didn't like their tone. Sam, I had hoped this subject would never come up again," she said. "He scared me then and just the thought of him still scares me."

"I can see no reason why he'd ever come back here," Sam said reassuringly. If the truth be known Sam could think of fifteen reasons why Frank would come back to Deer Isle. He didn't think that Julia Henderson figured into that, but you could never be sure.

"I hope you're right," she said.

Julia's phone rang and she got it on the first ring. Sam may have been there investigating murder but her ringing phone was a potential sale. "Over The Rainbow Realty," she said. A surprised look came over her face and Sam wondered what bad news she was getting.

"It's for you," she said as she handed him the phone. It was PCO Andrea Hunt from the Augusta Regional Communication Center.

"Hello detective," she said with her cool professional voice. "Lt. Thorsen needs you to go to Rockland on a tactical call."

Sam was a member of the State Police Hostage Negotiation Team. The team worked in conjunction with the State Police

Tactical Team on calls that involved armed felons who refused to submit to arrest and suicidal people who posed a risk to others as well as themselves. Occasionally they actually had a hostage situation but usually it was a single very distraught and desperate person that the negotiators would try to wear down until they were rational enough to surrender. Then there were the times that no amount of talking was going to help and the tactical team members had to employ various degrees of violence to end the siege and maintain public safety. Sam was very good at talking and finding a theme that held the interest of the troubled person. The only violence the tactical team needed to employ on Sam's calls was the linebacker-style tackle of the now submissive citizen.

"What do they have?" he asked.

"A fisherman out of Massachusetts is barricaded in a room at the Navigator Hotel with a handgun," she stated.

"What's his problem?" Sam asked.

"He shot a Knox County Deputy during an arrest. The Rockland PD officer with the deputy returned fire but it's unknown if the suspect was hit," she said, still just as cool as if she were giving a weather report.

"I'm on my way," Sam said unable to hide his excitement. "Do we have a name?"

"Hector Ramirez," she said. "It was a drug warrant."

Sam was stunned and Julia could see it on his face.

"Tell Lt. Thorsen, travel time from Deer Isle," Sam said and hung up the phone.

"It's something bad, isn't it?" Julia asked.

Sam was lost in thought. This is very bad he thought.

"Sam?" Julia said.

"Oh, sorry," he said. "Yeah. A deputy in Rockland got shot and I've got to go and help talk the shooter into giving up," he said. Sam started for the door.

"Is it dangerous?" Julia asked.

"Nah," Sam said nonchalantly. "I'm usually on a phone out of harm's way."

"See you later," he said as the door closed behind him.

"Be careful," Julia said to the closed door. Julia hadn't had the same feelings for Sam as he had for her but the thought was just crossing her mind.

Chapter Nineteen

Sam had eighty miles to travel to get to Rockland. A trip that should normally take two hours would take Sam an hour with the help of blue lights and siren. You could see Rockland from Deer Isle. It was only twenty-three miles across Penobscot Bay but other than a fast boat or plane there was no other quick way to get there from Deer Isle. Sam had access to neither. What he did have was an hour to think of what he would say to a man who had just shot a police officer. That was definitely a big hurdle to overcome. Sam had just an hour to come up with an effective theme to convince the man that this little incident was just a bump in the road of life and nothing to lose sleep over. But this man holds a secret that could help destroy my family, Sam thought. As Sam sped across the Waldo-Hancock Bridge into the town of Prospect he knew what he would do to take care of both problems. All he had to do was be the primary negotiator on the call. He spent the rest of the trip running scenarios through his head. If he were asked later he would have no recollection of speeding through Bucksport, Searsport, Belfast or Northport. He did have to stop in Lincolnville as tourists casually walked across Route 1. This brought Sam out of his mental planning briefly. Several of the strolling tourists were very attractive women that probably made a habit out of distracting men from their very important thoughts. But only for a moment in Sam's case. The Chief of Police in Camden received several irate calls about the unmarked police car that went through town at least 40 mph. He would placate them and curse the state police in his thoughts. Sam arrived at the command post that had been set up at the ferry terminal. It was in sight of the hotel but at reasonably safe distance away. Sam was the last one to arrive. Detective Stanley Griffin was on the phone with Ramirez and Lt. Thorsen was his coach.

Thorsen looked at Sam and whispered, "About time you got here."

"Seventy-nine miles in fifty-five minutes isn't bad, L-T," Sam said.

"You're on as soon as you get up to speed," Thorsen said.

Sam read the activity board. He scanned down through the times of events, background information and units that had been assigned. That's when Sam saw the bad news for Ramirez and the good news for Sam.

"Deputy Chuck Dow deceased 11:22 hours." It was written in the upper left hand corner of the board in red marker. I'm sorry, Chuck, but you just made my job a lot easier, Sam thought.

Det. Griffin was a good guy but he just didn't think on his feet fast enough to be a primary negotiator. He was good at gathering background information and was a decent coach but that was the extent of his usefulness and he knew it. Det. Griffin breathed a sigh of relief when he handed the headset to Sam. Ramirez had just hung up the phone for the tenth time and each time he yelled at Griffin, "Screw you, pig! I am not coming out and I'll kill anyone who tries to come in." That was a pretty common threat that Sam had heard a number of times from people who eventually walked out of their hiding places with tears in their eyes. Sam did not want that result this time. Ramirez picked up the phone on the sixth ring. Sam saw Thorsen turn on the tape recorder. Every word that Sam uttered was going to be recorded and then reviewed whether the outcome was good or bad. Sam would not be able to deviate far from accepted procedure.

"Hi, Hector," Sam said in a pleasant and relaxed voice. "I'm Sam. It seems that you plan on staying in there. Is there anything you need?"

Thorsen gave Sam a puzzled and concerned look. You didn't give the barricaded person anything unless you got something first and you certainly didn't offer anything until they asked. At least you didn't this early in the negotiation. Sam gave Thorsen a reassuring nod.

"Where's Stan?" a very agitated Hector asked.

"He had a personal problem he had to take care of," Sam said.

"What kind of problem?" Hector demanded.

Sam smiled. "If he wanted you to know he would have told you," Sam said.

"Listen, pig, I'm in charge here and you better do what I damn well tell you to do," he demanded.

"You're right, Hector. You are in control over what happens to you."

God, I'm tip toeing on a tight wire Sam thought. Thorsen was staring at Sam now and wondering why he sounded like he was trying to piss this guy off.

"Nothing is gonna happen to me, man," Hector barked. "Now put Stan on the phone."

"I'm sorry, Hector, but he can't," Sam lied sincerely. "His colostomy bag sprung a leak."

Thorsen almost fell out of his chair.

"Shit, man," Hector said.

"Exactly," Sam said with a smile. "Damn that's awful,"

Hector said in a somewhat calmer tone. "Sorry I asked."

"That's OK," Sam said. "You had a right to know but it's just something Stan doesn't like to talk about."

Thorsen looked at Sam with a smile and gave him the thumb up sign. Sam smiled and concentrated on how to end this.

"I guess you're pretty worried about how this is going to end," Sam said.

"I'm not worried," Hector said. "I know exactly how it's going to end." Hector was threatening but his voice was calm.

Sam was confident. "How?" Sam asked.

"You're gonna send someone up here to get me and I'm going to kill them," Hector said confidently. "And when I run out of bullets you'll kill me."

"How many bullets do you have?" Sam asked.

Three shots rang out in quick succession and the window of the hotel room shattered spraying broken glass on the parking area below the room.

"Three less than I had a second ago," Hector said sardonically.

Sgt. Bob Silver was the sniper today and a smile came across his face. That idiot just showed me what room he was in and removed the window for me, Sgt. Silver thought. The police knew his room number and that it was on the second floor but that didn't always translate well when trying to identify the room from the outside. Sam thought this was going to be easy and then he remembered his plan was for Hector to die, not surrender. Killing Hector would be much easier than talking him out. Deputy Dow's family would prefer it that way. The entire Knox County Sheriff's Department's only disappointment in that outcome would be that none of them had the opportunity to do it. The majority of the public wouldn't understand why we didn't kill him sooner. Then there was the noisy minority who would condemn the act and wring their hands over how poor drug dealer turned cop killer, Hector Ramirez, was denied the right of a trial. Society had let him down. Sam's only concern was with his own conscience. This wasn't the right thing to do but it was the necessary thing to do for several valid reasons. A person can rationalize anything, Sam thought, as he beat away the last of the guilt that was trying to stop him.

"Are you OK, Hector?" Sam asked with feigned worry in his voice.

"Yeah. I'm fine," Hector said. "I just needed to show you that you're wasting your time."

Thank you, Sam thought. "I don't think it's a waste of time to help you through this," Sam lied.

"I shot a cop you fool!" Hector growled. "You aren't letting me get out of here alive."

You're right about that Sam thought. "I can see why you'd think that," Sam said. "But it's not that bad. The cop had a bullet proof vest on. All he has is a little bruise. He's at his office writing his report as we speak," Sam said.

"You're shitting me," Hector said.

"Swear to God," Sam said.

Thorsen rolled his eyes. You're going to Hell, Sam, Thorsen thought. Stan Griffin was totally spellbound at how easily Sam talked to Hector. Griffin thought Sam was so cool it was as if he wasn't worried about this going to shit. Sam wasn't worried about it going to shit, he was counting on it.

"I want to see him," Hector said.

"That wouldn't be a good idea," Sam said. "He would probably shoot you."

"He'd probably try," a cocky Hector said.

"Wouldn't you?" Sam asked.

"Hell, yeah," Hector said.

"So why do you want to see him?" Sam asked.

"To see for myself," Hector said.

"You can trust me," Sam said. "He's fine. A little pissed off but fine."

"If he's OK what the hell are all these pigs doing here?" Hector asked.

"Geez, Hector," Sam said. "You did shoot someone. You know that you're gonna have to be arrested," Sam added.

"It doesn't take thirty frigging cops to arrest one person," Hector said sarcastically.

"You've got a point," Sam said. "What do you suggest?"

"I've got to take a piss," Hector said.

The line went dead. Thorsen looked at Sam.

"It looks like you're gonna talk him out but you've got a strange way of doing it," Thorsen said.

"I've got a feel for this guy," Sam said. "I think this will be over soon."

Sam gave Hector two minutes then he called him back. Hector picked up the phone on the twelfth ring.

"I told you I had to piss," Hector barked.

"Sorry," Sam said.

"I want all the cops the hell out of here," Hector demanded. "And I want to see you."

"I don't know, Hector," Sam said. "I'll see what I can do but I'm not hopeful that they will leave."

"You tell them if they want me to come out they'll have to leave and you can come to get me," Hector said.

"Give me a couple of minutes," Sam said. "I'll call you back with an answer as quick as I can."

"Don't bother calling unless it's the right answer," Hector said. Sam hung up.

"We can get them out of sight but you're not going out there," Thorsen said.

"L-T," Sam said. "I'll be fine. Just tell Lt. Fallon to have his sniper ready."

"Is that what you're working towards?" Thorsen asked.

"No L-T," Sam said, "I just think I've hooked him and this display of trust will close the deal."

"And if it doesn't?" Thorsen asked.

"Then the sniper will be doing society and the Dow family a favor," Sam said in a deadly serious tone.

"Are you that sure?" Thorsen asked.

"No sir, I'm not," Sam said. "But I've got a feeling about this and Sgt. Silver is as good as they get if I'm wrong."

It took all of five minutes to get the police and their cars out of sight. Sgt. Silver was given the discretion to take the shot if and when he thought it was necessary. Sam was given permission to walk out alone and talk to Hector face to face.

Sam called Hector back. Hector picked up on the first ring. Sam smiled.

"They're all gone and I'm coming out to meet with you," Sam said.

"How do I know they're not just out of my sight?" Hector asked.

"Look out the damn window," Sam said. "I'm hanging up the phone and I'm coming out."

Sam stepped out of the air conditioned ferry terminal and into the bright sun. The temperature was in the seventies but the paved parking lot felt more like ninety. Sam walked up the hill towards the hotel. He could see the shadows of the circling seagulls on the pavement but he didn't look up at them. He just stared at the broken window on the second floor of the hotel as he walked. Hector walked to the broken window and peered out.

"I have the target," Silver said into his radio. "He has a hand gun in his right hand."

"Copy," Lt. Fallon responded.

Sam walked closer and he could see Ramirez standing in the window and he could see the hand gun pointing at the floor. There were several lines of vehicles that had been waiting for the ferry. The police shut down the area and evacuated the occupants of the vehicles. Hector was looking at Sam now. Sam walked between a dump truck and an electrician's service van. Lt. Thorsen could only see the top of Sam's head from where he was standing. Sam was temporarily out of the sight of the tactical team members to his right and left. Hector was the only one who could see Sam clearly. Sam had a four second window of opportunity before he would be visible again. Sam reached inside the left side of his jacket with his right hand. Hector immediately raised his firearm thinking, as Sam wanted him to, that Sam was about to draw his weapon. Sam's weapon was actually on his right hip. Hector had his right hand extended with the blued Raven Arms .357 revolver aimed at

Sam. Sam started to bring his right hand back out now clutching a stick of gum. Come on Bob, Sam thought. The cylinder of the revolver began to turn as Hector squeezed the trigger. The deafening sound of gunfire echoed off the buildings. The right side of Hector's head spewed out its contents as the .308 caliber bullet from Sgt. Silver's rifle penetrated his left temple and quickly exited the right side of his head. An instant later, pieces of pavement sprayed up on Sam's legs from the impact of the .357 caliber bullet that struck the parking lot one foot in front of Sam. Sam began peeling the wrapper from the gum as he watched Hector Ramirez's body crumple to the floor of the hotel room. That was just too damned close, Sam thought as he stuffed the wrapper into his pants pocket. Sam looked up now but the seagulls were gone. Sam had been visited by fate and was able to take advantage of the opportunity. Ramirez would never be able to repeat his story about what he saw and heard on March 17 and 18, 1970. Lt. Thorsen knew this was what Sam had planned all along but he didn't know the real reason. Lt. Thorsen wasn't even upset about it. He secretly wanted the same outcome but for a much more noble reason. This is how cop killers should be dealt with, Thorsen thought. By cops.

The after-incident briefing was conducted in the ferry terminal. The travelers waiting for the ferry were allowed back to their vehicles after Lt. Thorsen filled a twenty-four exposure film of the parking area and vehicles where Sam had been standing. The first part of the briefing included the tactical team members, the negotiators, members of Knox SO and Rockland PD. There was no critique. Each involved officer was asked to give a brief synopsis of their actions and what they saw and heard. The sheriff and the Rockland chief expressed their appreciation for the State Police help. Sheriff Daniels joked that he was pleased that Sam had failed in his efforts to bring Ramirez out alive.

Lt. Thorsen looked down at his shuffling feet and Sam nodded and smiled at the sheriff. Sgt. Silver chose to save his brief for the private tactical team meeting that took place after everyone else was invited to leave. This was the meeting where each aspect of the incident was openly and honestly discussed and nothing held back.

"Thorsen, Peterson, wait up a minute," Lt. Fallon said as they were leaving the terminal. "I would like to think that what happened out there was not planned," Fallon said in an accusatory voice. "Because if it was, the next time I'd like to be in on it."

Sam started to speak but Lt. Fallon raised the palm of his hand. Sam stopped before he started.

"Unless you can talk to me without lying, don't speak," he said calmly. "We didn't plan on it ending that way," Lt. Thorsen said. Sam may have but he didn't tell me, he thought. Fallon put his arm around Sam's shoulder as he walked him to the door. Thorsen walked behind them but he couldn't hear what Fallon said to Sam. Fallon smiled, patted Sam on the back and walked back to the group. The investigators from the attorney general's office were just arriving. They would interview the negotiators and listen to the tape of the negotiation with Ramirez while they waited for the tactical team members meeting to get over. Sam and Lt. Thorsen were twenty feet away from the terminal door when it opened and Sgt. Silver called out, "Peterson."

Sam turned.

"What did you do to get him to shoot at you?" Silver asked.

No one saw me Sam thought with much relief. Lt. Thorsen was staring at the back of Sam's head waiting for the answer.

"I guess I have one of those faces that people just want to shoot at," Sam said with a smile.

"You've got that right," Silver said as he turned and went back inside the terminal.

Sam turned and faced Lt. Thorsen.

"Was what happened here a bad thing?" Sam asked.

"Not really," Thorsen said. "Not really."

The lieutenant was not sure but it felt like it ended the way it should have, he thought. He was concerned at what Sam did to help it along and if he had helped it along by not reigning Sam in.

"What did Fallon say to you?" Thorsen asked.

"He just commented that my balls were bigger than my brain and I should be careful," Sam said.

"I agree with him," Lt. Thorsen said.

The attorney general's investigation went like they always did. Sgt. Silver was placed on administrative leave for a month. He finished his deck and went striper fishing with his two sons. The attorney general announced that the death of Hector Ramirez was justified and Deputy Chuck Dow was given a hero's funeral. The news of Hector's death traveled south and quickly reached the Crow's Nest in Gloucester, Massachusetts. Capt. Jackson Lowe sat at the bar by himself and raised a mug of beer in a silent toast to the trooper that killed Hector Ramirez.

Chapter Twenty

Sam kept busy with a steady load of child abuse cases and those took priority over the seventeen-year-old murders of fifteen drug smugglers. He had talked only to Julia Henderson and Carl before putting the case file back on the shelf. The case was always on his mind and he needed to get back to it but today was Sunday and all he had on his mind was whether or not Bill Elliot was going to be able to get by Rick Wilson and win the Pepsi Firecracker 400 at Daytona. Sam was not obsessed with Winston Cup racing but it would probably take a catastrophe of biblical proportions to divert his attention from the race. Elliot was his favorite driver and victory was at hand. The phone rang from a table two feet from Sam and he didn't hear it. The race had one lap to go and Elliot was in second place. Todd and Mike were at his side and watched with enthusiasm. Sharon answered the phone and then walked towards Sam holding the phone out away from her as if it were a dirty diaper. Sam glanced up at her and then back to the television. Elliot had just passed Wilson in turn four and they were about to cross the finish line. If looks could kill, Sam would be dead. Elliot won the race by about three feet and the boys cheered.

"Who is it?" Sam asked.

Sam usually got work calls on his day off and he always was polite and did the best he could to take care of whatever problem that couldn't wait until Monday morning.

"Are you buying a house?" she said sarcastically.

Sam didn't have a clue what she was talking about and didn't try to figure it out. Sam took the phone and Sharon stood there and watched him.

"Hi, Sam," Julia said. "I'm sorry to bother you at home but I thought you'd want to know this."

"Not a problem," Sam said. He always said not a problem whether it was or not. Sam thought by the look on his wife's face it was a problem this time. "What's up, Julia?" Sam asked.

"I had an appointment with Ronald and Judy Grover today," she said. "Do you know them?"

"Yes," Sam said. "My brother Carl was friends with their son Gary."

"They want me to list their home," Julia said. "But most of my appointment with them was taken up by Judy talking about how her son was killed for what he knew about drug dealers and the Walker Estate murders."

"Gary was killed in a motorcycle accident in New Hampshire," Sam said.

"Yes, I know," she said. "The strange thing is that she said Gary told her that the killer was a local man and he and his family still live on Deer Isle."

Sam could feel his heart rate increase and Sharon noticed the change in his voice.

"Did she say who they were?" Sam asked.

Sharon was still staring at Sam with an intensity that Sam feared would melt the phone in his hand. Sam glanced at her and walked into the kitchen. Sharon followed him.

"Judy said he couldn't tell her but it was someone she knew," she said.

Sam started to relax. "That's interesting," he said. "I'm glad you called."

Sam wanted this conversation over as quickly as possible. He didn't want to spend the rest of this beautiful July afternoon explaining to Sharon why an attractive single woman was calling him at home. Especially an attractive single woman who Sam couldn't wait to see again.

"That's not all, Sam," she said. "Osnoe Haskell told me a long time ago that he knew who had done it because he saw them that night."

Sam could not respond. He remembered Osnoe driving by and almost running into his father's truck. Sam had always thought that he was so drunk he couldn't remember what he saw. Sam recalled the police report indicated that Det. Aronson had tried several times to interview him but he was always so drunk that it wasn't possible.

"Did he tell you who?" Sam asked not wanting to know the answer.

"No," she said. "I thought it was just the ramblings of a drunk and never thought any more about it."

Thank God, Sam thought.

"I'm sorry I didn't tell you last month when you stopped in," she said. "I never thought about what Osnoe said until Judy brought it up."

"That's OK," he said. "You would have remembered eventually."

"Do you think it could be true?" she asked.

"It would be hard to keep a secret like that on the island," Sam said.

"I suppose you're right," she said. "I'll do some digging," she said. "Why don't you stop by in a couple of days?"

"Thanks," Sam said. "I will."

"Bye, Sam," Julia said in a sweet voice that wasn't there a few minutes ago. "Have a nice Fourth of July."

"Thanks," Sam said. "You too."

Julia hung up the phone.

"Thanks, you too," Sharon mocked. "What did she want?" she asked.

"She thought she had information on the Walker Estate murders and wanted to let me know," Sam said with no emotion.

"How does she know you're working on that case?" Sharon asked. She's not going to let go of this, Sam thought. "I questioned her about a month ago about what she remembered," Sam explained.

"Really," Sharon said. "When was that?"

"The day I got shot at in Rockland," Sam snapped back.

Sharon was going to continue the inquisition but Mike walked into the kitchen.

"Will you help Todd and me decorate our bikes for the parade?" Mike asked with those brown eyes that you couldn't say no to.

"Sure," Sam said. Sam looked at Sharon and smiled. "It's just work and nothing more," he lied.

"Right," Sharon said not believing him.

***

"Listen, Maria," Frank said. "It's the Fourth of July. There will be a lot of people there and no one will recognize me."

"I don't know, Frank," Maria said. "It sounds dangerous to me."

"I'll be safer there than I am here in Warwick," he said. "I'm tired of hiding in your house and I still can't believe that Jimmy O'Shea's son is a cop and he's actually looking for me."

"I know," Maria said apologetically. "He and Paul are friends."

"I can't stay here much longer and I'm not leaving until Peterson is dead," Frank said.

"We are just going to see if we can find him on this trip, right?" she asked. Maria loved Frank but she didn't trust him.

"Yeah," Frank lied as he turned away and walked to the fridge for a beer. He didn't like lying to his sister but he needed her for the trip to Maine. Maria made a couple of phone calls and then made reservations for the 2nd through the 5th of July.

"We have one room left but it's two twin beds," the motel clerk said. "Is that OK?"

Perfect, Maria thought. Maria made the reservation in the name of Mr. and Mrs. Alan Collins. Tonight brother and sister will be pretending to be husband and wife at the Bridge End Motel on Little Deer Isle.

"It's at the end of the bridge," the motel clerk said. "You can't miss it."

No shit, Maria thought.

"Thank you," she said.

"Bye," the clerk said.

Frank always wondered if this day would ever come. He had been so close on St. Kitts but once again fate, no not fate, bad luck intervened and both times it involved Peterson's kids. Maybe I should include them in my little project he thought. He thought that if the opportunity presented itself he would decide then. His priority was Arnold Peterson and he wouldn't miss him this time. He was going to end his nightmare where it all began. He was having second thoughts about bringing Maria along but he needed a good cover and he couldn't trust anyone else.

"Thank you, Maria," he said as he gave her a one-armed hug and sipped his beer.

Maria let him hug but she didn't hug back. The only reason she was going along with this was because her two other brothers were murdered and Frank promised her that nothing was going to happen on this trip. She had actually enjoyed having him in her home. It gave her that family connection that was cruelly taken away from her seventeen years ago. She knew he would be gone as soon as this was over but she would worry about that when it happened and make the most of it now. Funny, she thought, I'm still mad at him but it feels good to have him around. Brother's suck, she thought. She needed a sister or even a sister-in-law. That wouldn't happen either, thanks to Arnold Peterson.

"Do you suppose Paul and I could move to St. Kitts with you?" Maria asked.

Frank looked at her and said nothing for a moment. It would be nice to have family around but would it be smart. He didn't know.

"You know," Frank said. "That might work. You should probably wait a month or two after I go back."

"It would take that long to sell the house and get everything in order," she said with excitement in her voice for the first time in a long, long time.

Maybe it would work, he thought.

Chapter Twenty-One

Officer Brandon O'Shea walked to the office of Captain Jonas Simpson, Chief of Detectives at Warwick PD. Brandon knocked on the frame of the open door. Captain Simpson was cleaning his glasses. He had been reading reports for two hours and was taking a much needed break. He liked to come in on Sunday afternoons and catch up on work when things were quiet. There never seemed to be enough time during the week. "Come in," he said without looking up. Brandon entered the spacious but dark office. Captain Simpson looked like he could play center for any pro football team in the country and no one would guess he was fifty-six years old. He was a cop's cop, old school and the end never justified the means. Honor and integrity were more than just words to him. His office had the usual police artifacts of thirty-five years on the job but it was the portraits of Malcolm X and Winston Churchill on the wall behind his desk that caught O'Shea's eye. O'Shea had no idea who they were or what they represented and they looked odd side by side. Officer O'Shea was only twenty-two years old and had been on the force for just over a year and that included his academy training. O'Shea was looking for someone who remembered the old days of Warwick, Rhode Island, and his sergeant recommended Captain Simpson.

"What can I do for you?" Simpson asked.

"Good morning, sir," O'Shea said nervously. "I was wondering if you knew Frank Silveira."

Simpson set his glasses down on his desk and leaned back in his well-worn leather chair. He studied O'Shea for a moment.

"I didn't get your name," he said.

"Brandon O'Shea."

Simpson folded his arms across his chest.

"Have a seat, O'Shea," he said.

O'Shea sat down immediately. It was clear he was still under the influence of his academy training. Simpson hadn't seen many people sit at attention.

"Yeah, I remember him," he said. "And I remember a friend of his named James O'Shea."

"That would be my father," O'Shea said. "I was five when he died."

"Son, your father didn't just die. He was murdered with fourteen other members of the Slayers motorcycle gang during the commission of a crime," Simpson said like a judge passing sentence.

"I know," O'Shea said. "I don't remember him. He left Mom and me when I was two. She never had much good to say about him, but I always wondered what happened to all of them and why it's still unsolved."

"You'd have to take that up with the state police in Maine," Simpson said unmoved. "Why do you ask about Frank?"

"I've only been on patrol a few months but people from my old neighborhood talk to me," O'Shea explained. "I heard from a couple of different sources that Frank is in Warwick somewhere."

"Did you check with his sister?" Simpson asked.

"Yeah," O'Shea replied. "Her son, Paul, and I were friends in school. Not so much now though."

"The cop thing and all," he added. "Yes. The cop thing," Simpson said with a smile. It can test the best of friendships.

"What did Mrs. Santos say when you asked?" Simpson asked.

"She said she hadn't seen him since he left for Maine with the rest of them and she thinks he's dead," O'Shea said.

"What do you think?" Simpson asked.

"I think she lied to me and I think she knows where he is," he said.

"You're right about the first and probably right about the second. My sources in 1970 told me that Frank made a quick stop at the Silveira home, left enough money to bury fifteen men and then disappeared," Simpson said with authority.

"You seem to know him quite well," O'Shea said. "Is your division still working on him?"

"Nope," Simpson said. "I have not laid eyes on Frank since the day he left town to go to Maine."

"You saw him that day?" O'Shea said with surprise.

"I saw them all. My partner, Bill Johansson and I were doing a stakeout on the Slayers. They were involved with organized crime in Providence and Boston. Small stuff. Enforcement and drug dealing. But the crime families they worked for didn't always work together and we were hoping that something would go to shit and we would be there to pick up the pieces and maybe an informant," Simpson told the story like it had all happened yesterday and O'Shea hung on his every word. "That day, Bill and I watched eight new Ford trucks and campers leave Narragansett Drywall and head towards Providence," Simpson continued. "We had permission to follow them into Mass but we were told to come home when they crossed into New Hampshire. My captain notified New Hampshire SP and the FBI and we came home. I guess no one thought to let Maine know," Simpson said.

"And that was it?" O'Shea asked.

"The Maine detectives came down here and we told them what we knew," Simpson said. "Which really wasn't a lot. We took them around to the relatives and that didn't go very well either. Your mom wouldn't let them in the door," he added with a smile.

"Did the Maine detectives have any leads at all?" O'Shea asked.

"Nothing that went anywhere," he said. "I've kept in contact with a detective named Dan Gervais. He had a local informant that said it was a local man who was rescuing his sons that just happened to stumble onto whatever your father and his friends were doing," Simpson said.

"I take it no names went with that information," O'Shea said already knowing the answer.

"Right you are," Simpson said.

Captain Simpson was enjoying this trip down memory lane and it certainly was a welcome diversion from report reading.

"And if my memory serves me correctly the informant was killed in a motorcycle accident a short time later," he added.

"Was that suspicious?" O'Shea asked.

"No," Simpson said. "It happened in New Hampshire, he was drunk and it was witnessed by several people including a New Hampshire trooper."

"Is there anything you don't know about this case?" O'Shea asked with a smile.

"I don't know who killed them. I know there was no evidence that Frank was killed with them and there is no reason to believe Frank would have killed his two brothers, his cousin and his friends. Frank was charged with felony murder because it was Frank's show and he was there. His fingerprints were on the murder weapon, too," Simpson explained.

"So I guess I should continue to follow up on my Frank leads," O'Shea said.

"I think watching Santos would be a good start," Simpson said.

"I want to, but Sarge said it's not happening," he said.

"When do you get off shift?" Simpson asked.

O'Shea looked at his watch. "Ten minutes," he said.

"Meet me in the parking lot in fifteen minutes," Simpson said with a smile. "I need something to do instead of reading what someone else did."

Thirty minutes later the rookie and the veteran were parked in Simpson's 1987 Buick Park Avenue on the street four houses from Maria Santos' home. Nice car, O'Shea thought. Captains must do all right. Neither man was on the clock. They were doing police work for no pay because they liked doing police work. O'Shea thought he was making the world a safer place. Well at least Warwick, Rhode Island. Simpson was reliving his glory days. Whatever their reasons, they were going to be involved in more than they bargained for and that is the reason they both were police officers. O'Shea sipped a cran-apple drink while Simpson drank coffee. They both stared at the house. A white 1982 Camaro backed out of the driveway and accelerated up the street towards the two men. Paul Santos didn't even look their way.

"Maria's son?" Simpson asked.

"Yep," O'Shea replied.

Twenty minutes later Maria's Ford Taurus backed out and traveled in the opposite direction.

"There's a man on the passenger side of the car," O'Shea said.

"I see him," Simpson said with a hint of excitement.

"Do you think it's Frank?" O'Shea asked.

"We won't ever know sitting here," Simpson said as he started his car. The two men followed Maria's Taurus across town and to Interstate 95 northbound.

"How far are we going to follow them?" O'Shea asked.

Simpson looked at his gas gauge and saw he had a little more than a half tank.

"At least 150 miles," he said with a grin. "Why, do you have some place you have to be?"

"No sir," O'Shea said.

Two hours and one hundred and twenty miles later both cars left the interstate in Portsmouth, New Hampshire. Simpson pulled up to the gas pumps three islands over from Maria's car. He handed O'Shea a twenty dollar bill.

"Fill it and get back in behind the wheel," Simpson said. "You're driving."

"What are you going to do?" O'Shea asked.

"Piss," he said as he got out of the car. Simpson walked into the restroom thirty seconds ahead of Frank. Frank didn't make eye contact. No one ever made eye contact in a men's room. Well, almost no one. Simpson stayed at the corner urinal until Frank left. The nasty bastard didn't even wash his hands, Simpson thought. Simpson got back to his Buick just as Maria and Frank were leaving the gas pumps.

"Where to?" O'Shea asked.

"Follow them," Simpson said.

"That was Frank Silveira, wasn't it?" O'Shea asked.

"Yes, it was," Simpson said masking his glee. "And this time I'm not turning around and going home."

O'Shea smiled and drove north. Running a one-car surveillance on an interstate is reasonably easy. There is usually a lot of traffic to hide behind, you have plenty of warning before an exit and the road is usually clear except for construction and the work crews were not out on a Sunday evening two days before the Fourth of July.

"This doesn't look good," O'Shea said waking Simpson from his nap. Traffic was nearly at a standstill near the Freeport exit.

"I don't think they're all waiting to go to L.L. Bean," Simpson said.

O'Shea smiled. "Where's our fellow travelers," he asked.

"Two cars ahead and in the left lane," O'Shea said. They were traveling about ten miles per hour and two cars behind Maria and Frank. A trooper parked on the side of the highway got out of his car and walked towards Maria's Taurus. He smiled and waved at Maria and then, as if the patron saint of wanted felons saw an opportunity to do a good deed, walked behind her car and stopped both lanes of traffic just by raising his right hand. O'Shea and Simpson just looked at each other in disbelief. The trooper signaled for a tow truck to come through the crossover as Maria and Frank slowly drove out of sight.

"You might as well relax," Simpson said. "We're going to be here a while."

"How will we find them again?" O'Shea asked.

"Do you act on your hunches, your intuition?" Simpson asked.

"All the time," O'Shea said.

"How often were you right?" Simpson asked.

"Probably nine out of ten times," O'Shea said proudly.

"I've got a hunch about where they're going," Simpson said, as he reclined the seat and closed his eyes.

Fifteen minutes later O'Shea and Simpson were northbound again. Simpson woke up as O'Shea was entering the toll booth in Augusta.

"Where are we?" a sleepy Simpson asked.

"The last sign I saw said Augusta," O'Shea said.

"Take the next exit," Simpson said as he got his bearings. "How long were we stopped in Freeport?" Simpson asked.

"About fifteen minutes," O'Shea said.

"If they stop to eat we may catch them," Simpson said. "Watch the restaurant parking lots."

Simpson knew the odds were against them finding the green Taurus just by driving by but he didn't want to take the time to check every restaurant. He knew where Silveira was going. He didn't know why he was so sure. It was a cop thing and he always paid attention to what his hunches told him. Simpson was confident if they missed them here they would find them on Deer Isle. O'Shea and Simpson traveled down Western Avenue checking every parking area at or near a restaurant, around the traffic rotary across the bridge through the next rotary and down Bangor Street. O'Shea was good at driving and looking Simpson noted. O'Shea only had three close calls at rear ending the car in front of him. Simpson thought it was a lot like teaching his kids to drive. He kept calm and only yelled out once.

"Why do you think they're going to Deer Isle?" O'Shea asked.

"Just a feeling," Simpson said. "He hasn't been seen for over seventeen years and by coming back, he's risking arrest and spending the rest of his life in a Maine prison. It had to be something important to him and there is only one thing in Maine important to him."

"What's that?" O'Shea asked.

"Revenge," Simpson said.

"You mean he knows who killed my father and the rest of them?" O'Shea asked.

"He either knows or thinks he knows," Simpson said.

"What are we going to do if we find him?" O'Shea asked.

"When we find him we'll call Det. Gervais and then sit back and watch," Simpson said wistfully. "And when Dan arrests him, I will be there to smile at him and he'll know I was the reason he was arrested."

"I take it that there is a lot more history between you and Frank than you have let on," O'Shea said.

"Nothing sinister or life changing," Simpson said with a smile.

"Well, what then?" O'Shea asked.

"The day they left for Maine, Frank looked over at me." Simpson said. "He knew we were watching him. We were in a covert surveillance van. No way could he have made us. Someone had to have tipped him off and it had to be someone at Warwick PD," Simpson said and was getting stressed just talking about it. The tick in his right eye that had not been present for five years started again and Simpson could feel it.

"He just looked at you," O'Shea said. "That doesn't mean he knew it was you."

"He gave me the finger," Simpson said flatly. "Don't you think it was funny that New Hampshire and the FBI were notified and not any police agencies in Maine?" Simpson asked.

"I didn't think much about it," O'Shea said. "Someone just dropped the ball."

"No," Simpson said. "No one dropped the ball. What ever happened was on purpose and it came from within our department."

"Did you ever suspect anyone in particular?" O'Shea asked.

"I didn't then and after seventeen years of thinking about it, I still don't have a clue," Simpson said.

O'Shea just looked at Simpson like the obsessed paranoid man he sounded like.

"I know what you're thinking," Simpson said. "But I always trust my hunches."

"When are we going to call your friend Dan?" O'Shea asked.

"When we find Frank," Simpson said.

O'Shea thought it would have been a good idea to tell the trooper in Freeport but Simpson hadn't suggested it. Rookies weren't in the habit of suggesting investigative ideas to criminal division captains. It would probably be good for the investigation and that is why a fresh perspective is good but it was usually bad for the rookie who seemed to have forgotten his place. O'Shea was still aware of his place. This was going to be interesting, O'Shea thought. They drove and scanned parking areas from Augusta to Belfast and then to Searsport. They admired the coastal views as they traveled the winding stretch of Route 1 through Stockton Springs and Prospect. O'Shea was commenting on the Waldo-Hancock Bridge as they approached and Simpson interrupted him with a, "Gotcha."

"What?" O'Shea said.

"Frank and his sister are having dinner at the Sail Inn Restaurant," Simpson said with no emotion. "Keep going across the bridge and we'll wait on the other side," Simpson said.

Maria gestured for Frank to wipe the tartar sauce from the corner of his mouth. Frank was finishing the last of his haddock sandwich and gave Maria a confused look.

"You've got food on your face," Maria said.

Frank instinctively wiped the wrong side of his face with a napkin. Elise, their server for their visit to the Sail Inn Restaurant, was walking by the booth and pointed at the corner of her own mouth and Frank wiped the tartar sauce away per Elise's directions. Maria smiled and rolled her eyes.

Elise enjoyed her waitress job. She liked meeting new people and the personal interaction, however brief, made her feel as though she was a part of her guest's lives. She needed adult conversation now more than ever. The 28-year-old reasonably attractive mother of two boys ages four and six was recently made a widow thanks to a drunk driver who killed her husband as he returned home from the Champion Paper Mill in Bucksport early one Sunday morning just eight months ago. When Elise wasn't working she doted on her boys and tried to get over her and her boys' loss. This year she had promised the boys that they would see the fireworks in Stonington. There were closer fireworks displays but a nice young man from Vinalhaven, who just happened to own a lobster boat, invited her and her boys aboard his boat. Elise's inclination was to decline but in the end the charm of Peter Ames was more than she could resist. Elise had met many very nice people working at the Sail Inn Restaurant and mistakenly thought that Frank and Maria fit that group. Elise had no way of knowing that this seemingly nice couple from Rhode Island had murder on their agenda.

Frank finished his water as Maria patiently waited. Elise offered a dessert menu that Maria declined for both of them. Maria was tired and she wanted to be in the motel bed as soon as she could. Elise presented the bill to Frank, wished them a nice visit to Maine and quickly walked to her new customer three booths away. Elise sat down next to Peter Ames and presented him with the menu.

"We didn't get that kind of service," Frank groused.

"They appear to be an item, Frank," Maria said.

"Showing favoritism may affect her tip," Frank joked.

Frank left a twenty-five percent tip despite his complaint of favoritism.

"That's quite a tip," Maria said.

"She has a nice ass," Frank responded dryly.

Maria sighed, they paid their bill and left.

"You're a pig," Maria said as they walked to the car.

"Oink. Oink," was Frank's only reply.

Frank and Maria crossed the bridge onto Verona Island and O'Shea and Simpson pulled out of the pool and spa store and followed them into Bucksport. The ride to Deer Isle was uneventful. Frank and Maria made the right turn at the Bridge End Motel and Restaurant as O'Shea and Simpson drove by then doubled back and pulled into the parking lot. Maria and Frank were just walking through the door of the rental unit with their overnight bags when O'Shea and Simpson drove into the parking area.

"Well, they're here," O'Shea said.

"Now what?" he asked.

"We find Gervais and watch," Simpson said. Simpson located the pay phone and called the state police barracks in Orono. Simpson returned to his car. O'Shea noted that Simpson looked concerned.

"What's wrong?" O'Shea asked.

"Gervais has retired," Simpson said. "Well, not actually retired yet but he's using up his vacation until his retirement date. They are going to try to reach the detective in the area but hc's on day off also."

Sharon answered the phone.

"I'm sorry he's not here right now but I'll tell him you called," Sharon lied.

Sam was walking in the door as she hung up the phone.

"Who was that?" he asked.

"Wrong number," Sharon said. Sam went to the bathroom and went back out to the garage and helped his boys decorate their bikes.

Maria fell onto the twin bed and quickly fell asleep. Frank left in the Taurus to revisit the place that was the beginning of the end of his life as he knew it. Frank drove within ten feet of O'Shea and Simpson as O'Shea was getting back into the car after getting two clam baskets for Simpson and himself.

"He's leaving and he's alone," O'Shea said.

"I hope you can eat and drive," Simpson said.

O'Shea smiled and started the Buick.

Frank picked just that moment to adjust the dial on the radio. He had discovered an FM station at 102.5 and "Cocaine" by Eric Clapton had just begun. Frank turned it up and looked down the road as he drove. Had Frank looked left as he passed the ranch-style home with the two-car garage he would have seen Arnold Peterson waxing the 1969 Roadrunner in preparation for the parade on the fourth. He didn't look and had no reason to. He knew where he was going and that's where his thoughts already were. O'Shea noticed the man in the T-shirt waxing the muscle car but that was all. O'Shea didn't know the significance of what he was looking at. The man that had killed his father and the car that the man's two boys were in on that March evening was seventy feet away and he didn't have any idea who the man was or what the car represented. He would soon enough.

"Nice car," O'Shea said.

"It's a car," Simpson said.

Frank came down over the winding hill that came into Deer Isle village. As Frank continued left on Route 15 he glanced over and saw that Over The Rainbow Realty was still in business. He saw a triple black 1987 Mustang GT convertible parked out front. His eyes lingered a little too long and he started to drift into the intersection. Frank noticed his problem and jerked the car back into the driving lane.

"Something on that street got his attention," Simpson said.

"Yeah," O'Shea replied. "Probably the Mustang."

"Not everybody gets a sexual experience from cars," Simpson chided.

"They don't?" O'Shea said, with a sarcastic smile.

"No, they don't," Simpson said. "But I bet that's the real estate company where Frank leased the property," Simpson said. "We should stop later and warn them that Frank's in town."

"Do you think that's a good idea?" O'Shea asked.

"I know Frank and it's a bad idea if we don't warn whoever is left at that company," Simpson said.

"You're probably right," O'Shea said.

Simpson looked at O'Shea. "Probably?" Simpson asked.

"Definitely right, sir," O'Shea said nervously.

Simpson sighed and turned his attention to Frank.

Julia tried not to work seven days a week but when people want to spend six figures on a real estate deal, Julia would work on Christmas. Julia left the office just as Simpson's Buick went out of sight around the corner and up the hill by the old high school. Julia started up her Mustang and drove down the west side of the island to do some grocery shopping.

Frank turned left onto the Sunshine Road and Simpson instructed O'Shea to turn into the Mobil Station, wait a few seconds and then turn down the Sunshine Road. This is a simple maneuver that keeps the surveillance car out of the mirror of the car being followed. O'Shea caught up with Frank just as Frank turned down the driveway to the Walker Estate. O'Shea drove by.

"That's where it happened," Simpson said.

"How do you know?" O'Shea asked.

"Where else would he be going?" Simpson said in a matter of fact tone. "Besides, the mailbox said Walker," Simpson added.

Frank came down the tree-lined driveway and entered the semi-circular driveway just as he had done seventeen years ago. Just like then, there were cars and people already there. Frank continued around the driveway and drove out without stopping. Frank felt nothing, no fear, no hate, no remorse, no nothing. He didn't think about it much but he did think about the woman who first brought him to this place. She would know the Petersons and she would help him. Frank would see to that. Frank came out of the Walker driveway before O'Shea and Simpson got back into position. Simpson instructed O'Shea to wait. About twenty minutes later a car, not Frank's, came out of the driveway. There was no sense of urgency. Just a family on vacation.

"He's gone," Simpson said.

"How do you know?" O'Shea asked. Simpson was getting tired of O'Shea's, "how do you knows".

"Because he wouldn't have stayed if people were there and if he did stay those people would not have been so relaxed," Simpson said like an elementary school teacher.

"Sorry," O'Shea said.

Simpson did not reply. O'Shea drove back towards the Bridge End Motel without being told by Simpson. Frank was not there. O'Shea inquired about a room and there was one available.

"You're lucky," the clerk said. "That room was booked a month ago and they just cancelled an hour ago."

O'Shea didn't feel lucky. It was a room with just one double bed and O'Shea knew who was getting the bed.

Frank drove to the post office and parked so he could watch Over The Rainbow Realty. The sun was going down but he would stay as long as it took. He didn't know if she would be back or not. Frank was relying on luck. Julia had packed her six bags of groceries into the back seat and started back up the island to go home. Julia drove slowly through the village. She saw the lone car in the post office parking lot but did not give it a second look. Julia stopped at the office to check for a fax that was supposed to come for her latest deal. Frank smiled. He would remind himself to visit Atlantic City on his way south this time. Julia had left the door ajar and didn't hear Frank walk into the office. Julia turned from the fax machine just as Frank was a step behind her. Frank struck Julia in the forehead with the heel of his hand, knocking Julia to the floor and sending papers flying. Julia was momentarily stunned and her first thought was to pull her skirt down to a more modest position. Frank laughed to himself. Julia looked up at her attacker and froze. She recognized him immediately.

"What's wrong, Julia?" Frank mocked. "You look like you've seen a ghost."

Julia did not respond.

"Get up," Frank demanded.

Julia felt tears welling up. This was the day she had feared for seventeen years. Where are you Sam, Julia thought to herself. Frank removed a 9mm pistol from his waistband. Julia thought of herself as a strong and confident person, but she had to use all her strength to keep from throwing up when she saw Frank pull out a gun and point it at her.

"I need another place to rent," Frank said calmly.

"I only have one," Julia said fighting back the tears.

"Well, get the keys and let's go," Frank barked.

Julia clumsily rose to her feet and went to the key case and removed the numbered keys to a cottage on the Reach Road. Frank grabbed Julia by the hair at the back of her head and guided her to the map on the wall. Julia stared at the floor as Frank found the corresponding number on the map.

"Where are your car keys?" Frank asked.

"In it," Julia said.

225

Frank paused and pushed Julia back to her desk. Frank didn't trust Julia to continue to be submissive. Frank suspected she was a survivor and that type of person could be unpredictable. He found some packing tape in a drawer and bound her hands behind her back and then pushed her out the door. He put her into the front seat of her Mustang and leaned in to fasten her seat belt so she couldn't move. Julia lunged forward and sunk her teeth into the back of Frank's neck. Frank lurched away striking the back of his head on the convertible roof frame. Julia did not release her grip and ended up with flesh and hair still in her teeth. Frank staggered backwards as he was momentarily stunned by the pain. Julia spit out the divot from Frank's neck and tried to scramble over the console into the driver's seat but Frank reached in and grabbed her by the shoulder of her blouse. As Frank pulled her back to the passenger seat the blouse ripped open in front and tore down the back. Julia was wide eyed and opened her mouth to scream just as Frank landed the first of three violent blows to Julia's face. The first punch knocked her unconscious. The other two were to placate Frank's rage. This time Frank was able to seat belt her into her seat without any interruption. Julia's head slumped forward and blood streamed from her broken nose. Frank sped away from the village and traveled north to the Reach Road. The back of Frank's neck was throbbing and he could feel the blood dripping down his back. The cottage was easy to find. The owners saw fit to place one of those carved signs with their name emblazoned in gold paint for all to see and admire. Frank stopped to unlock the chain that was suspended between two large oak trees. When Frank got back into the car Julia was staring at him with one eye. Her right eye was already swollen shut and looked like a little ripe plum. Her left eye was focused on his face but she still looked a little dazed. The blood had slowed from her swollen nose and her upper lip was swollen on the right side and split. Her mouth, neck and breasts were covered in blood. What had been a blouse was now a tattered cotton shawl and her white lace bra was now crimson.

"Why?" Julia mumbled.

Frank noticed what had been a very attractive woman now looked like an extra from Dawn of the Dead. Even her breasts didn't look appealing to Frank now that they were covered in blood.

"Shut up," Frank snapped at her.

Julia was still dazed but she was lucid enough to realize that she was probably not going to live through this.

"Don't give up," she said.

"What?" Frank said.

Julia didn't respond. She needed to say it out loud. She needed to hear her own voice to give her strength. Her entire life she had relied on no one but herself. It would be no different tonight and she would have to start thinking before she did anything that stupid again if she was going to survive. Frank stopped the Mustang near the front porch of the relatively small one-and-a-half story cedar-shingled cottage. He unlocked the door, found the light and looked around. Julia stared out the windshield of her car and watched the bright moonlight sparkle and sway on the water in front of the cottage. She looked towards the cottage and saw Frank as he moved in and out of view while checking out the rooms. Julia tried in vain to bring her taped hands around her side to reach the seat belt. Frank came back to the car, opened her door and unbuckled her seat belt.

"Don't do anything unless I tell you to or you will get more of the same," Frank said.

Julia didn't speak. She just turned her head almost owl like so she could see his face with her left eye. She gave him a look of contempt which he recognized. Frank grabbed her hair at the top of her head and pulled her out of the car. Julia fell as she came out of the car and the pea stone driveway dug into her knees with excruciating pain. Frank pulled Julia to her feet by her hair and pushed her towards the door. The screen door shut behind them and Frank continued to push Julia towards the master bath. Julia could hear the shower running as they entered the room. Frank stopped at the edge of the tub and cut the tape from her wrists with a pair of scissors.

"Get in," he barked.

Julia stepped into the tub and the warm water stung her face. She watched as the water and blood mixed then swirled down the drain. Frank pulled the curtain shut and sat on the closed seat of the toilet. Julia noticed that the flower patterned shower curtain was not see-through. Thank God for small favors, Julia thought.

"Don't take all night," Frank said. "I found a man's t-shirt for you and there's a first aid kit here too."

Julia did not respond. She removed what was left of her blouse and draped it over the shower rod. She took off her bra and squeezed the blood from it and used the remnants of a well-used piece of Ivory soap that the house cleaner had missed to clean it further. The bra was hung next to the blouse. Julia did the same with her navy blue skirt and her white cotton panties. Julia tried to wash her face but it hurt all over. She dabbed gently at her nose and lip. Julia washed her hair with the same piece of soap, rinsed it and turned the shower off. Julia just stood there without speaking and waited for Frank's next move. Frank tossed a towel over the curtain and Julia caught it before it landed in the bottom of the tub. Julia dried her hair and her body the best she could and wrapped the towel around her as modestly as the towel would allow. Julia opened the shower curtain and carefully stepped out of the tub. Normally Frank would have found the sight of Julia Henderson in nothing but a towel to be a pleasing sight. It was, for the most part, but he had inflicted terrible injuries to her once pretty face. Frank felt a little remorse until the throbbing neck pain reminded him how she earned her battle wounds. Julia still did not speak. She just stared at Frank with her left eye. No emotion and no fear either he noticed. Frank handed her a white, men's large t-shirt that had paint stains on it.

"I think it was a rag but it's clean," Frank said.

Julia took the t-shirt from Frank and turned her back to him. She pulled the shirt over her head and let the towel drop. Her butt was briefly displayed for Frank's inspection but at this point she really didn't care. The shirt hung like a short dress a few inches below her butt. Frank did notice and his thoughts drifted for a moment until she turned around. Her battered face subdued the sexual thoughts he was having. Once my bra and panties are dry I should be quite comfortable, Julia thought. Julia pulled her bra, skirt and panties from the shower curtain rod and looked back at Frank. She left the tattered blouse. She hoped his presence while she showered was to make sure she didn't try anything and not so he could try something.

"You're going to clean and bandage my wound," Frank said. "And I'll see to yours."

Frank handed Julia the first-aid kit he had found in the bathroom. Julia placed her clothes on the edge of the tub and opened the kit. Frank held up the scissors and tweezers and gave her a knowing smile. Julia didn't think he was that stupid but she had hoped for a few seconds.

"You stay here and keep an eye on their room," Simpson said. "I'm going to drive around and see if I can find him."

O'Shea nodded, "You want me to take notes on what happens while you're gone?" he said.

Simpson smiled. There wasn't much more that he could do. A police radio would be awfully nice to have, Simpson thought.

"That's a good idea," Simpson said. "I won't be gone long."

Simpson drove off in his Buick and O'Shea sat on a porch chair by his front door. It was a pleasant July evening on the coast of Maine. O'Shea marveled at how quiet it was. He could hear the television in the next cottage and the sounds of the cars as they traveled across the bridge. The sounds of the waves gently lapping at the beach were some of the most soothing sounds he had ever heard. O'Shea thought that as soon as this adventure was over he was going to look into becoming a police officer in Maine. Just then, Maria came outside, just two cottages down from where O'Shea relaxed. He had a Yankees hat pulled low so the brim covered his eyes. Maria had known O'Shea since he was born and he had been at her house just four days ago. She lit a cigarette and stared at the ocean. O'Shea watched her as she walked towards the water and kicked at the sea weed. Headlights lit up the area. The triple black Mustang that O'Shea had seen earlier pulled up to the rear of Maria's cottage. A man got out and walked to the ocean side door. O'Shea couldn't see the man clearly but he knew it was Frank. Frank went inside not seeing Maria on the beach. Maria walked up the beach towards the cottage as Frank came back out.

"Come with me," Frank said.

"Where are we going?" Maria asked.

"Just come on," Frank said impatiently. The two disappeared behind the cottage.

"Whose car is this?" a surprised Maria said.

Frank did not respond. O'Shea walked to the edge of his cabin in time to see the Mustang back around and leave. O'Shea didn't have a problem memorizing the license plate. TOTO. Vanity plates make a police officer's job much easier.

Frank had placed a towel on the blood-soaked passenger seat but he hadn't cleaned the blood off the console and dashboard.

"What in hell happened in here and where is my car?" Maria demanded.

"Your car is fine. I'm taking you to it," Frank said.

"What about the blood?" Maria asked.

"Never mind," Frank said. "No one is dead. OK?" he added.

Maria noticed the lipstick in the console and the Chip and Dale male stripper air freshener hanging from the mirror.

"Where's the woman that owns this car, Frank?" Maria asked.

"She's fine," Frank said.

Maria thought about more questions but let them go. She didn't want to know and she was going to separate herself from Frank as quickly as possible. Frank drove to the post office and told Maria to take her car back to the Bridge End Motel and wait there for him.

"How long do I wait?" Maria asked sarcastically.

"As long as it takes," Frank snapped back.

Maria got in and drove back up the island. Frank followed her and Simpson followed a half mile back behind them both. It is a winding road through North Deer Isle and Simpson lost sight of the Mustang several times and he did not notice it turn right onto the Reach Road. Simpson didn't realize that he was only following one car now until he started down Hardy's Hill toward the causeway that connects Deer Isle with Little Deer Isle.

Frank locked the chain behind him this time. He was not planning any more trips this evening. Frank entered the cottage and flipped on the light as he entered the living room. Everything looked the same, he thought. Frank walked upstairs and the telltale creak of the steps alerted Julia. Julia was able to count to thirteen before Frank opened the bedroom door. Frank turned on the overhead light. He had drawn the shades before he had left and Julia had been in total darkness. It took her a few seconds to adjust her one good eye to the light. Julia looked at Frank without speaking but this time it was because Frank had taped her mouth shut. Her broken and blood-clogged nose had made it difficult to breath and she had managed to moisten the tape enough to loosen it and allow her to breathe through her mouth. Frank had taped her ankles to the legs of the chair he sat her in. It was an old wide cushioned chair and it had left her in a very un-lady like position considering her attire and lack of underwear. Julia had watched as Frank taped her ankles and noted with loathing as he glanced between her legs. He was now doing it again. You bastard, she thought. Frank had taped her wrists tightly to the arms of the chair and there was no wiggle room whatsoever. Julia's head and face still throbbed with pain but she did her best not to let Frank know.

"Comfy?" he asked.

The chair actually was comfortable and even though she was taped tightly to the chair's appendages it wasn't painful. Julia did not respond. Frank pulled another chair around to face her and sat down with his knees touching hers. Here we go, she thought. Frank reached towards Julia and she turned her head away. Frank grabbed the corner of the tape on her mouth and ripped it off in one quick motion.

"They say it doesn't hurt as much if you do it quickly," Frank said with a smile.

They didn't know what they were talking about, Julia thought. She wanted to scream but wouldn't give him the satisfaction. The lip that had stopped bleeding started again.

"I need to know where Arnold Peterson lives," Frank said calmly.

Frank could see the recognition register in Julia's left eye and also puzzlement.

"I know you know who he is," Frank said. "Tell me where he lives."

Julia just stared at Frank. Frank pulled his 9 mm pistol from the waist band at the small of his back and pushed it against Julia's forehead. Julia winced in anticipation. Frank smiled.

"Where does he live," Frank said, enunciating each word very slowly. Julia could feel herself start to tremble but said nothing. Suddenly Frank whipped the gun away from her head and slammed the barrel across the knuckles of her right hand. Julia screamed out and began to sob. Frank was an equal opportunity torturer. This was a ritual he had performed many times when he was making collections for his mob friends. This was the first woman he had treated in this fashion but it made no difference to him. She was just another bitch and she would tell him what he wanted to know. It was up to her how many of her bones had to be broken before she complied. Julia could add a broken index finger to her already broken nose.

"Why?" Julia whimpered.

Frank slapped her already bruised face with his left hand. Julia hung her head and cried uncontrollably.

"Just tell me where Peterson lives and I'll leave you alone," Frank said.

Julia looked up at Frank and tried to stop her sobs. Frank was not a patient man and he enjoyed what he was doing. Frank reached over with his left hand and with his thumb and index finger slowly squeezed Julia's swollen bleeding lip. Julia cried out again.

"Okay! Okay!" she cried. "He lives about three miles from here near the ice cream store," Julia said between sobs. "A blue house," she added.

Frank nearly shot Julia but thought he should make sure she hadn't lied to him first. Another day wouldn't matter. Frank smiled, got up, turned off the light, and closed the door as he left the room. The darkness was almost soothing, Julia thought.

"I lost him near this intersection," Simpson said as they turned down the Reach Road. O'Shea and Simpson were looking for Frank and the black Mustang. Maria was back in her room and she was alone. Simpson and O'Shea drove around for two hours. Nothing but gated roads and dark houses.

"We're going to have to call someone," O'Shea said. "You know he stole the car or worse," he added.

"I know," Simpson said. Simpson called the Orono State Police barracks and learned that Det. Peterson had not called in. Simpson was told that Peterson would be off tomorrow and asked if he would like contact with another detective or trooper. Simpson declined and stated he would check back tomorrow.

"We need some sleep," Simpson said.

"Whatever you say, Captain," O'Shea said.

It was a little after midnight and Frank had just fallen asleep. Julia nodded in and out and finally had given up her fight to suppress her urge to urinate. It felt so good to let it out that she barely gave a thought that she was now sitting in her own urine. O'Shea nodded off to the sounds of Simpson's snoring. Thirty minutes later Maria got into her green Ford Taurus and left Deer Isle for home. Four hours later Arnold Peterson left his home near the ice cream store for a long day of hauling his lobster pots off Stonington. Anne slept soundly.

Julia was awake when Frank got up. She knew that as soon as Frank found the Petersons she would be dead. Julia was not a physically strong woman but she was in good shape and it was an old chair. She had spent the night carefully and quietly flexing her arms back and forth against the arms of the chair. She had successfully loosened them to the point that all she needed was a couple of violent jerks and the arms would break away from the chair and that would be a start. Julia heard Frank cough and then heard the toilet flush. Two minutes later the stairs sent out their signal. Julia leaned her head forward and feigned a light snore. Frank looked in and did not turn on the light. The light from the hallway let in a bright shaft of the morning sun and showed him all he needed to see. A sleeping woman with her legs spread revealing the place on her body that Frank would like to visit. Maybe I'll take care of that before I punch her ticket to paradise, Frank thought. Frank closed the door and walked down the stairs and out the front door. Julia heard the throaty rumble as her Mustang came to life and then the sound disappeared. Please don't be home, Julia thought.

Anne had just placed the last of the breakfast dishes into the dishwasher where they joined last night's supper dishes when the phone rang.

"Hi Sue," Anne said. "Sure. I'll meet you there in fifteen minutes. Bye."

Anne's golf clubs were already in her car and all she had to do was grab her golf shoes and out the door she went. It was a beautiful day and she was going to enjoy every minute of it. Anne was rounding the corner south of her home as Frank was rounding the corner north of her home.

Simpson woke up swearing. He had not planned on sleeping in and 8:30 a.m. was a much later start than he had wanted. He looked around and saw O'Shea was gone. A moment later the door opened and O'Shea came in with coffee and breakfast.

"Bacon and scrambled eggs," he said with a smile.

"Thanks," Simpson said.

"Bad news," O'Shea said.

Simpson just looked at him.

"The green Taurus is gone," O'Shea said.

"Well, of course it's gone," Simpson said. "It's 8:30 in the morning. We should be gone too."

O'Shea looked away and sat down on the edge of the bed to eat.

***

Julia needed only three jerks of her left arm and two with her right and she broke the chair arms free. She peeled away the tape from her right hand first. The index finger was swollen and it hurt. She painfully removed the tape from her left hand and repeated the process with her legs. Julia stood and was a little unsteady. Her hips were sore from sitting in the same position for at least twelve hours. Julia made her way down the stairs and into the bathroom. She began to cry as she saw herself in the bathroom mirror for the first time since her ordeal. She wanted to shower off the urine smell but she didn't know when Frank would return and she was sure he would return. She quickly pulled on her underpants and skirt. She had only one shoe so she left it behind. The sunshine was bright, warm and invigorating.

Chapter Twenty-Two

Julia trudged up the dirt driveway and was stepping over the chain at the end of the driveway as O'Shea and Simpson drove slowly by.

"That didn't look right," O'Shea said.

"No shit," Simpson said.

"Turn around."

Julia saw the big Buick drive by. She was still a little dazed and her head and nose still hurt. Her only concern now was that it wasn't Frank in her Mustang. Julia started walking towards Route 15 and didn't see the Buick turn around and approach her from behind. She walked in the roadway as it was easier on her feet than the gravel shoulder. O'Shea pulled alongside and Simpson rolled down his window.

"Are you okay, Miss?" Simpson asked.

Julia turned and faced Simpson. That answered his question. There were tears leaking from her left eye and her swollen lips trembled.

"No," she said. "Will you help me?"

Simpson was already getting out of the car and helped her into the front seat. Simpson got into the back seat.

"I need to get to a phone so I can call the police," Julia said in a monotone.

"We're police officers," O'Shea said. "And you need a hospital."

"You're police officers?" Julia asked.

"Yes," Simpson said.

"Warwick, Rhode Island Police Department at your service," O'Shea chimed in.

It took a few seconds to register with Julia where they were from but when it did she knew why they were on Deer Isle.

"You're looking for Frank Silveira," Julia said.

O'Shea looked at Simpson in the rear view mirror. Simpson nodded.

"Yeah, we are," O'Shea said.

"He has my black Mustang and he's looking for Arnold Peterson," Julia said.

"I take it that your injuries are from Frank," Simpson said.

"I think he was going to kill me," Julia said. "He had to make sure I hadn't lied to him first. I'm afraid the Petersons are in danger."

"Who are the Petersons?" Simpson asked.

"Arnold and Anne Peterson," Julia said. "He's a fisherman and Anne's a school teacher."

"Any relation to Trooper Sam Peterson?" Simpson asked.

"Yeah," Julia said. "They're his parents."

"Did he say why he wanted to find them?" Simpson asked.

"He didn't say much," Julia said. "And he only asked about Arnold."

"Did you know Frank before last night?" O'Shea asked.

"I was the one that leased the property to him where all those men were killed in 1970," Julia said. "I guess he remembered me."

"It looks like it wasn't a happy memory for him," Simpson said carelessly.

Julia looked at Simpson in the mirror. Even through her injuries, Simpson could tell that he had misspoken.

"I'm sorry, Miss," Simpson said. "I meant no disrespect."

"He did this to me because I bit a hole in the back of his neck when he kidnapped me and stole my car," Julia said defiantly. "If I'm lucky, he'll get an infection to go with the bite."

"A black Mustang with TOTO for a plate?" O'Shea asked.

"That would be my car," she said. "This is the Petersons house," Julia said.

O'Shea pulled in the driveway. Simpson got out and checked the doors and found them locked.

"There doesn't look to be anyone home," Simpson said.

"Arnold's probably fishing," Julia said. "Anne could be most anywhere on a nice day like this."

O'Shea backed out of the driveway and Julia gave him directions to the Island Medical Center.

***

"That damn bitch," Frank said out loud. "I should have killed her when I had the chance."

Frank had backed Julia's Mustang in the garage next to the Roadrunner and was waiting for Arnold to come home. The garage was not attached to the house and was rarely, if ever, locked. Frank had intended on staying there no matter how long it took. He wasn't sure what to do now and he couldn't believe Jonas Simpson was here too.

"I know he's on his day off but I think he'd be interested that a wanted murderer was looking for his parents," Simpson said trying to keep his cool.

"Who did you say you were?" Dispatcher Wood asked.

"Captain Jonas Simpson of the Warwick, Rhode Island Police Department," he said.

"And you said that you're at the Island Medical Center in Stonington with a kidnap and assault victim?" Wood asked.

"Yes," Simpson said. "Her name is Julia Henderson."

"Please hold," Wood said and the line went silent.

"Hi Sharon," Wood said. "Is Sam there?"

"Why?" a cool Sharon responded. Wood had dealt with Sharon screening Sam's calls before and she was sure Sam didn't know about it.

"I've got a Rhode Island detective on the other line that needs to talk to Sam," Wood said.

"I'm sure it can wait until Wednesday when he's back to work," Sharon said.

"I'm sure it can't," Wood said.

Sharon was momentarily at a loss for words. Usually the dispatchers just say okay and hang up.

"Excuse me?" Sharon said.

"It can't wait," Wood said. "This guy needs to talk to Sam now. It involves his parents."

"Well, why didn't you say so?" Sharon said indignantly.

Bitch, Wood thought.

"Sam," Sharon called out. "The barracks is on the phone."

Sharon set the phone on the kitchen counter and left the room. A short time later Sam picked up the phone.

"Peterson," he said.

"Hi Sam," Wood said. Wood explained the situation as Simpson had explained it.

"You guys should have called me last night," Sam said.

"We did," Wood said.

"Oh," Sam said, knowing why he didn't get the message. "Sorry," he added.

"I'll connect you to Simpson," Wood said and the line was quiet. "Okay, Captain Simpson," Wood said. "You're on with Detective Peterson."

Wood disconnected her end and waited for the next call.

"Hello, Captain," Sam said.

"Call me Jonas," he said sincerely.

O'Shea heard this part of the exchange and wondered why he couldn't call him Jonas. Simpson saw the look on O'Shea's face and smiled. Someday, Simpson thought. A CNA wheeled Julia into the waiting room. Simpson motioned to O'Shea to see how she was doing.

"I was told that Silveira is on Deer Isle and may be looking for my father," Sam said. "Do you know why?" he added.

"Sam," Simpson said. "All I can tell you is that I followed Frank to Maine with the intention of having Dan Gervais arrest him here and I could watch. I didn't know he had retired and your dispatch couldn't find you."

Sam could feel his heart begin to pound. He was home and Sharon didn't give him the message.

"How's Julia?" Sam asked.

"Just a second," Simpson said. "I'll ask her."

Simpson was back on the phone a minute later.

"She's in worse shape than we thought," Simpson said. "Her skull is fractured and brain fluid is leaking out her nose. They're taking her to Bangor by ambulance."

"What happened to her?" Sam asked.

"Frank beat her pretty badly when he stole her car. And beat her again when he questioned her about your father."

"Where can I meet you?" Sam asked.

"Cabin 2 at the Bridge End Motel," he said.

"I'll be there in twenty minutes," Sam said. He hung up the phone, changed out of his shorts and got his service weapon from the top of the closet.

"Where are you going?" Sharon asked.

"Deer Isle," Sam said. "Where I should have been last night," he added.

"Is there anything wrong?" Sharon asked.

"If you call a murderer looking for my parents and a woman nearly beat to death something wrong. Then yeah, there's something wrong," Sam said.

"Who was beaten?" she asked.

"Julia Henderson," he said. Sharon rolled her eyes and turned away as Sam went out the door.

"Where's Dad going, Mom?" Todd asked.

"I don't know. I guess work is more important than you and Mike," Sharon said.

"1251 Orono. 10-8," Sam said.

"10-4 1251," Wood responded.

Simpson and O'Shea walked out to the ambulance with Julia. In spite of her condition she told them to be careful and wished them good luck.

"She's a strong woman," Simpson said as the ambulance drove off.

"Amazing," O'Shea agreed.

Sam didn't have his emergency lights on or his siren but he was driving to the edge of his car's ability, the road's ability to handle the car, and his own ability to handle the car and the road. He shouldn't have been but he was.

Anne Peterson loaded her golf clubs into the trunk of her car as she said good-bye to Sue. They had played eighteen holes and enjoyed each other's company in the warm July sun.

Arnold was sitting on the washboard of his boat with his legs crossed thinking about the cigarettes he had given up ten years ago. That is what these moments were for. Take a break between the strings of pots that had been hauled and the ones that had yet to yield their catch. Take a break and enjoy the beautiful scenery of the coast of Maine. This would be so much better with a cigarette, he thought. A twelve-ounce bottle of Sprite would have to do now. Arnold looked off towards Shingle Island where a small pleasure boat was moored. The small waves caused the vessel to gently bob up and down and occasionally the sun would reflect off the windshield like a signal mirror or like the reflection from a sniper's scope on an opposite hill in Korea. Arnold was no longer thinking about his longing for Pall Malls. He was mesmerized by the twirling, falling Kennedy half dollar. Arnold could hear his own voice but he wasn't speaking.

"Go to your car," he had said. "Stay in the shadows."

Arnold wasn't on a battlefield with his fellow soldiers. He was with his two oldest sons and they were at the Walker Estate. He felt his finger squeeze the trigger, he heard the deafening blast for the ninth time and he saw Sammy Sangelo fall to the floor with his pants down around his ankles. Then he saw him. It was a dark-haired and dark-eyed man staring back at him through the kitchen window. Arnold was out of ammunition and he had to retreat. The man looked familiar now. The half dollar landed on the seat of a Mercedes taxi between Arnold and Anne. Arnold looked into the rear view mirror and saw the dark-haired and dark-eyed man and now saw the recognition in the man's eyes. Arnold lurched backwards and flailed his arms wildly to regain his balance. Arnold's boat had drifted against a granite ledge that was part of the shoreline of Saddleback Island. He jumped to his feet and backed his boat away from the ledge. He looked at his watch. It had been forty-five minutes since he sat down to drink his bottle of Sprite. Arnold now had the answers to the nagging questions of the last seventeen years. He now knew, or more appropriately, was now aware of what Carl and Sam had known all along. Arnold had one hundred more traps to haul but they would have to wait for another day. Arnold turned his lobster boat towards Stonington and pushed the throttle all the way forward.

Sam had miraculously made it to the Bridge End Motel but there was no one at Cabin 2. He continued on towards his parents' home and met the ambulance carrying Julia as they crossed the causeway. He also met Simpson's Buick but did not recognize them and all they noticed of Sam's car was some idiot driving way too fast on the narrow rock-lined causeway. Simpson and O'Shea arrived at their cabin at the same time Sam pulled in behind his mother's car at the Peterson residence.

Frank was out of the Mustang and at the side garage door when Sam drove in. Anne was in the bathroom. Sam bounded up the steps and through the door.

"Mom," he called out. "I'm in the bathroom," she said. "I'll be out in a minute."

Sam paced the kitchen floor. He heard the toilet flush and then water run in the sink.

"Hi, sweetheart," she said. "To what do I owe this surprise visit?"

"Sit down, Mom," Sam said.

Anne could see the concern in her son's eyes.

"What's wrong, Sam?" she asked as she sat at the kitchen table.

"Mom, do you remember the night Dad had to look for Carl and me? The night those men were killed at the Walker Estate?"

"Yes Sam, I do," she said. "I think everyone on the island remembers that night or at least the next day. Why do you ask?"

"Dad found Carl and me at the Walker Estate," Sam said.

Anne's eyes got wide and she began to tremble.

"What are you saying?" Anne said as she began to cry. Anne had suspected this all along. Arnold had revealed as much unknowingly in his nightmares but she never dared ask him about it.

"Carl and I were there to meet with Gary to buy some pot when these guys showed up," Sam explained. "They kidnapped us and during the scuffle Carl hit one of them hard enough to kill him."

Anne gasped and covered her mouth with her hand at the horror of learning that her son had killed someone.

"A little while later Dad showed up and killed all of them except one man who evidently got away," Sam explained with the calm of a veteran police officer. He no longer recalled the events of March 17, 1970, through the eyes of a 14-year-old boy.

"The man that they charged with the murders," Anne recalled. "Silver something."

"Frank Silveira," Sam said. "And he's on the island now looking for Dad."

"He's here!" Anne exclaimed.

"Yes mom," Sam said. "And he has Julia Henderson's black Mustang. Have you seen it today?"

"Julia's car," Anne said puzzled. "Why does he have her car?"

"I don't know, Mom," Sam said a little impatiently. "He just has it. He beat up Julia very badly and she's on her way to EMMC."

"Oh, my God!" Anne cried. "What are we going to do?"

Suddenly they both heard the roar of a car engine and Sam saw the black Mustang streak past the kitchen window. Sam ran outside with his 9mm in hand. All he saw was dust and heard the sound of the Mustang being put through the gears as it traveled towards Stonington. Frank was not leaving Deer Isle until he found Arnold Peterson. Sam noticed the garage door was open and saw where the driveway had been spun up by the Mustang as it left the garage. He was there all along, Sam thought. Sam ran to his car only to find that both passenger side tires were flat. The tires on his mother's car were in the same condition. The tires had been cut while Sam and his mother sat in the kitchen.

"Mom, open the garage door so we can get the Roadrunner out and then get in," Sam ordered.

Anne was still in shock but she complied without hesitation. Sam notified the Orono barracks of the situation and gave them a description of Julia's Mustang and the name of the man driving it.

"10-4 1251," Wood said.

Jesus. That guy's a shit magnet, Sgt. Cohen thought after hearing the broadcast. Sam grabbed his portable radio and ran to the garage. Arnold had washed and waxed the Roadrunner for the Fourth of July parade and, more importantly, he had filled the gas tank. The 383 fired immediately as it had just been driven the day before. Sam eased it out of the garage and then north on Route 15.

"Where are we going?" Anne asked.

"There are two Rhode Island police officers waiting for me at the Bridge End," Sam said. "You're going to stay there while I look for Silveira."

"Oh," was all Anne could manage as Sam brought the Roadrunner past one hundred miles per hour as they approached the causeway. Anne was grateful that Sam slowed to seventy five on the causeway even though that was still way too fast for her.

"Mom," Sam said urgently. "You cannot tell these guys what I just told you."

"Don't worry, Sam," she said. "I suspected all along that your father was the demise of those men. I just didn't know how you and Carl were involved or what you knew."

"I'm sorry, Mom," Sam said. "Now I have to return the favor to Dad."

Arnold had found an AM radio station when he was cleaning the car and the radio came to life when Sam had started the engine. "Sleepwalk" was playing as they crossed the causeway and Sam thought the song was as surreal as the moment. "That was 'Sleepwalk' by Santos and Johnny," the static-shrouded AM radio voice said. "And now for one of my favorites, 'Bad Moon Rising' by CCR." Sam and Anne pulled into the Bridge End and stopped behind Simpson's Buick. Sam reached for the ignition key to turn off the engine but hesitated and listened to the haunting lyrics.

"Hope you got your things together. Hope you are quite prepared to die. Looks like we're in for nasty weather. One eye is taken for an eye." Sam turned the switch and looked at his mother.

"Remember," he said. "Not a word."

Anne nodded and wiped away her tears.

Sam found Simpson and O'Shea in their cabin and quickly brought them up to speed. Simpson went with Sam and O'Shea and Anne stayed at the cabin.

"You guys are armed?" Sam asked.

Simpson hesitated, "Yes, but we aren't advertising it," he said. Sam realized that Simpson and O'Shea's visit to Maine was likely not sanctioned by the Warwick PD administration.

Captain of Detectives or not, Simpson still had to answer to someone.

"I understand," Sam said with a smile. "I don't think Silveira cares about rules, laws and department policies."

Both O'Shea and Simpson nodded in agreement. Nothing needed to be said. All would do what they had to do to protect the citizens of Maine from Frank Silveira.

***

"Short day," Norm Wallace said. "I filled my barrel and it's a nice day," Arnold lied.

Arnold topped off the fuel tank, put his boat on the mooring and rowed ashore. Frank drove down Indian Point Road while checking all the docks along Stonington's working waterfront. He saw the big man rowing the little rowboat towards the dock but did not know it was Arnold. Frank had made cursory passes through several parking areas but didn't know what he hoped to find. He did the same at the Co-op parking lot. He drove between two lines of vehicles and a blue bumper sticker on a Ford pickup caught his eye. "Support Maine's Troopers". Frank had not noticed any other vehicles with a sticker like that and decided to wait and watch. Arnold secured his rowboat and walked to the office. Frank saw him walk across the parking lot and up the steps. He had found Arnold Peterson again.

"Nice car," Simpson said.

"It's my brother's," Sam said.

Simpson was trying to break the ice but Sam was focused on other matters. The radio was playing "Top of the World" by the Carpenters. Sam turned off the radio.

"Why is Frank looking for your father?" Simpson asked.

"I don't know," Sam lied.

"I think Frank came back here for revenge," Simpson said. "I think Frank figured out who killed his crew."

Sam did not respond.

"He was so sure that he convinced his sister to come with him," Simpson added.

Sam shifted down to second gear as he navigated the S turns known as "Lover's Lane" just across the Stonington – Deer Isle town line.

"Where is she?" Sam asked.

"I don't know," Simpson admitted. "Her car is gone and she's not in their cabin."

Sam's portable radio picked up a transmission between Sgt. Cohen and Dispatcher Wood.

"1205 Orono, have you heard from 1251?"

"Negative," Wood replied.

"Have a marked unit set up on the mainland side of the bridge and send another unit down to look for him," Cohen said.

"922 and 902 are already en route," Wood said.

"10-4," Cohen said. "I'm on my way, too."

Sgt. Cohen was on his day off and he had been in his police car to visit his wife for lunch at her work. Off duty use of the state vehicle was a perk but it often meant that the user would get called to work. Sgt. Cohen hadn't been called yet but with Peterson's recent track record he knew the call was inevitable.

"Notify the OD and call Unit 11," Sgt Cohen added.

"10-4, 1205," Wood responded. "The OD has been notified and Unit 11 was unavailable." Wood didn't seem to need a sergeant giving her instructions, Sgt. Cohen thought.

"10-4 Orono, thanks," Cohen said. Sam looked at the radio on the seat and smiled.

"They cover your back well," Simpson said.

"They've had a lot of practice," Sam said. The two men drove in silence for a few minutes. No sounds except for the low throbbing rumble of the car's exhaust and the wind whistling around the weathered car door seals.

"You asked me on the phone if I knew why Frank was looking for your father," Simpson said. "And I didn't exactly answer you. And I just asked you if you knew why and you didn't answer at all."

Sam looked out the windshield looking for the right words. "Frank probably has good reason to be looking for my father," Sam said reluctantly.

"We'll leave it at that," Simpson said.

"Thanks," Sam said.

"You look so young to be a police officer," Anne said.

"I am young," O'Shea admitted. "But it's a young man's job."

"I suppose you're right," Anne said. "Sam was your age when he joined the state police. I guess I shouldn't be surprised. I can't believe this man is here looking for Arnold," she added.

"Frank thinks your husband killed his friends back in 1970," O'Shea said. "My father was one of them."

Anne looked at O'Shea and was unable to mask her grief.

"Excuse me," she said as she walked to the doorway and stared at the bridge.

That hit a nerve, O'Shea thought. O'Shea walked outside and stopped alongside Anne. O'Shea watched the waves gently broke on the beach.

"My father was not a good person," O'Shea said. "If he didn't die there, then it would have been somewhere else and in a similar fashion."

Anne's shoulders bobbed up and down as she tried to stifle her tears.

"I'm well aware they were involved in drug smuggling. What I don't know is how your husband fits into this," O'Shea continued. "I'm just a little curious. It may be morbid and I may not want to hear it, but I want to know what happened."

"You're not here for revenge, too?" Anne asked.

"No, Mrs. Peterson. I'm not. I'm here to help arrest Frank. I was hoping he would tell me the story of that night. Now I'm hoping your husband will tell me the story," O'Shea said.

"I hope you are prepared," Anne said. "Because I'm not."

Arnold came out of the office and walked to his truck. He was opening the door as he saw the black fender move by the rear of his truck. Frank lowered the passenger side power window and raised the 9mm handgun to bear on Arnold. Arnold directed his attention back to the interior of his truck. Frank's first shot struck Arnold in the right thigh causing Arnold to buckle and fall back against the open door. The next shot struck Arnold in the right chest and punctured his lung. Arnold tried to climb into the truck as the third bullet grazed his back and lodged in the truck door. Frank fired four more times with only one reaching its intended mark. Frank sped out of the parking area and nearly struck Sam and Jonas as he skidded through the intersection next to R. L. Greenlaw's. Sam quickly turned to follow Frank. The Roadrunner was fast but it didn't handle the winding roads as well as the Mustang. Simpson pulled his seatbelt a little tighter. It reminded him of the poor bastard in the black Dodge Charger that was chasing Steve McQueen in *Bullitt*. Simpson hoped that he and Sam wouldn't come to the same end but it was eerily similar. It was just a movie, Simpson thought to himself. Sam hadn't seen the movie and only concentrated on the rear of the Mustang that he glimpsed occasionally as they sped towards Deer Isle. Traffic was light and both Frank and Sam maneuvered around the other motorists easily. Sam used up the entire road going back around "Lover's Lane". Simpson now held on to the arm rest and the seat much the same way as Sam used to when riding with Carl.

"You know what you're doing?" Simpson said nervously.

"Nope," Sam replied.

"Great," Simpson mumbled.

Sam could not understand how anyone could drive a car like this on anything but a straight road. It handled awful and he was losing the Mustang.

"Orono 1251," Wood said.

"I'll get that," Simpson said. "You concentrate on driving."

Sam smiled but the smile would be short lived.

"Go ahead for him Orono," Simpson said.

Wood didn't recognize the voice but he sounded like a cop.

"10-32 at the Stonington Lobster Co-op on Indian Point Road," Wood advised. "Several shots fired. One person wounded. Suspect vehicle is a black Mustang."

"We're in pursuit of the black Mustang now," Simpson said.

"10-20?" Wood asked.

"Where are we?" Simpson asked.

"Route 15, Northbound, Southeast Hills," Sam said.

"Route 15, Northbound, Southeast Hills," Simpson repeated into the radio.

"10-4," Wood said.

"902 Orono," Sgt. Wilson said. "I copied. I'm set up in Deer Isle village."

"922 Orono," Trooper Palmer said. "I'm still at the bridge."

"This should be over soon," Simpson said.

"I've heard that before," Sam said. Sam didn't have to ask who the wounded person was. The Roadrunner was gaining on the Mustang going up the last hill but Sam had to slow for the right turn at the top of the hill. As they crested the hill they saw a large cloud of dust on the left side of the road and skid marks on the pavement. The Mustang shot out of the dust and back onto the road. Sam slammed on the brakes and shifted into first gear. Sam shifted into second and was practically pushing the Mustang. Sam hit third gear and bumped the Mustang. The speedometer moved quickly past ninety. Frank lost control again on Long Cove Corner. Sam had slowed to make the corner but Frank sideswiped the Reverend Phister's Cadillac forcing the big car into the guard rails. The collision kept Frank on the road. Sam hit Frank again and caused him to fish tail as they went by Porter Brothers Mobil. Both cars were traveling over eighty as they approached Sgt. Wilson's cruiser. Sgt.

Wilson had blocked most of the road just beyond the old high school. He was still in the car.

"Hold on," Sam said. "I don't think Frank is going to stop."

Frank maneuvered onto the shoulder and clipped the front of Sgt. Wilson's car as he went by. Sam had slowed considerably and eased by Sgt. Wilson. The front left fender of the Mustang was rubbing on the tire but Frank didn't let up. Both cars rounded the corner at the monument and took off. The Roadrunner was in its element now and the 5.0 Mustang couldn't pull away. Both cars went airborne as they passed Carmen's Rock. They both hit hard and Sam grimaced at the thought of the damage he just caused to his brother's car. Both cars went airborne again at the other end of the straight stretch of road. Sam anticipated it and was able to maintain control. Frank and the Mustang did not touch down until they were nearly on the opposite shoulder. Through no help from Frank, the Mustang bounced back into the right lane and then Frank took over driving again. Frank was a little more cautious now and didn't go over eighty-five miles per hour. Sam kept bumping him but he wouldn't pull over. Sam called Orono and told them to advise Palmer that they would be coming over the bridge in less than a minute as both cars negotiated the causeway's turns. A young couple from Vermont in their Volkswagen Super Beetle convertible crossed the bridge at thirty miles an hour as they enjoyed the views. Trooper Palmer watched helplessly as they slowly came towards him. Palmer blocked the end of the bridge as soon as the couple drove by. Palmer exited his cruiser and ran as fast as he could away from it. The driver of the Super Beetle looked in his rearview mirror and stopped to see what the trooper was doing. Just then the black Mustang crested the top of the bridge at over a hundred miles per hour. Sam was already on the brakes and had slowed to seventy as he crested the top of the bridge. Frank saw the cruiser at the end of the bridge. There was nowhere to go. Frank hit the brake pedal with both feet. The front left tire was nearly worn through from the rubbing fender. The stress of the braking caused the tire to explode and caused the car to lurch to the left and strike the bridge. The Mustang ricocheted across to the other side and impacted the right side of the bridge. It then spun around backwards and hit the left side of the bridge again. The force caused the car to roll over and skid on the bridge surface on its convertible roof. The metal frame of the roof strained under the weight of the car and collapsed. Frank's head and shoulders were pressed into the cloth roof and that quickly gave way as the car slid along the pavement. Frank was conscious briefly. Very briefly. Just long enough for him to feel the pavement grind through the muscle and bone of this left shoulder and then the left side of his skull. The front of the Mustang, now upside down, struck the side of the bridge with enough force to raise the car above the deck of the bridge and then drop violently back down. Frank was dying as the car hit the bridge for the last time and was dead when the car finally ceased to move.

Trooper Palmer wrote down the plate number of the Volkswagen on his hand as the yellow car sped away. They didn't want to be involved but a detective from the Vermont State Police would track them down and take their statement a week later. Sam backed the Roadrunner back to the top of the bridge and activated the emergency flashers to warn approaching vehicles. Trooper Palmer returned to his cruiser and notified the Orono barracks as to what had just transpired. Sgt. Wilson was able to drive his damaged police car to the bridge and stopped traffic so the scene would not be disturbed. Anne Peterson and Officer O'Shea had seen the cars start across the bridge and they heard the crashing sounds as the black Mustang ricocheted off the sides of the bridge. Anne would never forget the sights and sounds of that moment. She was not yet aware that her husband had been shot and that news would dominate her thoughts when she found out.

The Vermont detective would learn that the passenger in the Volkswagen, a professional photographer, managed to get three pictures of the Mustang including one that showed it rolling over. More importantly, the photographs showed that Sam and the Roadrunner were several car lengths behind the Mustang and did not ram him as Maria Santos' attorney would suggest.

Arnold's ambulance crossed the bridge about twenty minutes after the Mustang crashed. There was only six inches to spare as the ambulance crept by the flattened Mustang. Sam learned that his father had been shot four times and his brother Carl was in the ambulance with him. Sgt. Cohen arrived and told Sam to get his mother and take her to the hospital to be with Arnold. Sgt. Cohen gave him his car. Sam reluctantly left. He wanted to be there when Frank was pulled from the wreckage. He needed to see him dead just as a bird dog needs to bite the dead bird. Part reward. Part closure. Sam stopped at a pay phone at the Eggemoggin Store and called Sharon. Sharon seemed appropriately concerned but he couldn't tell.

"I'll call you when I know more," he said.

"Thanks," she said.

Simpson sat down with Sgt. Cohen in Cabin 2 of the Bridge End Motel and gave a lengthy and detailed statement about what had happened and why he and O'Shea were in Maine. Sgt. Cohen did not have to ask one question. Captain Simpson knew the drill and was thorough. After the statement, Simpson called his chief and Sgt. Cohen called the attorney general's office. A seventeen-year-old unsolved homicide had been solved and the AG needed to be notified. Simpson's chief said that he would see him on Wednesday and to save the details for then. The bridge was closed for two hours. There was no place to divert the holiday traffic so the travelers just waited at either side of the bridge and enjoyed the summer day. The Bridge End Take Out window benefited from some extra between-mealtime business and several people on the mainland side engaged in a game of Frisbee football. It was hard to imagine what had actually happened here, given the happy and unconcerned faces on both sides of the bridge. There was some morbid curiosity as the Mustang was rolled back onto its now deflated tires. Frank was still seat belted in the driver's seat and he was left there for the trip to Augusta. An EMT was able to reach into the wreckage and check for vital signs. She found none. Frank's face was uninjured but the pain that had been there was still evident in the features that were frozen there by death. The funeral home people tried to make Frank look peaceful for the viewing but it was difficult. Frank had never been at peace in his life and it didn't appear that death would change that.

Sam and his mother got to the hospital to find out that Arnold was already in surgery. Carl was waiting for them in the lobby and explained that Arnold was awake all the way to the hospital. Carl told them that Arnold had been shot four times and still had bullets in his chest, leg and his butt. Carl and his mother sat down and Sam called Sharon with the news. Sharon told Sam that she thought it best for her and the boys to wait until tomorrow to visit Arnold.

Sam went to the front desk to find another patient. He made his way to ICU and was greeted by Julia's mother. Julia's father had died of a heart attack two years ago and Julia and Claire Henderson were now like sisters.

"Come in, Sam," Claire said.

"How is she?" Sam asked as he stood in the doorway.

"Get in here and ask me yourself," Julia said.

Sam walked in and saw a bandaged and bruised but smiling Julia. The only exposed part of her face was her left eye and her swollen lips. If you sat down at the end of her bed you could see her nostrils but that wasn't Julia's best view.

"Well, what I can see looks good," Sam said. "And what I hear sounds better. What's the verdict," he asked.

"The doctors set my nose and that stopped my brain from leaking out. They had to cut my right eyelid to stop the swelling and speed up the healing," Julia said in her usual upbeat manner. "They said I'm going to be fine but I might have vision problems in my right eye. Did you get my car back?" she asked.

"You haven't heard?" Sam asked.

"Heard what?" Julia and Claire said in unison.

"Silveira crashed your car on the bridge," Sam said quickly. Julia just stared at him.

"I was chasing him in Carl's Roadrunner," Sam added to fill the silence. Claire was the first to speak.

"That man is dead?" she asked.

"Yes," Sam said.

"Your dad and mom?" Julia asked.

"Mom's fine but Silveira shot Dad," Sam said. "He's in surgery now but the doctors said he should be OK."

"I'm so sorry," Julia said.

"Thanks," Sam said. "I'm sorry this happened to you," he added.

"There's nothing you could have done, Sam," she said.

Sam walked over and kissed Julia on the cheek below her left eye. A tear came and went and then she smiled.

"I've got to get back to Mom and Carl," Sam said. "I'll stop back and let you know how he is."

"Thanks, Sam," Julia said.

Claire said nothing but gave Sam a hug before he left the room.

"Why are all the good ones taken?" Julia asked.

"Because they're good ones," Claire said. "He's too young for you anyway dear."

"No such thing," Julia said with a laugh.

"Do you want to spend another night or go back to Rhode Island?" Simpson asked.

"Do I get to call you Jonas?" O'Shea asked.

"As long as we're in this cabin, on this beach you can call me Jonas," he said with a smile.

"I guess we're staying," O'Shea said as he walked to Simpson's car.

"Where are you going?" Jonas asked. "Look around you," O'Shea said gesturing at the view and the sky. "This calls for some cold beer."

"I'll get the burgers," Jonas said with a smile.

Sgt. Cohen arrived at the hospital about an hour and a half later. He found Sam and handed him the keys to the Roadrunner. Sam handed Sgt. Cohen the keys to his car.

"That's quite a car," Sgt. Cohen said.

"It certainly is," Carl said. "Did he hurt it any?"

"The front bumper is dinged up," Sgt. Cohen said.

"You'd better put it on a lift," Sam said. "I hit pretty hard at Carmen's Rock."

Carl started to speak but stopped as Arnold's doctor came through the door.

"How is he?" Anne asked.

"He had lost a lot of blood and his lung was collapsed," the doctor said. "We removed all the bullets and his lung is healing. He will be in the hospital a while but his prognosis is good."

"When can we see him?" Anne asked.

"About an hour should be fine," he said and then left as fast as he appeared.

"Sam," Sgt. Cohen said, "your tires have been replaced and a local garage fixed your mother's too."

"Thanks, Sarge," Sam said.

"You got a minute?" Sgt. Cohen asked Sam. Sam looked at his mother.

"Carl and I are going to get something to eat," she said. "We'll see you back here in an hour."

"I'm all yours, Sarge," Sam said lightheartedly but knew this was going to be a serious conversation.

"This is not official," Sgt. Cohen said, "but the AG is going to present a case against your father to the grand jury."

"What about me?" Sam asked.

"This is official," Sgt. Cohen said. "You are being officially notified of an Internal Affairs investigation that has been opened. You're being investigated for obstruction of justice." Sam just nodded. "Can you meet me at my office Friday?" Sgt. Cohen asked.

"Yep," was Sam's reply.

"Hang in there, Sam," Sgt. Cohen said. They shook hands and Sgt. Cohen left.

Sam was afraid this day would come the moment Det. Gervais gave him the case file. It didn't take long. A couple of months was all. Sam guessed he'd be looking for a job in a month or so and he hoped that would be the worst of it. The thought of jail did not appeal to Sam. He paced the waiting room floor for a few minutes and then went back to ICU. Julia was reading a *Reader's Digest* and put it down as he walked in.

"Couldn't stay away?" she said.

"Nope," he said. "Where's your mother?"

"She had to get some food and I sent her home," she said. "Where's yours?"

"She and Carl went to eat," he said. "They'll be back in a little while to see Dad."

"How is he?" she asked.

"The doc said he's going to be fine," Sam said. "He's in recovery now."

"Things sound good, Sam, but you don't look good," Julia said.

"I'm in trouble," Sam said.

"Why?" Julia asked, though she thought she knew.

"I've known for seventeen years who killed those men and why," Sam said. "This wasn't a problem until I joined the state police and it became an even bigger problem when I was assigned the case."

"So because you didn't turn your father in you're the bad guy," she said.

"That's about it," he said. "At the time it happened I thought my father was a hero and I didn't understand why he didn't come forward with what he did. I learned early on that Dad had little or no recollection of what he did," Sam explained. "It was like he flipped out and then didn't remember."

"Sam," Julia said. "This may sound too simple but all you need to do now is go with the flow. It's out of your hands and whatever happens, happens. I have faith in you and I believe this will work out in your favor."

Sam looked at Julia but he wasn't hearing her. He was remembering all the times since he was fourteen years old that he saw her or spoke to her. Wishing he had been old enough to have had a relationship and even a life with her. Sam wanted to tell her how he felt about her but he knew he never could.

"... you can't control fate but you can guide it sometimes," Julia said.

Sam just looked at her.

"What, is my brain leaking out my nose again?" she asked with a smile.

"No," Sam said. "I was just amazed at how beautiful you are even with half your face bandaged."

Sam couldn't believe he just said that out loud but there was no taking it back and he didn't want to. Julia studied him very carefully before speaking.

"If that was some bullshit line you can leave my room and don't come back," Julia said sternly. "But," she smiled. "If you are as sincere as you sounded you better come over here and kiss me."

Sam walked to her side, leaned and kissed her softly on the lips.

"That's what I thought," she said. "Sam, this is going to get real complicated," she said. "You're going to have to get some things in your life straightened out and then we can talk. In the meantime we are just good friends."

"You're right," Sam said.

Sam sat in the chair next to her bed and held her hand until she fell asleep.

Carl came to ICU looking for Sam.

"We've got to go," he said. "Mom's waiting in the car."

"What about Dad?" Sam asked.

"He's fine and he's sleeping and so is she," Carl said gesturing towards Julia.

Sam released her hand and kissed her while Carl watched. They both left the hospital together and didn't say a word. Just like that night so many years ago.

Chapter Twenty-Three

The Warwick Rhode Island police cruiser glided along West Shore Road. It was a clear and cool morning. More like the end of October rather than the beginning of September. The bright sun was deceiving. Officer O'Shea turned into the narrow driveway of the white two-story house. O'Shea had been on duty for two hours and it was time for his coffee break. There was nothing in department policy that said it had to be at a coffee shop. Jonas Simpson, retired all of one month, smiled and greeted O'Shea.

"Slummin'?" Simpson said.

"You live in a much nicer neighborhood than I grew up in," O'Shea said.

"Wasn't always this way," Simpson countered.

"I thought you might need to catch up on your reading," O'Shea said as he handed Simpson the current *Boston Globe.* "Front page but below the fold," O'Shea said. "I guess it was too old a story to be given much more prestige than that but pretty good just the same," he added.

MYSTERY OF MURDERED BIKERS SOLVED the headline read. Just below was a smaller headline, "Maine State Police Detective Disciplined During Investigation." O'Shea prepared coffee in Simpson's kitchen as if he lived there and Simpson sat at the kitchen table and read.

A Hancock County Maine Grand Jury failed to return an indictment against a 55-year-old lobster fisherman from Deer Isle. Arnold Peterson testified on his own behalf as did his son Det. Samuel Peterson of the Maine State Police. Assistant Attorney General Hebert LaRoche would not comment on the testimony or evidence presented but did say that the state presented a compelling case to the panel as to what happened at the Walker Estate on March 17, 1970. "The case is closed now." LaRoche said. Real Estate Broker Julia Henderson, the agent that leased the Walker Estate to Warwick, Rhode Island resident, Frank Silveira, testified at the four-hour hearing. When asked if she thought justice had been served Henderson stated, "I don't disagree with the Grand Juror's findings. I'm glad it's over."

"I'd say by the picture that Miss Henderson healed up well from her encounter with Frank," Simpson said. The Globe had a picture of Julia opening the door to a new Mustang convertible that was parked in front of the granite courthouse steps. She had that same disarming smile but was now wearing glasses.

"Sam told me that she needs glasses now because of the injury to her right eye," O'Shea said. "A detached retina or something like that," he added with a shrug.

The story went on to relate the history of the case. There was no mention of why Arnold Peterson was the suspect and what his motivation may have been. There were the usual unnamed sources that alleged that Mr. Peterson was protecting his family from the men he killed.

"Who's the unnamed source?" Simpson asked.

"I don't know," O'Shea said. "But Sam's boss, Sgt. Cohen, is a pretty cool guy and the reporters seemed to like him."

"You still put four sugars in your coffee?" O'Shea asked.

"Yes," Simpson snapped. "And stop being my doctor."

"Someone has to," O'Shea said. "'Cause he's not having very good luck with you."

O'Shea put two and a half sugars into Simpson's cup. Simpson continued reading. The Globe had managed to come up with Sam's academy picture.

"He looks younger than you do," Simpson said.

"He looks like a girl wearing his dad's uniform in that picture," O'Shea laughed.

Sources close to the investigation revealed that Det. Peterson had been disciplined for his involvement in the investigation. Lt. Col. Skofield stated that it was a personnel matter and he could not comment.

"What'd he get?" Simpson asked.

"Thirty day suspension," O'Shea said. "No pay. No bennies."

"Holy shit," was the only reply.

"Don't worry about him," O'Shea said. "He's making more money working for his dad. He said he couldn't wait to get back, though," O'Shea said. "He told me he felt lucky it was only thirty days."

Simpson didn't comment. He turned the page. On page two were pictures of sixteen men. Every one was a mug shot except for Anthony Silveira. Anthony had never been arrested and had never done anything to be arrested for. That night with his brothers was his first and last criminal involvement. Simpson studied James O'Shea's picture and was amazed how little O'Shea looked like his father. A good thing, he thought. Simpson read on.

"Christ all mighty!" Simpson swore.

"I thought you'd like that part," O'Shea said.

"How do you know what part I'm reading?" he asked.

"Just psychic, I guess," O'Shea laughed.

The investigation revealed that a now retired Warwick PD lieutenant, turned federal informant, had helped the Slayers in the planning stages of what was supposed to have been a marijuana smuggling operation. A source close to the FBI stated that the officer's involvement was minimal but what he had to offer was extremely valuable. The US Attorney in Providence would not comment.

"That was a hard story to swallow when the chief told me and it still doesn't go down any easier seeing it in print," Simpson said.

"Weren't you the one who told me you thought there was someone dirty in the department and was involved with Frank?" O'Shea asked.

"Yeah," Simpson admitted. "But I didn't think it was my partner."

The rest of the story consisted of brief biographies of each of the sixteen dead men and ended with a picture of Simpson when he was promoted to Captain and a paragraph of how he had been honored by the Maine State Police and the City of Warwick for his work and bravery in bringing this case to a close.

"That bravery part was on the money," Simpson said. "If Sam ever offers you a ride in that Roadrunner, just politely say no and walk away."

"Don't worry," O'Shea laughed. "His brother has the car back now and he said that Sam would never drive it again."

Simpson took a sip of his coffee. "You shorted me," Simpson said."

O'Shea gave him a "what are you talking about" look.

"There's barely three sugars in this," Simpson said as he got up and went to the kitchen. O'Shea just shook his head and looked at the picture of his father in the paper.

"Thanks for keeping me out of this," O'Shea said.

"It was easy," Simpson said with a smile. "You didn't do anything."

They both knew that wasn't true. The Globe reported that Simpson *"doggedly pursued the investigation for nearly two decades"* but the truth was he occasionally thought about Frank and who his WPD contact was but he didn't lose any sleep over it until O'Shea walked through his door on that Sunday in July.

"My mom was relieved that my name was not mentioned in the story," O'Shea said. "She still lives in the old neighborhood and Grandma O'Shea visits often."

"The chief knows what your role was," Simpson said.

"I know, Jonas," O'Shea said. "Thanks."

Simpson smiled. "I heard that Maria's son has resurrected Narragansett Drywall and Painting," Simpson said.

"Yeah, he has," O'Shea said with a sigh. "He also resurrected Frank's contacts in the mob."

"Life goes on," Simpson said wistfully.

"That reminds me," O'Shea said. "Grandma O'Shea said that Maria packed her bags and headed south."

"How far south?" Simpson asked.

"She wasn't sure," O'Shea said. "All she knew was that it was some island somewhere and she was living in Frank's house there."

"Good for her," Simpson said. "If Frank had been living there it was probably some Caribbean Island that doesn't extradite to the United States," O'Shea said.

"Likely," was Simpson's reply. "You still up for your golf lesson today?" Simpson asked.

"Soon as I get off shift," O'Shea said. Simpson folded the newspaper and tossed it in the trash.

"Now this is how coffee should taste," Simpson said.

About the Author

Stephen Pickering grew up on Deer Isle, Maine, where his family has lived for several generations. He served in the US Navy and joined the Maine State Police shortly after his discharge. His twenty-eight year career ended in 2006 with his retirement as a sergeant in the Criminal Investigation Division. Upon his retirement he began his second career as a private investigator and continues to work in that capacity. He resides in Blue Hill, Maine, with his wife, Betty.

CPSIA information can be obtained at www.ICGtesting.com
Printed in the USA
BVOW03s0859080615

403444BV00001B/1/P